Educ
V.50

# Constructing
## Evaluation Instruments

# Constructing
# Evaluation Instruments

BY   EDWARD  J.  FURST

DEPARTMENT OF PSYCHOLOGY, UNIVERSITY OF IDAHO

FORMERLY CHIEF,

EVALUATION AND EXAMINATIONS DIVISION

UNIVERSITY OF MICHIGAN

LONGMANS, GREEN AND CO.

NEW YORK          LONDON          TORONTO

LONGMANS, GREEN AND CO., INC.
119 WEST 40TH STREET, NEW YORK 18

LONGMANS, GREEN AND CO., LTD.
6 & 7 CLIFFORD STREET, LONDON W 1

LONGMANS, GREEN AND CO.
137 BOND STREET, TORONTO 2

CONSTRUCTING EVALUATION INSTRUMENTS

PUBLISHED SIMULTANEOUSLY IN THE DOMINION OF CANADA BY
LONGMANS, GREEN AND CO., TORONTO

FIRST EDITION MARCH 1958
REPRINTED APRIL 1961

LIBRARY OF CONGRESS CATALOG CARD NUMBER 57–14528

PRINTED IN THE UNITED STATES OF AMERICA

To
*Helene*

# Preface

Of all the competencies an instructor needs, probably none is as neglected as that of evaluating student progress. It is not unusual to find instructors who lack a grasp of basic principles of evaluation or who lack the skill necessary to produce a good classroom test.

At the same time, the fields of evaluation and test construction show a rather high state of development. A substantial body of theoretical and technical literature, representing the thinking of minds fully as able as those in the older disciplines, now exists. But it is, to be sure, not always readily accessible nor in a form useful to the instructor.

How bridge the gap between the apparent need and these potential resources? It was partly this question—this challenge—that prompted me to begin this book. Yet I did have a more personal interest, and that was to explore an approach that had intrigued me for quite some time. Might not there be considerable value in isolating from a variety of techniques the *really fundamental problems* and then subjecting these to intensive study? I thought there was, and so I plunged ahead. The results of these efforts constitute Part I.

While a book built around such basic problems would be of value in its own right, it could not go very far in the treatment of a specific technique. Nor would it be safe to assume that the typical instructor could readily apply the general principles to special techniques such as the essay and multiple-choice types of test. Such devices have their own peculiar technical problems for which special suggestions can be offered, and accordingly they require special skills on the part of instructors. Hence, in order to increase the potential usefulness of the book, I decided to supplement the original core on basic problems with a part on the construction of achievement tests. This supplement constitutes Part II.

In writing this book, I have intended it mainly for teachers and prospective teachers in our schools and colleges. But I have not been unmindful of the growing number of professionals in business, industry, government, and the military services who must also be concerned with the evaluation of instruction, with the measurement of proficiency, and with test development. I hope that they, too, will find the book stimulating and useful. Certainly their problems in this area are as challenging as those found in public education.

The major purposes of this book are to help such persons (a) acquire an understanding of the several basic problems involved in developing any evaluation technique, (b) further their understanding of principles of test construction, (c) become familiar with some of the best references in the field, and (d) broaden their understanding of the purposes which can be served by tests and other techniques of appraisal.

With such groups and purposes in mind, I have tried to make the book as functional as possible. Throughout most of the chapters there appear questions and exercises which challenge the reader to tease out implications, to search for illustrations from his own experience, and to apply principles previously discussed. Since these questions and exercises tie in so closely with the text, they have been incorporated right in each chapter rather than listed at the end. In a very real sense, they are part of the text. Another feature intended to make the book functional is the style of writing. I have worked toward a fairly simple, direct exposition which I hope is both interesting and readable. This choice of style accounts for the frequent use of the active rather than the passive voice, and of the pronoun "you" rather than the more distant third person.

Most of the illustrative materials have come to me directly or indirectly from other persons, to whom I am naturally most grateful. I wish to thank, first of all, the many authors, editors, and publishers who have generously permitted me to quote from their materials; then the numerous individuals whose contributions remain for the most part anonymous. I owe special thanks to Ralph W. Tyler, from whose many writings I have drawn quite liberally; and to Ray Loree, for allowing me to reproduce several excerpts from his doctoral dissertation. I do not know whom to thank for the figure which appears on the cover and again on page 3, but along with so many other excellent materials it has come to me from the Board of Examinations of the University of Chicago. Many of the anonymous contributions referred to above have been produced by instructors who have served with the board in the capacity of examiner. They have carried the art of examining to a high level and certainly deserve more credit than this passing mention.

An author's heaviest obligations are necessarily to those individuals whose teaching, research, and writing in the field have had the greatest impact upon him. In my case these obligations are again to Ralph W. Tyler, and to Benjamin S. Bloom, Chester W. Harris, and Herbert A. Thelen, all four of whom were on the faculty of the University of Chicago during my residence there as a graduate student. They have been extraordinarily effective in helping students to raise fundamental questions and seek the answers for themselves. In no small way, this book is an outgrowth of the curiosity which they have helped to kindle.

My remaining obligations are to William Clark Trow, Russell E. Diener, and, again, Benjamin S. Bloom, for their careful reading and criticism of major sections of the manuscript; to Miss Dorothy McKim, Mrs. Esther Rentschler, and Mrs. Carolyn Gott, for their expert typing of the manuscript; and finally, to my wife, Helene, for her devotion and forbearance while this writing was going on.

EDWARD J. FURST

*May, 1957*

# Contents

# Figures

# Tables

# CHAPTER 1

# Introduction

THE CONCEPT OF EVALUATION

PURPOSES SERVED BY MEASUREMENT AND EVALUATION

> Determining the Effectiveness of Courses and Programs
> Testing Assumptions about Given Practices
> Clarifying Objectives
> Selecting and Appraising Objectives
> Discovering and Understanding Learning Difficulties
> Planning Instruction
> Motivating Learning
> Guidance
> Selection
> Placement
> Certification
> In-service Development of Staff

TECHNIQUES FOR ACCOMPLISHING THE PURPOSES

PROBLEMS BASIC TO A VARIETY OF TECHNIQUES

This is a book on the development of evaluation instruments. It deals with basic problems and principles. Neither the problems nor the principles, however, can be adequately considered without reference to some larger context. To do so would be to reduce the discussion to the merely technical and to lose some larger values. It is for this reason that this introductory chapter has been written. Consideration will be given to the concept of evaluation, and to the variety of purposes served by tests and other techniques for appraisal.

## THE CONCEPT OF EVALUATION

Techniques for the appraisal of human behavior have a long history. Performance tests of physical strength and endurance, such as are common in primitive societies, must surely go back many thousands of years. Even such formal devices as written tests are old as far as recorded history goes. Thus, the Chinese had a highly organized examination system before the time of Christ.

In contrast, the notion of evaluation is of quite recent origin. The germ of the concept is certainly embodied in the work of Rice, who in the 1890's sought empirical data to challenge the mechanical teaching and learning of the three R's (8). Rice felt the amount of drill devoted to subjects like spelling was excessive, and that the time wasted could better be spent working toward other objectives. Consequently, he devised a spelling test and administered it on a large scale in order to compare the achievement of pupils who had spent varying amounts of time on drill. On the basis of the test data, he concluded that the actual time spent on drill was the least important factor in determining the pupil's spelling skill (8).

But Rice was ahead of his time and it was not until decades later that the evaluation movement began to influence formal education. Since his day there have been several large-scale evaluation studies in American education and thousands of research studies on teaching and learning. Moreover, leaders in the movement have been explicit in formulating the purposes and assumptions underlying evaluation and educational research. There exist excellent statements on evaluation which make it unnecessary here to develop this viewpoint at any great length.

According to one view, evaluation is a basic task of the educator. It is one of four basic tasks in the development of a curriculum or a plan of instruction that we may distinguish (11). These four are:

1. To determine the objectives which the course or program should seek to attain.
2. To select learning experiences which will help to bring about the attainment of these objectives.
3. To organize these learning experiences so as to provide continuity and sequence for the student and to help him integrate what might otherwise appear as isolated experiences.
4. To determine the extent to which the objectives are being attained.

This view rests on the assumption that education is a process for changing the behavior patterns of human beings. As a result of this process, it is expected that individuals will acquire ideas they did not have before, improve their ways of thinking, develop tastes and sensitivities, modify their attitudes, and improve in other desired ways.

It follows from this conception of education that the kinds of changes which an educator seeks to bring about constitute his educational objectives. The fundamental purposes of an education are to effect *changes* in the way the individual thinks, feels, and acts.

The process of evaluation is one of determining the effectiveness of the course or program in bringing about such desired changes. According to the view above, evaluation is an integral aspect of curriculum development and instruction. This is shown schematically in the following figure, which brings out the reciprocal relations between the main elements in a well-planned program of education.

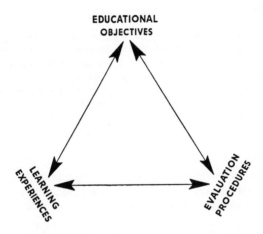

Thus, the objectives serve as the bases for developing both learning experiences and evaluation procedures. The learning experiences and evaluation procedures, in turn, help to clarify the objectives. Furthermore, situations used for instruction provide parallels for evaluation, and indeed may suggest good leads for the latter. Correspondingly, the evaluation procedures provide evidence on the effectiveness of the learning experiences, and ultimately on the attainability of the objectives themselves. There thus exists the possibility of interaction among these different factors, each having a potential influence on the others.

Recently, Dressel has experimented with ways of relating evaluation and instruction (4). He has made a conscientious effort to show instructors how they can tie in evaluation more closely with instruction. His listing of the parallel elements in these two processes is worth reproducing (after 4, pp. 23–24):

| *Instruction* | *Evaluation* |
|---|---|
| 1. Instruction is effective as it leads to desired changes in students. | 1. Evaluation is effective as it provides evidence of the extent of the changes in students. |
| 2. New behavior patterns are best learned by students when the inadequacy of present behavior is understood and the significance of the new behavior patterns thereby made clear. | 2. Evaluation is most conducive to learning when it provides for and encourages self-evaluation. |
| 3. New behavior patterns can be more efficiently developed by teachers who know the existing behavior patterns of individual students and the reasons for them. | 3. Evaluation is conducive to good instruction when it reveals major types of inadequate behavior and the contributory causes. |
| 4. Learning is encouraged by problems and activities which require thought and/or action by each individual student. | 4. Evaluation is most significant in learning when it permits and encourages the exercise of individual initiative. |
| 5. Activities which provide the basis for the teaching and learning of specified behavior are also the most suitable activities for evoking and evaluating the adequacy of that behavior. | 5. Activities or exercises developed for the purposes of evaluating specified behavior are also useful for the teaching and learning of that behavior. |

He concludes:

Evaluation does not differ from instruction in purposes, in methods, or in materials and can be differentiated from instruction only when the primary purpose is that of passing judgment on the achievement of a student at the close of a period of instruction (4, p. 24).

## PURPOSES SERVED BY MEASUREMENT AND EVALUATION

Evaluation can serve a variety of purposes, some central and others only peripheral or incidental. The central purposes are to determine the effectiveness of courses and educational programs and to provide a basis for improving them. But the techniques developed for these central purposes, the data collected, and indeed the entire process, lend themselves to other important uses. It is true, however, that some of the tasks which we are about to review are usually performed independently of any formal evaluation program.

### Determining the effectiveness of courses and programs

The need for evaluation was never greater than it is today. A number of forces have given impetus to this need: attacks on contemporary education, mounting enrollments, and increasing costs. Forces such as these will compel educators to seek evidence on the effectiveness of existing programs and on new ways of doing the job.

The need for evaluation is especially great when a school or college introduces a new curriculum. At that point there is likely to be much uncertainty—and some misgivings—about the potential effectiveness of the new program. Such conditions no doubt were present when the College of the University of Chicago introduced a new program of general education in the early 1940's. The faculty there abandoned survey courses emphasizing information in favor of a curriculum emphasizing the intellectual arts and abilities (1). They wished to have students learn methods of attacking a great variety of problems of general significance to educated adults. As the faculty sharpened their conceptions of what they wanted to accomplish by means of general education, they experimented with new methods of teaching, new types of instructional materials, and new ways of organizing courses. For each of these major innovations, the faculty wanted evidence of effectiveness in bringing about the desired changes in students. This they obtained from reports on comprehensive examinations and from special studies conducted from time to time. These reports helped them to determine the strengths and weaknesses of particular courses and practices, and to make continual improvements.

## Testing assumptions about given practices

Every program, indeed every course as it is taught, rests upon certain assumptions. A major purpose of evaluation is to test the validity of these assumptions so that sound practices may be continued and unsound abandoned.

The scope of such assumptions varies considerably, as shown in the following list of examples:

Students will develop effective writing habits and skills if this responsibility is left entirely to the English classes.

An introductory laboratory course in a science will develop a good understanding and appreciation of scientific method.

The reading of biographies of outstanding historical personages inculcates in students the values embodied in the lives of these personages.

Once students have learned to read a foreign language they can easily be taught to speak it.

Adoption of the elective system will provide adequately for differences in the needs of individual students and will provide as well a balanced liberal education.

Students who have acquired a good fund of information on everyday natural phenomena will develop an ability to explain these phenomena in terms of scientific principles.

An informational course in vocational orientation given to high school seniors or college freshmen will foster sound vocational choices.

Courses which emphasize interpretation and analysis of original works in the field also enable the student to acquire a fund of significant knowledge about that field.

Assumptions such as these have been tested through formal research, and there are data on their validity. Such evidence as is available suggests that most of the above assumptions cannot be sustained; the last is an exception. However, the important point is not the findings on this particular list of assumptions. *It is rather that such beliefs can be tested in school situations by educators who are able and willing to take the time to collect the right evidence.*

The educator's first thought is perhaps that this kind of inquiry is none of his business, that it is too technical for him to conduct, and that his findings can hardly have any validity. Nothing can be farther from the truth, if we look to the experiences of practitioners who have engaged in such "action research" (3). The educator can test many of his practices through such methods and, although these may lack the rigor of formal research methods, they can help him to improve his own practices.

## Clarifying objectives

It is true that good teaching can go on without instructors having clearly defined their aims in terms of student behavior. The aims are there— implicit in the activities carried on—but not written down. Or they may be written down in general terms only. Neither of these conditions is satisfactory for purposes of evaluation.

To evaluate any course or program, or to devise any kind of evaluation procedure, it is essential that the aims be defined in terms of student behavior. Otherwise it is not possible to know precisely what evidence to seek. Evaluation thus provides both a challenge and an opportunity to clarify educational objectives.

## Selecting and appraising objectives

One of the major tasks of the educator is to determine educational objectives. Evaluation can aid him here by providing data on the status or progress of students.

Achievement tests given before a course of study can reveal deficiencies about which something should be done. It may turn out, for example, that students have many misconceptions about the Bill of Rights or that their reading interests are unusually narrow. Such "gaps" in development provide suggestions for educational goals.

At the end of a course or program, data may be collected, which, when compared with earlier data, give an indication of the progress of the group. Data on the extent of improvement help to show whether the desired changes (objectives) are realistic. Attainability is one important criterion which must be considered in choosing or judging an educational goal. This and other considerations are discussed in detail in Chapter 2.

### Discovering and understanding learning difficulties

Almost any evaluation device can help to discover learning difficulties, and some devices can even help to diagnose them. Evaluation, if it is carried on regularly, can provide data on the weaknesses of individual students and the group as a whole. It may reveal, for instance, that many students in a course are having difficulty detecting the underlying assumptions in arguments, and that many are confusing opinion with fact as evidence for conclusions. These specific objectives, then, are not being realized.

The discovery of such specific difficulties makes possible a kind of feedback process for both students and instructor alike. The feeding back of such information to students gives them some idea of how they are doing, so that those who are falling short can know what deficiencies need correcting. Correspondingly, the feeding back of such information to the instructor gives him a sounder basis for modifying instruction.

This process of discovering specific difficulties has implications for the choice of goals. The fact that a substantial number of students are having difficulty reaching certain goals does not necessarily mean that those goals are unattainable, and therefore inappropriate for them. It only means that under the *particular* conditions of instruction the goals were not fully attained. The attainability of a specific goal is always relative to the methods of instruction as well as to the potentialities of the group. It may well be that subsequent modifications of instruction will bring the goals within reach of most of the students.

### Planning instruction

Although the interrelations of evaluation and instruction have already been discussed, they need further emphasis and illustration.

The collection of data for the purpose of planning instruction can take place at almost any point in instruction, even before it or some time after.

The great advantage of pretesting is that it lets the instructor know where he's starting from (or really, where his students are starting from). It tells him about their present status—the extent and precision of their knowledge about the subject, misconceptions which they hold, their mastery of prerequisite skills, and so on. With such information at his disposal, he is in a much better position to plan instruction than otherwise.

In a college course on the evaluation of student progress, the writer found through pretesting that a substantial proportion of students had deficiencies in their mathematical background as well as an aversion to anything mathematical. Many students could no longer compute a square root; and, if they had had elementary algebra at all, they were rusty on that. Since elementary statistics came into the course at many points, it was clear that such deficiencies would handicap students and that a disregard of them would only aggravate the students' aversion further. Rather than devote extra time to the upgrading of computational skills, however, the instructor chose to emphasize the interpretation of test data in various forms. The strategy was partly to show the importance of statistical concepts, and partly to emphasize what really was more central to the purposes of the course. Interpretation of data became one important focus, and computational procedures were introduced primarily to promote an understanding of elementary statistical concepts. Students were not required to memorize formulas, but to be able to translate them and to follow a computing guide in a standard textbook. Moreover, they were urged to use computational aids such as Barlow's Tables to get squares, square roots, and the like. These adaptations represent one solution to the problem, and another instructor may have done otherwise.

A similar problem arises in other courses which require some facility with elementary mathematics. Physics, chemistry, statistics, and other courses with a quantitative emphasis can well profit from pretesting to determine students' present facility in mathematics. A common weakness is the inability to express quantitative relationships in mathematical form. But even the most elementary operations, such as ability to work with fractions, percentages, ratios, and proportions, may prove a stumbling block to some students. When an instructor has detailed information beforehand on such student weaknesses, he can take steps to work the necessary experiences into his course as it unfolds.

During the course of instruction itself, careful evaluation will reveal how a group is progressing and where it is falling short. In a basic course on engineering materials and processes, one instructor soon found that students tended to think that there was always *one* "right" answer for each problem. Perhaps this attitude was a carry-over from their earlier schooling in which problems in mathematics or science did in fact have one correct answer. The engineering student has to realize that typically several major factors determine the solution to an engineering problem, not the least of which is cost, and that typically there is more than one acceptable solution. The recognition of the above attitude prompted the instructor to lay more stress on engineering as an *art*. This viewpoint he emphasized through lecture-discussion and through analysis of alternative solutions to typical problems worked by the class.

At the end of a period of instruction also, evaluation can provide data useful for planning. The advantage of posttesting is brought out well elsewhere (12, pp. 78–80). In a high school course on contemporary social problems, it was found that, at the end of a full year, students had acquired a great deal more information about these problems; that they had shifted their attitudes slightly in the direction of greater social and less selfish attitudes, but that their attitudes were much more confused and inconsistent than before; that they had not gained any skill in analyzing social problems; and that their ability to interpret social data was worse because they were drawing more unwarranted conclusions than before. After examining these results, the staff concluded that too much material was being covered (over six thousand pages) and not enough time spent in critical interpretation, analysis, and application. For the following year, therefore, the staff decided to reduce the number of major problems from twenty-one to seven and to reduce the amount of reading by more than half so as to utilize more time in analyzing and otherwise treating the material dealt with. An evaluation conducted at the end of the next year revealed that, although students had not gained quite so much in range of information acquired, they had gained greater consistency in social attitudes, had gained greater skill in analyzing social problems, and had become able to draw better generalizations from the data presented to them. These results supported the hypothesis that the course during the previous year covered too much ground. This rather dramatic instance shows clearly how evaluation can help to improve the curriculum and instruction.

### Motivating learning

Repeatedly it has been shown that testing influences learning. What students emphasize in their studying undoubtedly depends more upon what they expect on examinations than upon any formal statement of course aims. Thus, in one institution it was found that when comprehensive examinations consisted of knowledge questions while the instruction emphasized problem-solving skills, students tended to memorize information (and ignore much of the instruction) in order to pass the examinations (1, p. 306). On the other hand, when the examinations were of the open-book type in which notes and materials were allowed, students did not try to cram but rather in their preparation sought to apply the methods and principles of the course to new situations and problems.

Evidently testing can have undesirable effects on learning, so that it is of the utmost importance that examinations be consistent with objectives, instructional methods, and materials. When they are thus consistent, examinations and other evaluation procedures can help to motivate students in the right direction.

The process of evaluation can help to motivate learning in at least two important ways:

1. By encouraging instructors to clarify goals so that students know *what to spend their time doing*. Students are much more likely to accept, and to work toward, goals which are clear to them than toward those which are vague. Clear goals give meaning and direction to learning.

2. By giving students frequent evidence of their progress so that they know *how they are doing*. Knowledge of progress shows students how they have improved and encourages them to move confidently on toward further goals. Correspondingly, as students discover inadequacies in their behavior, they are more likely to feel impelled to overcome them.

### Guidance

Certainly one of the most important purposes of evaluation is to provide data useful for the guidance of the individual student. The discovery of learning difficulties, the clarification of educational goals, and the feedback of evidence on progress toward short-term goals, all constitute forms of guidance. But beyond these services are still others which help the individual through the continuing, pervasive processes of adjustment and growth. It is this kind of development which is at the heart of guidance, as conceived here.

In this view, guidance is a process of helping the student to clarify his interests and long-range goals, to work through his own difficulties, to learn to satisfy his own needs, and in general to achieve a reasonable degree of self-direction. At one level, this means helping the student to plan his education in relation to his own needs, to choose a field of specialization, and to work toward important educational goals.

A continuing program of evaluation will concern itself with these broader aspects of development—broader in the sense of transcending any given area or point in the student's education. It can throw light on the student's pattern of development and on the factors, especially emotional, that impede his optimum development. Such a program can seek answers to questions of the following sorts (after 6, pp. 16–17):

What kind of person is the student? What kind is he likely to become? What role or roles is he likely to play in the years ahead?

How do the interests and goals he expresses at this point fit in with his kind of person? Can his probable abilities sustain them? Will these interests or goals prove sufficient challenge to stimulate his growth?

What aspects of his personality can be counted on to keep him in the pursuit of these goals, and what obstacles is he likely to confront within himself?

What can this school contribute to the fullest development of his strengths, and the overcoming of his weaknesses? What materials, activities, and personalities in the school are likely to be most helpful to his development?

The answers to such broad questions must come from fairly specific information on the individual student. They cannot come from conventional letter grades or other such summary indexes. Only a comprehensive, continuing program of evaluation can provide the data needed for the kind of guidance envisioned here.

### Selection

To some extent, every school must exercise some selection of its students. Concern for selection is much more likely in higher education, where institutions conceive of their role as that of providing advanced education to a more capable student body than exists at the high school level. The prevailing philosophy of education at the elementary and secondary levels contrasts sharply with this, for selection is rejected as being inconsistent with the belief that every child or youth is entitled to the *opportunity* for the optimum development of his potentialities. Yet many high schools, particularly private, do exercise selection because they prefer to cater to the needs of the intellectually able, the technically inclined,

or the artistically talented. In a democracy there should be no objection
to this sort of special purpose. Nor to the practice of selecting students
for courses which require superior qualifications, even in schools which
attempt to meet the needs of all youth.

Evaluation can contribute to selection by providing data on the kinds
of growth to be expected of students at different levels of aptitude or
potentiality and with different patterns of personality. To fulfill this purpose, evaluation requires much data on the differential aptitudes and
personality make-up of students. It is necessary to know the kinds of
changes taking place in *particular types of students,* so that an institution
can distinguish those types of students who will profit from instruction
from those who will not. Surely an institution is justified in selecting those
students in whom its goals can be attained.

### Placement

Even when students are selected for a particular school or program, as
a group they will tend to show a wide range of individual differences in
characteristics of educational significance. This range will argue for adjustments in the pattern of courses and in the rate at which students are
allowed to progress. In a sense, such adjustments are a form of guidance
and, in another sense, they are a form of selection. Because of their importance, they deserve separate mention here.

Placement is a process of starting a student at that point in a program
or sequence of courses at which his aptitude or demonstrated competence
merits. This process is perhaps most common at the college level. Many
colleges place their entering students in courses such as English composition, mathematics, chemistry, and foreign languages. The great majority
of students will be placed in regular sections of the introductory course,
but some will be placed in advanced sections or given complete exemption
from the requirement. The poorly qualified may even be placed in remedial sections.

There are two rather different approaches to placement (2, p. 111). One
emphasizes aptitude for learning; the other, demonstrated learning. The
appropriateness of either approach depends upon the course or sequence.
In freshman mathematics, the first approach is common. Students may
come with roughly comparable backgrounds in mathematics, so that a
general test of their mathematical understandings and skills gives a good
indication of their aptitude for learning freshman mathematics. The test
score indicates probable *rate* of learning. In foreign languages, the other

approach is common. It rests upon carefully established norms showing the level of competency expected of students at the end of the several courses in the sequence. Here, evidence on *proficiency* (demonstrated learning) determines the point at which the student will be placed.

By cumulating data on the levels of competency normally attained at different points in a sequence, an evaluation program can provide a sound basis for placement procedures. Placement, in turn, can contribute to the better articulation of secondary and higher education by accelerating the student who has already attained some of the major objectives of the college curriculum. Acceleration of the well-qualified student is one of the most urgent needs in American higher education (7).

Dramatic evidence for the values of guidance-placement examinations comes from a twenty-year experiment involving 12,450 students of French and Spanish at the University of Wisconsin (9). The administration of such examinations enabled 52 per cent of the students to achieve the traditional standards with an average saving of 10 credits in elementary and intermediate courses. These they were then free to apply either in work in other fields or to more advanced courses in the languages themselves. Moreover, by reducing the per cent of failures and dropouts, the use of the tests helped the not-so-well-qualified student too.

### Certification

It is fair to say that the certification of student accomplishment is not a major purpose of evaluation as defined here. Yet it is true that the data collected in such an undertaking can serve various administrative purposes: grading, promotion, graduation, reports to parents, reports to other schools and to prospective employers.

Even here, the philosophy behind evaluation can lead to improvements in traditional certification practices. It can, in the first instance, encourage the reporting of grades which indicate demonstrated level of competency rather than relative standing in a group. With its concern for many aspects of student development, evaluation can also encourage the analytic reporting of the student's accomplishments in place of, or supplementary to, the usual letter grades or single scores.

### In-service development of staff

While the pursuit of such purposes as have been outlined benefits the individual student, it can also benefit the instructor. Evaluation provides a powerful means for the continuing in-service development of staff.

The activities required by an evaluation approach provide superb opportunities for an instructor to grow professionally. It is a real challenge to have to state one's teaching aims as changes expected in student behavior, to justify the worth of these aims over other possibilities, to relate one's teaching as closely as possible to the stated aims, to seek situations which will give valid evidence of their attainment, and to seek ways of improving a course or program. The responses which an instructor or staff makes to these challenges provide major experiences for growth.

A real advantage of an evaluation approach is that it fosters an objective, creative approach to teaching. The above challenges now become the focus of attention, and not the instructor and his personality. In this way they help to prevent defensiveness on his part and to foster creative thinking about his work. When an instructor continually raises good questions about instruction and its effects on students, and when he continually seeks good answers to these questions, he has adopted *evaluation as a way of thinking and acting*. And when he has done this, he has released within himself forces which will assure his continued growth.

## TECHNIQUES FOR ACCOMPLISHING THE PURPOSES

A wide variety of techniques is necessary to serve so broad a range of purposes as those just reviewed. Reliance upon a few time-honored devices such as the paper-and-pencil test will hardly do. A many-sided picture of student development requires the use of many kinds of evidence-gathering techniques.

To obtain evidence on methods of thinking, for instance, requires not only paper-and-pencil tests of ability to make correct judgments, but other techniques designed to discover the student's characteristic methods of arriving at his judgments. Additional techniques might include an interview in which the student tries to retrace his thinking, or sound recordings of his utterances as he tries to solve the problems or answer the questions out loud. These additional techniques are necessary in order to get at mental processes which are incompletely revealed in any paper-and-pencil test.

Among the more important types of technique are the following: paper-and-pencil tests, performance tests (of motor skills and the like), motion-picture tests, observation of behavior in lifelike situations, observation of behavior in test situations, and interview and questonnaire methods. This is not a complete list but it serves to give some idea of the range of possibilities.

## PROBLEMS BASIC TO A VARIETY OF TECHNIQUES

Despite the differences among the various techniques in use, they do have much in common. Regardless of their form or intended purpose, techniques intended to measure, describe, or evaluate human behavior must deal with certain basic problems. These problems are to:

1. *Determine what to evaluate—that is, the attributes or properties of human behavior or its effects.*
2. *Define the what in terms of behavior.*
3. *Select appropriate situations for calling forth this behavior.*
4. *Devise some method for getting a record of this behavior.*
5. *Devise some method for summarizing or evaluating the behavior so recorded.*

The strategy behind Part I is to single out these several basic problems for intensive study. This contrasts with the approach of concentrating on a single technique at a time, such as the essay examination or the method of direct observation, and going into great detail on the problems connected with its development and use. This latter approach has values, of course, for the reader interested in a specific technique. Particularly good illustrations may be found in volumes describing the development of instruments used in certain formal evaluation programs, such as the Eight-Year Study (10) and the more recent Cooperative Study of general education (5).

Our approach in Part I will be to take up each of these several basic problems in turn. We will go into each one intensively, exploring ways in which it may be attacked, drawing upon illustrations from different areas and techniques, and considering the requirements which must be met if the problem is to be successfully solved.

It is hoped that this approach will sensitize us to the similarities as well as to the differences among various techniques, and, especially, that it will deepen our understanding of those basic concepts and principles which are widely applicable.

## REFERENCES

1. Bloom, B. S. Changing conceptions of examining at the University of Chicago. In P. L. Dressel (Ed.), *Evaluation in general education.* Dubuque: Wm. C. Brown, 1954. Pp. 297–321.

2. Chauncey, H., and Frederiksen, N. The functions of measurement in educational placement. In E. F. Lindquist (Ed.), *Educational measurement*. Washington, D.C.: Amer. Coun. on Educ., 1951. Pp. 85–116.
3. Corey, S. M. *Action research to improve school practices*. New York: Columbia Univer., 1953.
4. Dressel, P. L. Evaluation as instruction. In *Proc. 1953 Invit. Conf. on Test. Probs*. Princeton: Educ. Test. Serv., 1954. Pp. 23–34.
5. Dressel, P. L., and Mayhew, L. B. Selected chapters. *General education:* explorations in evaluation. Washington: Amer. Coun. on Educ., 1954.
6. Murphy, Lois B., and Ladd, H. *Emotional factors in learning*. New York: Columbia Univer., 1946.
7. Pressey, S. L. *Educational acceleration:* Appraisals and basic problems. Bur. of Educ. Res. Monogr., No. 31. Columbus: Ohio State Univer., 1949.
8. Rice, J. M. The futility of the spelling grind. *Forum,* 1897, **23,** 163–172, 410–419.
9. Schenck, Ethel A. *Studies of testing and teaching in modern foreign languages*. Madison: Dembar Publications, 1952.
10. Smith, E. R., and Tyler, R. W., and others. *Appraising and recording student progress*. New York: McGraw-Hill, 1942.
11. Tyler, R. W. Achievement testing and curriculum construction. In E. G. Williamson (Ed.), *Trends in student personnel work*. Minneapolis: Univer. of Minnesota, 1949. Pp. 391–407.
12. Tyler, R. W. *Basic principles of curriculum and instruction*. Chicago: Univer. of Chicago, 1950. Copyright 1950 by the University of Chicago.

## FURTHER READINGS

Corey, S. M. *Action research to improve school practices*. New York: Columbia Univer., 1953.
Dressel, P. L. (Ed.). Selected chapters. *Evaluation in general education*. Dubuque: Wm. C. Brown, 1954.
Tyler, R. W. The functions of measurement in improving instruction. In E. F. Lindquist (Ed.), *Educational measurement*. Washington: Amer. Coun. on Educ., 1951. Pp. 47–67.

PART I

*Basic Problems*

# CHAPTER 2

# Determining What to Evaluate

GENERAL APPROACHES AND CONSIDERATIONS

Empirical Approaches
Job or activity analysis. Critical incident technique.
Diagnostic studies of performance. Statistical methods.
The Importance of Values

DETERMINING EDUCATIONAL OBJECTIVES

What Is an Educational Objective?
A Generalized Procedure for Determining Objectives
Getting Ideas for Objectives
Studies of the learner. Studies of contemporary life.
Suggestions from curriculum specialists. The taxonomy of educational objectives. Review of evaluation instruments.
Screening the Suggested Objectives
Using philosophy. Using the psychology of learning.
Teacher-Student Planning and Self-Selection

STATING THE OBJECTIVES IN GENERAL TERMS

Illustrations of General Objectives
Suggestions for Stating Objectives

Any attempt to develop an evaluation technique or to study human behavior requires that we determine those properties of behavior which are significant for the purpose at hand. For evaluating a course or curriculum, we must determine those characteristics which we feel are worth developing in students; for conducting a guidance program, we must determine those characteristics on which it is desirable to cumulate data; and for instituting a selection program, we must determine those characteristics desirable for individuals to possess.

All this is to say that we must have some concept of the significant behavior and its characteristics. This concept is crucial in at least two respects. First, it restricts the domain of behavior.[1] It singles out, from the broad and extremely varied range of human behavior, the area or areas that most concern us. Second, it specifies the aspects of this behavior that are to be studied. This second step is necessary because there are many characteristics that one can look for in a given sample of behavior. In the area of reading, for instance, we may study the pupil's attitude toward what he is reading, the number of eye fixations per line of print, the rate of reading, the level at which he comprehends, and so on. These are important characteristics of reading, and they are often studied. The particular characteristics we choose for study will determine, to a great extent, the kind of evaluation technique we develop.

The distinction drawn in the previous paragraph is a subtle one, and a single illustration may not get it across. What we have said is that, to evaluate any kind of human behavior, we must both define that behavior clearly *and* specify what characteristics of that behavior we are to evaluate. In other words, to *know* what to evaluate is to know both the nature of the behavior and the characteristics of that behavior to be evaluated.

There is good reason for emphasizing this distinction because we find so many statements of purpose that are incomplete in one or both of these respects. The statement: "To evaluate the student's logical reasoning . . ." is incomplete in both respects. It singles out an area, but this area is much too vague because there are different kinds of reasoning processes. It does not mention any characteristics of reasoning that are to be evaluated, although ability or skill seems to be implied. The latter terms are common in statements of educational aims, and, while they do indicate a general focus, they do not indicate what specific characteristics are to be used as a basis for judging ability or skill. The statement: "To assess the student's originality . . ." specifies a characteristic of behavior but it tells nothing about the kind of behavior or the field of endeavor. We are led to assume here that originality is a trait that characterizes a person's behavior in a wide variety of fields. But this assumption seems unsound, for it is unlikely that a person can be expected to show originality in more than a few fields at best.

In short, to determine what to evaluate is to determine both the behavior and the characteristics of that behavior which are significant for the given purpose. It is sometimes possible to postpone the decision about characteristics until after the sample of behavior has been obtained, and then

[1] In this book we will use the term "behavior" very broadly to include feeling and thinking as well as overt actions.

to determine what specific characteristics to look for. But for purposes of developing an evaluation technique it seems sounder to begin with as clear a concept of what one wants to evaluate as is possible. This helps to aim the technique in the right direction, and to build into it those features that are consistent with its intended use.

The next two chapters deal respectively with the problems of determining and defining what to evaluate. In this chapter we will discuss the problem of determining what to evaluate, first from a general standpoint and then from the standpoint of choosing educational goals.

## GENERAL APPROACHES AND CONSIDERATIONS

In the evaluation of human behavior, everything goes back—or should go back—to purpose. What aspects of behavior should you evaluate? It depends upon your purpose. The aspects of behavior that you decide to evaluate should help you attain that purpose.

Even when one has a clear-cut purpose, however, it is often difficult to know precisely what data to gather. There are instances in which people have gathered data on certain characteristics without really knowing whether those characteristics were the most important. At one time some people thought that general intelligence provided the key to an understanding of juvenile delinquency. It was assumed that the young delinquent had too much or too little intelligence, generally the latter, and that this condition led to the bad conduct. Present views on juvenile delinquency challenge this earlier preoccupation with general intelligence and place more emphasis upon emotional and environmental factors. This merely illustrates that, in the absence of definite knowledge about the significant attributes, the personal judgments and convictions of the investigator play a large role. These are often necessary, but they may be susceptible to a wide margin of error.

It may be necessary, then, to go ahead on the basis of some sort of logical, or "armchair," analysis as to what is important. But where time and resources permit, it is desirable to check these ideas through experiment or through a review of what others have done who have faced a similar problem.

There are available a number of such empirical techniques for isolating critical aspects of behavior. These techniques are widely applicable in education and in personnel research. Despite minor variations, many of them amount to the same thing—job analysis. As such they share the advantages and limitations of this basic approach. Because of their wide applicability as well as their similarity, these techniques deserve separate treatment in this general section.

## Empirical approaches

### Job or activity analysis

The question of what to evaluate can often be answered after a thorough study of the activity for which people are being selected or trained. Indeed, job or activity analysis may provide the *only* sure way of identifying the important attributes needed by the performer.

The utility of job analysis in business, industrial, and governmental settings is well established. Its utility in strictly educational settings has yet to be widely demonstrated, although the method is just as applicable there. Thus, educators might analyze the job of being a good consumer and use these results for the planning of units or courses in consumership. Or, getting closer to the school, they might analyze the job of being a good student. What does the task of being a graduate student in the X department involve, and what are the characteristics which make for successful performance of this role? This is rather a different approach than that of listing desirable traits "off the cuff."

A job analysis grows out of a job description, or statement of what the person does and the conditions under which he does it. The analyst seeks to discover the demands made upon the performer, and then to organize these into a set of critical requirements. The latter provide the basis for choosing or developing evaluation techniques.

### Critical-incident technique

A promising refinement of job analysis is the critical-incident technique. Developed in wartime studies of air crews, it has since been applied to studies of airline pilots, scientists, dentists, doctors, teachers, and executives (9).

The technique assumes that a job consists of two types of tasks, or behaviors: *critical and noncritical.* Critical behaviors are defined as those that *make the difference between success and failure in carrying out important parts of the job.* Hence, they represent either very effective or very ineffective on-the-job behaviors, as judged by a qualified observer. Noncritical behaviors, on the other hand, derive from two sorts of tasks:

(1) *those having so little relation to success on the total job that the way in which they are performed is of little consequence;* (2) *those done well by most workers, so that they are not a source of judgments on individual effectiveness.* As one would expect, the technique focuses on the critical behaviors and ignores the noncritical.

The heart of the technique lies in the collection of a large and representative sample of critical incidents. The investigator gets these reports from persons best able to observe and evaluate on-the-job behavior— supervisors, workers, coworkers, and even clientele (when practitioners in medicine and dentistry are being studied). He must take several steps to insure that the sample of incidents will be representative by (1) getting reports from observers in a variety of situations; (2) collecting incidents until no new types of behavior are reported in significant numbers; (3) having each observer report only on those individuals whom he has observed closely and at some length; and (4) having each observer report only those incidents from the recent past, so as not to select only the most dramatic or outstanding from his past experience.

Each incident is a description of either effective or ineffective on-the-job behavior. It should give details of the circumstances. However, *it should not be a rating of traits nor an interpretation of behavior.* The first incident below describes effective behavior by one research worker, while the second gives an example of ineffective behavior by another.

This engineer applied a system for standardizing the steps involved in accomplishing the various types of projects assigned to his section of the laboratory. This was effective because he applied it consistently so that it served as a continuous guide to subordinate engineers. The system consisted of requiring a series of conferences at important points common to all projects, such as procedures, progress, and report conferences. At each conference, so far as possible, subordinate engineers presented their plans of work and decisions were made as needed to provide a firm definite path to the next important stage of the project (**27,** p. 19).

. . . An electronics engineer had quite an elaborate device designed and built which later proved to be obsolete by the discovery of information which was available from the first, had the originating engineer taken the trouble to find it. The device was to be rushed to completion before a demonstration instead of waiting the week or two necessary to gather the complete information on what was required by the ultimate user of the unit. Work was pushed ahead by guessing what the user was most likely to want in order to have something to show for a rather meaningless demonstration. The demonstration, incidentally, never took place (**10,** p. 77).

The investigator makes sure that he gets a large and representative sample of such incidents. He then does two things. First, he studies each incident, abstracting the critical behaviors. Thus, in the first example above, two critical behaviors were identified:

1. Devised standard procedure for subordinates to follow on projects, involving conferences at key points and resulting in definite work outlines for each stage.
2. Applied procedure consistently, so it was a continuous guide to subordinates.

Next, he groups related behaviors into categories. This step involves the derivation of a classification scheme. In the study of research personnel, thirty-six categories were needed to classify more than three thousand critical behaviors. These categories were grouped into eight main areas as follows:

I. Formulating problems and hypotheses
II. Planning and designing the investigation
III. Conducting the investigation
IV. Interpreting research results
V. Preparing reports
VI. Administering research projects
VII. Accepting organizational responsibility
VIII. Accepting personal responsibility

Since an outline with as many as three thousand specifics would be too unwieldy to use, the investigator has to boil it down. He does this by studying all the behaviors within a category, and grouping together all "duplicate" behaviors (those which are so similar that they may be considered identical for practical purposes). He then writes a descriptive statement for each group of duplicates, omitting specific details that render each behavior unique. But even this number of statements is likely to be too large; so he must go through similar operations to reduce them. In the end, these new descriptive statements amount to a list of critical requirements for the job.

The list of critical requirements can then be used in various ways: for establishing goals for a training program or a course of study; for planning tests of aptitude or achievement; and for making a rating scale for appraising personnel. Although the critical requirements reflect some weighting, they are probably not of equal importance. Hence, when used as a basis for constructing an aptitude test, they must be checked against job performance to determine which are especially predictive.

1. Are noncritical behaviors essential parts of job performance?

2. Support the following statements:
    a) A critical incident should give details of the circumstances.
    b) It should not be a rating of traits, nor an interpretation of behavior.
3. Suppose we were to use the critical-incident technique to identify critical requirements for teaching. From whom should we get reports? Who would be in the best position to give reports?
4. Write a short descriptive statement for each critical behavior that you can abstract from the second incident on page 23.
5. In what sense are critical requirements weighted?

### Diagnostic studies of performance

Another form of activity analysis is represented in diagnostic studies of performance. Such studies aim at important activities learners are expected to carry out—arithmetic, reading, handwriting, written and oral expression, problem-solving, and others. A good recent study is one on the problem-solving of college students (1). The investigators had students "think out loud" as they tried to answer a variety of questions taken from comprehensive course examinations. Each student took part in several individual sessions, after first getting some practice in working problems out loud. The problems themselves were neither puzzles nor questions of specific facts, but problems that offered the possibility of being solved if they were systematically attacked. As the student thought out loud on each problem, the interviewer took as complete notes as possible on everything the student said or did. Occasionally, it was found necessary to supplement these notes by asking the student to recall what he had done after he had completed a problem. The record of one student's thinking on the problem below gives some idea of what the method yields (1, pp. 16–17).

*Problem 3*
Some economists feel that there is danger of an extreme inflationary boom after the war. It is the opinion of such economists that the government should control the boom in order to prevent a depression such as the one following the stock-market crash of 1929.

Below are a number of specific suggestions. For each of the following items, *blacken—*
answer space 1—if it would be consistent with the policy of controlling the boom;
answer space 2—if it is directly *inconsistent* with the policy.
    26. Lower the reserve that banks are required to hold against deposits.
    27. Reduce taxes considerably.
    28. Encourage the federal reserve banks to buy securities in the open market.

*       *       *       *       *       *

*Stephen N.* (*Score 1*): (Read the statements and the directions.)

(Read item 26.) "Forgot that reserve ratio—if you lower the reserve ratio would tend to control inflation—consistent, I think—would let less deposits out of the bank."

(Read item 27.) "Inconsistent—people would have more money for other things —would be runaway inflation."

(Read item 28.) "Forgot open market—if you buy in the open market—know three ways for banks to have more reserve on hand—reserve ratio, something else, and open market—would be consistent, I think—can't remember how it operates— have to study economics some more."

The interviewer comments as follows on the student's thinking:

This student attempted to remember relevant material he had studied at one time and made little effort to solve the problem on the basis of the given material. It is interesting to note that he translated the reserve into a reserve ratio. He did not, however, grasp the correct relation between changes in reserves and release of deposits from the bank. In Item 27 the student correctly related reduction in taxes to amount of money available and to inflation. In Item 28 the student attempted to remember particular subject matter rather than think through the consequences of the item. He had great difficulty in solving other problems presented to him; to a large extent, this difficulty can be accounted for by his lack of independent thinking. In attempting to solve most problems, he tried to remember specific answers from textbooks, lectures, and discussions rather than make an effort to think through each problem on the basis of the given material. This student was not at all confident about his problem-solving and apparently found it necessary to make several excuses about his lack of memory for certain specifics (1, p. 17).[2]

One problem, of course, could not yield a dependable record of a student's habitual ways of solving problems. However, two to three one-hour sessions in which a variety of problems were presented did seem to give a pretty reliable record. The investigators then analyzed these records, trying to identify the outstanding characteristics in each case. They also found it very helpful to compare different students, particularly the good and poor problem-solvers. These analyses and comparisons enabled them to produce a tentative, three-level check list of important problem-solving characteristics, which is reproduced here only to the second level (1, pp. 106–109).

  I. *Understanding of the nature of the problem*
    A. Ability to start the problem (comprehension of directions)
    B. Ability to understand the specific problem presented
    C. Other difficulties

[2] Reproduced by permission of the University of Chicago Press.

II. *Understanding of the ideas contained in the problem*
   A. Ability to bring relevant knowledge to bear on the problem
   B. Ability to comprehend the ideas in the form presented in the problem
III. *General approach to the solution of problems*
   A. Extent of thought about the problem
   B. Care and system in thinking about the problem
   C. Ability to follow through on a process of reasoning
IV. *Attitude toward the solution of problems*
   A. Attitude toward reasoning
   B. Confidence in ability to solve problems
   C. Introduction of personal considerations into problem-solving [3]

The third level of the check list is more specific, of course, and contains items like those for IV B, Confidence in ability to solve problems:

1. Makes little attempt to attack the problems which appear to be complex and abstract.
2. Makes only a superficial attempt to reason through a problem, then gives up and guesses.
3. Is unable to come to a definite conclusion as to the answer or to decide between two alternatives.
4. Has little confidence in the correctness of the solution selected.

Thus, through diagnostic studies of problem-solving, the investigators have come out with a very useful set of categories. The check list, though tentative, does identify some of the critical aspects of problem-solving.

Many diagnostic studies concentrate on personal products rather than on performance itself. Although this is usually done for the sake of economy, such studies often yield more information than would a study of performance itself. Teachers may study samples of handwriting, English themes, art work, mechanical drawings, products of shop work, food cooked in home economics classes, graduate dissertations, and many other products. A common approach is to compare the work of different students, abstracting the features that distinguish between the good and poor products. The list of features can then serve as a check list for observation, for rating, or for developing test materials.

### Statistical methods

You may have noticed a common element in the approaches just reviewed—namely, the use of contrast. An approach may contrast good and poor performers, effective and ineffective incidents, or good and poor

[3] Reproduced by permission of the University of Chicago Press.

products. To a certain extent, such approaches concentrate on the extremes in order to bring out more sharply the attributes that differentiate between them.

This practice is fairly common in studies of individual differences. Thus, differences between good and poor readers have been used as a basis for building diagnostic reading tests. So, too, for other diagnostic tests. Differences in the responses of good and poor students to a study-habits inventory have been used as a basis for choosing those statements to be kept in the inventory and for assigning numerical weights to different kinds of responses (25). The statements chosen for the final form of the inventory were those found to distinguish between good and poor students of the same intelligence level. In effect, the study habits listed in the inventory define the relevant characteristics. Essentially the same procedure has been used to build questionnaires on vocational interests and on personal adjustment.

Studies of this kind draw heavily upon statistical methods. It is probably fair to say that statistical methods come into such studies at a fairly late stage. By that time, the investigator has already singled out an area of behavior and has made a preliminary analysis of those characteristics he considers significant. Statistical methods then help check the soundness of that analysis.

Statistical methods are especially helpful in selection and prediction studies. There they can help identify and weight those variables that make a difference in performance. These methods also have much in common, but their complexity precludes any further treatment here.

### The importance of values

Empirical methods can be extremely useful tools. We wouldn't want to do without them any more than a doctor would his instruments. But we wouldn't want the tool to become our master rather than our servant. Unless we keep certain things in mind, this may well happen. The tool, and not we, will then determine what is important. Let us now search out these other things that we must consider before using the tool itself.

One thing to consider is the significance of the activity. Safecracking is a highly significant activity in one sense. Some people make a living out of it. Other people lose money because of it. Since both the winner and the loser have a stake in it, safecracking makes a difference in their lives. Although safecracking is socially significant in the sense that it affects the well-being of certain individuals and of the larger society, we would obviously not consider it socially desirable. Consequently, people don't go around making job analyses of safecracking so as to isolate the critical requirements of the job. Society isn't interested in promoting this activity, nor in training people for it, nor in developing tests to pick good safecrackers.

Well and good to this point. An activity should be socially desirable, and *at the same time* it should be good for the individual. That opens the door wide. There are all sorts of desirable activities going on in the world. What's more, they aren't of equal importance; all of which means that we have to make judgments of relative value. These are not always easy to make, and there are some pitfalls along the way.

In the first place, the ease with which an activity can be analyzed is no guarantee of its significance, nor of the significance of the characteristics isolated from the analysis. Diagnostic studies sometimes focus on the mechanical aspects of a school subject, apparently because these aspects can be easily studied. This seems likely to happen in such fields as mathematics and the language arts. A good illustration is the case of a high school mathematics teacher who was much interested in diagnostic work (21). She made careful studies of the difficulties students had in factoring algebraic expressions, such as the sum or the difference of two squares, as well as difficulties with other aspects of algebraic manipulation. However, she made no attempt to diagnose difficulties in representing the conditions of a problem by an algebraic expression. Most mathematics teachers would feel that the ability to express quantitative ideas in algebraic form is much more important as a goal of algebra teaching than is the ability to factor various types of complex algebraic expressions.

All too often have we done this sort of thing in our evaluation of student progress. We have looked for the outcomes that are easy to find, but have ignored important outcomes that are not easy to see nor easy to measure objectively.

In the second place, because a great many people do certain things, there is no guarantee that what they do is significant. Many people read comic books, listen to soap operas, watch boxing matches, or "play the horses." They like to do these things, and we could therefore justify them for certain segments of our population. Should the school study these activities so that it might teach people to get more out of them? Yes and no, we say. Somehow, we feel that there are more important things to teach, and we may even feel that there are more important things for people to be doing in their leisure time. Hence, why spend time trying to find out what it takes to be a skillful reader of comic books, a soap opera listener, a boxing spectator, or a gambler.

Third, because an activity is commonly carried out in a certain way, it must not *always* be carried out that way. When the millennium comes to education and instructors have smaller classes, teaching as an activity undoubtedly will undergo some change. We would then expect instructors to share more responsibility with students for planning activities. This shift would place greater demands upon instructors and students alike for ability to participate in, and to profit from, group efforts. Study habits inventories, if there be any, would have to be changed accordingly. Skill in stenographic skills such as notetaking would probably receive less emphasis.

We cannot dodge such questions of value. Whether an activity is desirable, whether an occupation should be differently organized, whether a given trait is individually or socially desirable, or whether a given attribute is worth testing, ultimately reduces to a question of values.

Whatever society values, ultimately determines the choices that we make. The importance of values is brought out clearly in the process of determining educational objectives, a problem to which we now turn.

## DETERMINING EDUCATIONAL OBJECTIVES

### What is an educational objective?

*An educational objective may be defined as a desired change in behavior.* It represents any change in a person that we try to bring about through education. This definition rules out the many changes that are not sought by the school—those that come about from other experiences or that arise incidentally from schooling. It also rules out certain other things which are often confused with educational objectives. An educational objective is *not* something the instructor does; it is *not* the same as course content; and it is *not* a fundamental life value.

Any statement of what the instructor is to do is a statement about means, not ends. "To illustrate through films the way of life in Paris"; "To trace the development of the industrial revolution in England"; "To discuss the works of contemporary American short-story writers"; "To show how maturation influences readiness for learning"—the foregoing are not statements of educational objectives as here defined; they are statements of what the instructor plans to do. But the aims of education are not to have the instructor (or the students for that matter) go through certain motions. The aims of education are the kinds of learning which all this activity should bring about.

Course content is also not an end in itself; it is a means to other ends. The following quotation helps to distinguish course content from educational objectives:

> . . . Specifying the content included in the course does not always make clear the objectives of that course. Content is used as a means to an end and does not always indicate the end. Some course material is used for illustrations. Other material may be used to provide experiences in ways of thinking where the important outcome desired is not to memorize the material but to develop certain ways of thinking through problems in this field. Other content may be used to clarify certain issues, again not with the idea that the content is necessarily to be remembered verbatim, but to help the student arrive at a consistent belief and point of view about the issues involved.
>
> The foregoing illustrations emphasize the dangers involved in the kind of test construction which merely samples the content of textbooks and courses of study without taking the necessary first steps of identifying objectives and defining them clearly in terms of behavior . . . (23).

This quotation should not be taken to mean that elements of content are not important as educational objectives. They are. In most courses, it is expected that students will acquire facts, concepts, and other elements of content. But these represent only a portion of the course content, and may usually be acquired from a variety of instructional materials.

Educational goals should also be distinguished from life values, or the essential elements of a good life. The following list of major values should find general acceptance (6).

1. *Life-maintenance*—Sheer physical survival on almost any terms, but preferably on a level at which the organism functions efficiently and comfortably. This value includes the necessities (food, clothing, shelter, etc.), and mental and physical health.
2. *A sense of worth or achievement*—Of amounting to something, of living up to one's picture of one's self, of being recognized and accepted, and of having accomplished something of importance.
3. *Friendly relations with others*—Relations of mutual respect, affection, courtesy, tolerance, etc.
4. *A free society*—A self-governing society with the maximum of individual liberty that is compatible with effective cooperation.
5. *Aesthetic experience*—A sensitive response to beauty in many forms.
6. *Meaning*—Knowledge and intellectual discipline, integrated in a view of life which gives orientation, direction, and security.

These values are not educational objectives. They are things we want to get out of life. Educational objectives are the *behavior patterns* that enable us to attain these values.

6. Many instructors if questioned about their course aims will reply, "We cover the text," or "We cover the course of study outline." What is un-satisfactory about such a reply?

7. In stating the aims for a course, a social studies staff listed certain "areas of concern," as, for example:
   a) The issue of equality versus privilege
   b) The issue of limited versus unlimited government
   c) Power distribution in a society

   Is this a statement of educational objectives?

8. To what extent are principles or generalizations of the following kind satisfactory as statements of specific aims?
   a) It is extremely difficult for a nation to become a great power without accessibility to supplies of coal, iron, and petroleum.
   b) Settlement of many parts of the world in the nineteenth century resulted from the markets created by rapidly growing industrial cities.

### A generalized procedure for determining objectives

An educational objective is the product of a value judgment. This follows because some person or group has decided that the goal is a worthy end. What makes the choice a value judgment is the preference for the particular goal over many other possible goals, and the commitment to work toward it.

However, the fact that an educational goal represents a value judgment does not guarantee that the choice is the best possible. Human judgment is fallible, and the goal may prove to be less worthy than others.

To insure that the choice is sound, those who plan a course or curriculum should really proceed in a systematic way so as to give balanced consideration to a number of things. What this involves will be our concern in the next two sections: "Getting ideas for objectives," and "Screening the suggested objectives." In the first of these, we will examine several sources of ideas for goals; in the second, the role that philosophical and psychological considerations can play in evaluating the suggested goals. It is important to recognize that these two sections are organized into a *generalized procedure for determining educational objectives*. For this rationale, the writer is indebted to a formulation by Tyler (24). The procedure is admittedly ideal and few instructors or committees will be as thorough in arriving at aims. It does, however, serve our purposes admirably in providing a framework for organizing these several major types of considerations.

## Getting ideas for objectives

### Studies of the learner

Studies of needs and interests provide valuable data for deriving educational goals. Such data may be obtained from studies of the learners themselves, or from available scientific studies on human development.

During the last twenty-five years, many studies have been carried out to identify student needs. These studies follow much the same pattern: first they try to find out present characteristics and ways of behaving; then they compare these findings against desirable standards of development. Any serious gap between the student's present development and the standard suggests an "educational need." [4] If the school decides to do something about the need, it then becomes an educational goal.

A good example of such a study is the one on problem-solving reviewed earlier (1). Again and again it was found that college students tended to avoid real problem-solving. They glossed over problems superficially, didn't try to reason them through, had little confidence in their own ability, and often arrived at answers on the basis of personal whim. When these habits are compared with good problem-solving, a serious gap is evident. The gap suggests a broad objective that the school might emphasize—the improvement of problem-solving.

Other studies point up the need for greater facility in written expression; for improved listening comprehension; for greater self-understanding; for a better philosophy of life; for more tolerance of minority groups and of different religious views, and so on.

The growing field of human development has many suggestions to offer that are of general significance. One writer has organized his suggestions around the concept of "developmental task" (12). A developmental task is a kind of mastery expected of all members of a society at about the same age. For example, during adolescence it is expected that each boy and girl master the following tasks:

1. Accepting one's physique and accepting a masculine or feminine role.
2. Achieving of new relations with age-mates of both sexes.

[4] This meaning of the term "need" should be kept distinct from another meaning current in psychological writings. The other meaning refers to a tension in the organism which must be relieved if the organism is to maintain a healthy condition of equilibrium.

3. Achieving a degree of emotional independence of parents and other adults.
4. Achieving assurance of economic independence.
5. Selecting and preparing for an occupation.
6. Developing intellectual skills and concepts necessary for civic competence.
7. Desiring and achieving socially responsible behavior.
8. Preparing for marriage and family life.
9. Building conscious values in harmony with an adequate scientific world picture.

The list of tasks thus suggests some important learnings that the high school might well try to foster.

Many studies focus on interests as a source of ideas for goals. They are based on the assumption that the individual learns best when he takes part in activities that interest him. If it turns out that these interests are undesirable, narrow, or limited, then this suggests gaps which need to be overcome if the student is to get a good education. If it turns out that these interests are desirable, then this suggests a good starting point for instruction.

A great variety of studies have been made of interests in reading, in science, in games and sports, in health problems, and in other fields. These data provide a basis for setting up goals for particular fields.

A few cautions are in order. First, collecting data on needs and interests does not automatically identify objectives. The data have to be interpreted in the light of desirable norms of development—a value system —before we can draw any such conclusions. Also, needs that are properly met by the school must be distinguished from needs that are best met through other social agencies.

9. Evaluate the following point of view: "The determination of teaching aims and materials should be left to the judgment of the teacher since he is in a better position to know what is worth teaching."
10. What possible values do you see in pretesting your students for the purpose of deriving educational goals?
11. What limitations can you see in deriving objectives solely from an analysis of student needs and interests?

### Studies of contemporary life

Studies of contemporary life outside the school provide a wealth of suggestions for educational goals. For the most part, these studies are based on a logic similar to that of job analysis. The idea is to analyze important adult activities or circumstances so as to identify critical requirements and needs.

All sorts of studies have been made, and are being made, of contemporary life. Some concentrate on aspects of individual life, such as health, family, recreation, vocation, religion, buying habits, and citizenship. Others examine social groups, such as a rural community or a minority group, to find out their dominant ideas, values, problems, and practices. Still others explore the factors conditioning life in particular communities or areas: natural resources, population changes, growth of slums, and so on.

The subsequent careers of graduates, for example, provide provocative data for a school to consider. Schools of engineering, as they trace their graduates into the world of work, find that many do not continue in the fields of their undergraduate specialization. A considerable proportion will shift to other specializations, and many will move into managerial positions. Moreover, so rapid have been technological advances that it is necessary for engineering graduates, as indeed for other technical personnel, to continue their educations while on the job. Technical education must be spread out over the span of a man's career. The increased leisure which characterizes our culture also makes it desirable that the engineer have experiences which give esthetic enjoyment and integration to living. Challenged by these trends, a number of schools of engineering have reoriented their programs toward a broader education. What they conclude is that the engineering student needs, first, a liberal education which will help to make him a *whole man*; second, a broad technical education which will give him greater flexibility in his vocational adjustment; and third, the cultivation of the ability and the desire to take responsibility for continuing his education beyond the period of formal schooling.

But again, as with studies of the learner, objectives do not follow automatically from the data. It is necessary to interpret the data in light of what *ought* to be.

12. What limitations can you see in deriving objectives solely from studies of contemporary life?

### Suggestions from curriculum specialists

By far the most common source of ideas for objectives is that body of materials and suggestions produced by curriculum specialists. Valuable ideas emerge from the reports of curriculum committees, from course of study outlines, and from instructional materials such as textbooks.

In the area of general education, subject specialists can make their best contributions if we ask them the right question: "What can your subject contribute to the education of students who are not going to be specialists in your field?" Then they are less likely to propose goals that are too specialized or technical for large numbers of students.

Some of the more recent reports do show that subject specialists can make helpful suggestions in answer to this question. Witness the several reports on general education put out by the Progressive Education Association's Commission on the Secondary Curriculum, *Science in General Education, Mathematics in General Education,* and similar volumes on the social studies, language, and the visual arts. Consider also the periodic reports published by such groups as the National Council of Mathematics Teachers, the National Council of Social Studies Teachers, and the National Council of English Teachers.

In addition to reports of this kind, there are available reports that cover large segments of the curriculum. Invariably, they reflect a consideration of student needs and the demands of contemporary life, as well as the contributions of the various subject fields. Representative reports, oriented toward general rather than specialized education, include the following:

*Elementary school objectives.* A report prepared for the Mid-Century Committee on Outcomes in Elementary Education by Noland C. Kearney. New York: Russell Sage Foundation, 1953.

*Developing a curriculum for modern living.* By F. B. Stratemeyer, H. L. Forkner, M. G. McKim, and others. New York: Bur. of Publications, Teachers College, Columbia Univer., 1947.

*A design for general education.* Edited by T. R. McConnell. Washington: Amer. Coun. on Educ., 1944.

*General education in a free society.* A report of the Harvard Committee of the Harvard University Commission on the Objectives of a General Education in a Free Society. Cambridge: Harvard Univer. Press, 1945.

*The idea and practice of general education: an account of the College of the University of Chicago.* By faculty of the College. Chicago: Univer. of Chicago Press, 1950. Copyright 1950 by the University of Chicago.

13. Examine a recent curriculum report in your field for possible aims.
14. What limitations can you see in deriving objectives solely from printed instructional materials and the ideas of subject specialists?

### The Taxonomy of Educational Objectives

A valuable source of ideas is *The Taxonomy of Educational Objectives,* one handbook of which has been worked out and is now available for a nominal sum (2). This reference contains a classification of objectives in the cognitive domain. It is assumed that the several categories form a progression from simple to complex, each category including the behaviors involved in those previous, yet going beyond them in complexity. The taxonomy for the cognitive domain appears below.

1.00  Knowledge
    1.10  Knowledge of specifics
        1.11  Knowledge of terminology
        1.12  Knowledge of specific facts
    1.20  Knowledge of ways and means of dealing with specifics
        1.21  Knowledge of conventions
        1.22  Knowledge of trends and sequences
        1.23  Knowledge of classifications and categories
        1.24  Knowledge of criteria
        1.25  Knowledge of methodology
    1.30  Knowledge of the universals and abstractions in a field
        1.31  Knowledge of principles and generalizations
        1.32  Knowledge of theories and structures
2.00  Comprehension
    2.10  Translation
    2.20  Interpretation
    2.30  Extrapolation
3.00  Application
4.00  Analysis
    4.10  Analysis of elements
    4.20  Analysis of relationships
    4.30  Analysis of organizational principles
5.00  Synthesis
    5.10  Production of a unique communication
    5.20  Production of a plan, or proposed set of operations
    5.30  Derivation of a set of abstract relations
6.00  Evaluation
    6.10  Judgments in terms of internal evidence
    6.20  Judgments in terms of external criteria

The handbook includes an analysis of these major categories, together with illustrative objectives and test items. Because of its comprehensiveness and because it describes objectives not widely emphasized, this reference should stimulate thinking about the range of possibilities for any course of study. It will have other important uses too.

### Review of evaluation instruments

One educator has described an achievement test as "an image of an image" (18). To him, not only is an educational objective a conception which is roughly approximate, but also the test designed to embody it.

With this characterization we can readily agree. In a very real sense, *an achievement test represents an attempt to translate abstract ideas about particular goals into concrete test situations.* The sample of test situations (exercises, items), together with the reactions they evoke, help define the goals in operational terms. Viewed in this way, tests can help us communicate more easily about particular objectives. Two instructors can generate a lot of heat in talking about the nature of "critical judgment in the arts," but they can avoid pointless discussion by agreeing upon the best sorts of exercises for revealing this ability.

Though an objective may be imperfectly conceived, it may be a highly significant one and the test of it an unusually good representation. If such is the case, there would be real value in examining the instrument to get a clearer conception of what the objective involves. A good test may thus prove to be an excellent source of ideas for instructional aims.

But how can an instructor know what a good test is in the first place? If the instrument is published, the chances are that it is reviewed in one of the *Mental Measurements Yearbooks* (3). These yearbooks contain fairly critical reviews of published instruments by two or more competent authorities. With few exceptions, reviewers pay special attention to the analysis and evaluation of *what* is being measured. Another source is the publisher's manual describing the instrument. Often this contains a helpful analysis of the objectives sampled. At the present time, however, these manuals fall short of the ideal. They do not contain all the information an instructor would need in order to judge adequately the nature of what is being measured. Ideally they should contain detailed information on the nature of the objectives sampled, their relative emphasis in the test, and the growth to be expected of various kinds of students (7). Such information can come only from more extensive research. All this is to say that the instructor needs also to use his own judgment when reviewing published tests. Many tests are so traditional or limited in conception that one can safely disregard them and pass on to newer types of instruments.

Additional ideas may be found in books on evaluation and in folios of problems and questions. Most of these sources contain analyses of objectives along with sample test materials. An annotated list of such references will be found on pages 233–36.

15. Below are two representative items from a recent test of arithmetic understanding (14).
   a) What sort of outcomes do these items emphasize?
   b) Are they different from those expected of you in your early schooling?
   c) Would these be desirable outcomes for a course in the teaching of arithmetic (intended for prospective elementary school teachers)?

Why can't you divide by zero?
   1. Zero is a place holder.
   2. You can't divide something by nothing. Zero is the same as nothing.
   3. Zero is not a quantity but a lack of it.
   4. In dividing you find how many times you can subtract the divisor from the dividend. If the divisor is zero, you have nothing to subtract.

The base of our number system is 10. What does that mean?
   1. After counting up to 10, all numbers have a constant relationship to each other.
   2. Each place in a number has a value 10 times as great as the one to the right of it.
   3. The basic unit of addition, subtraction, multiplication, and division is 10.
   4. All numbers revolve around 10.

16. A group of instructors responsible for teaching the same course has available a large and varied pool of examination questions.
   a) If the group has the problem of agreeing upon common objectives for the course, how could it use this pool to facilitate communication and agreement?
   b) What cautions must be observed in following such a procedure?

## Screening the suggested objectives

### Using philosophy

The preceding sources should yield a wealth of suggestions for objectives. In fact, they will normally yield many more goals than the school can possibly hope to attain. Furthermore, some of these goals will be more important than others; and some will be inconsistent with others in the sense that they call for contradictory patterns of behavior. Clearly the school must choose a smaller number of important and consistent goals than can be attained in the time available.

The educational and social philosophy to which the school is committed can serve as the first screen. Philosophy can help by providing a set of values against which particular objectives may be evaluated. Objectives that rank high on the scale of values stand a better chance of being selected than those that rank low or are inconsistent with it. But what are values in this case? In general, they are the essentials of a good life and a good society as the school conceives of these.

An educational and social philosophy, therefore, will answer several important questions of the following type:

What should be the essential elements of a good life?

Should the school prepare young people to accept the present social order, or should it encourage them to try to improve society?

Should different social groups or classes of society receive different kinds of education?

Should the school try to make people alike or should it cultivate idiosyncrasy?

Should the school emphasize general education, or should it aim at specific vocational preparation?

Different schools and social groups often answer these questions differently. The answers determine, to a large extent, how a school will value particular behavior patterns.

To see how philosophy can serve as a screen for choosing goals, let us consider the question: "Should the school prepare young people to accept the present social order, or should it encourage them to try to improve society?" If a school accepts the first alternative, it will emphasize conformity to the present forms and traditions, and skills in carrying on the present ways of living. Such a school may also emphasize mastery of fairly stable and well-organized bodies of subject matter on the assumption that there are certain essentials all pupils should acquire. If a school accepts the second alternative, it will emphasize sensitivity to social problems, skills in analyzing problems and proposing solutions, independence and self-direction, freedom of inquiry, and self-discipline. This issue, however, does not require an either-or commitment. Most schools will include objectives that help the student fit into society and some that enable him to take an active part in improving it. But in most American communities today there are strong feelings as to how far the school should go in either direction.

As a second, and more specific, illustration of how philosophy functions, let us refer to the program of general education of the College of the University of Chicago. There are several good reasons for referring to this program. It is, first of all, a program built upon an *explicit* philosophy of education (26, 29). This is, in itself, quite unusual in higher education. This philosophy permeates the entire program: in the choice of objectives, in the design of the curriculum, in the choice of teaching materials and methods, and in the development of comprehensive examinations for evaluating student progress. The program, moreover, represents so radical a departure from traditional programs of liberal education, with respect to *all* of the features listed above, that it deserves study on this account alone. Finally, it represents an important contribution to the general education movement. It has already influenced general education at the college level, and it should markedly influence general education at the high school level. This is not to say that it is an ideal program for all schools and colleges; only that there are many features in it worth adapting elsewhere.

What specifically are the philosophical tenets of this program, and to what educational ends and means do they lead? The three main tenets are as follows:

1. *A liberal, general education is desirable for everyone, whatever occupation or profession he expects to enter.* Back of this value judgment lie the usual arguments: that the success of our democracy depends ultimately upon the wisdom of our people (and hence that wisdom be widely possessed); and that to reach his fullest potentialities the individual needs more than a narrowly vocational education. These potentialities include: the development of social and political wisdom; the capacity to understand, appreciate, and enjoy the products of man's creative activity in literature, music, and art; and man's capacity for reflective thought concerning the nature of the universe, and of man's place and role in it (29, p. 7).

2. *The main purpose of a liberal, general education is to teach students how to think for themselves, rather than to provide them with a mass of information on a host of subjects or with a set of general truths.* To quote an official statement:

. . . It is not the purpose . . . to instruct members of the rising generation what to think but, rather, to teach them how to think. Its purpose is not indoctrination but the development of power to form sound judgments with respect to those questions which are the concern of everyone. . . . It has not been thought sufficient in the application of this principle to develop the student's powers of logic in the sense of teaching him either to avoid common logical fallacies or to analyze in terms of formal logic his own or other people's arguments. It is not a matter, so to speak, of developing a smartly functioning logical machine. What is required in general education can best be described by the term "wisdom" rather than by the popular term "straight thinking"; for what students need is not merely guidance in avoiding error, or even smoothness in mental operations, but the competence to establish an adequate relation of the mind to the things which it undertakes to grasp. This kind of competence, like skill in swimming, cannot be developed by learning rules but only by exercise; and, since the methods by which problems regarding the natural world are formulated and resolved differ from the formulation and resolution of problems in the interpretation of lyric poetry—and both of these differ from the methods of formulating ethical standards—education in the formation of sound judgments in these various areas requires practice in thinking about different subject matters (**29**, pp. 17–18).[5]

And again:

. . . A good college program must do more than provide a survey of the present state of knowledge. The body of that knowledge is not only vast but constantly changing. It is more important that a college student learn how knowledge is acquired and tested in any field than that he memorize a body of currently accepted information. It is more important, for example, that a college student learn what kinds of problems the physicist investigates, how he formulates them, and by what methods he seeks to solve them, than that he memorize a set of generally accepted facts or theories of physics. Knowledge worth the name must be more than a memory of facts and of favored interpretations of facts. It involves an understanding of the ways in which facts are acquired and the processes of reasoning by which they have been interpreted. All real knowledge includes a grasp of reasons.

The special function of a college is to teach people . . . how to reflect on what they read, how to discover and estimate the premises of arguments offered to them, and how to identify and test the conclusions of these arguments. Students do not fully understand a fact or theory until they have examined the reasons for holding it and are able to justify accepting or rejecting it . . . (**26**, p. 5).[6]

3. *A liberal, general education should deal with the major areas of human knowledge—the humanities, the social sciences, and the natural sciences—and with their interrelations.* This philosophy recognizes—

. . . that the subject matter, the methods, and the aims of disciplines which have come historically to be dealt with in separate academic departments fall into certain groups having fundamental and essential traits in common and that these common traits make possible a treatment broader than that of individual, academic departments. Physics and chemistry from this point of view fall together; so do anatomy, physiology, botany, and zoology; so, too, do political science, sociology, economics, and anthropology; so, likewise, do literature, art, and music. The members of these

[5] Reproduced by permission of the University of Chicago Press.
[6] Reproduced by permission of the University of Chicago Press.

groups fall together by reason of certain basic likenesses, while the groups themselves are separated by basic differences. The area of knowledge commonly assigned the social sciences is related to a subject matter different from that of the natural sciences, in that what is examined in the social sciences is the product of man's desires, intentions, thoughts, and activities, rather than the product of forces outside man. Moreover, a common purpose animates the work of the social sciences—that of determining what is best, or at least better, in human activities and in the institutions which men devise. The methods of the social sciences for acquiring knowledge of this subject for this purpose have, therefore, certain basic likenesses by contrast with those of the natural sciences (**29**, p. 15).[7]

Thus, it is believed that the approach through broad fields will bring about a broader and better integrated education, avoiding the fragmentation that comes from taking an array of departmentalized courses. It is further believed *essential* for the student to acquire a grasp of the problems, methods, and aims basic to *each* of these major areas. Therefore he pursues a *prescribed* curriculum designed to give the breadth and depth of education which this college values.

Language and mathematics are also a part of this prescribed curriculum, for it is believed that the educated man should have more than a passing competence in these forms of expression and communication. Here the student should master the *idea* of language and the *idea* of mathematics, the two disciplines which undergird the humanities, the social sciences, and the natural sciences.

So much for the philosophy of the college. Now for a review of the educational ends and means to which this philosophy leads.

   I. *ENDS*

      One all-embracing end is basic: the development of "the competence to establish an adequate relation of the mind to the things which it undertakes to grasp" (**29**, p. 17).

      From this, major objectives emerge in connection with each of the courses. Though not the primary objective, knowledge of facts, principles, and methods assumes an importance in every course in the program.

  II. *MEANS*

     A. *Curriculum*

      An integrated sequence of general courses required of all students in the basic college. (These are *not* survey courses; neither are they Great Books courses—although great books are studied in some of the courses.) The philosophy rejects the traditional highly specialized course for purposes of general education.

[7] Reproduced by permission of the University of Chicago Press.

B. *Instructional materials*

Original works in the major fields of human knowledge. This includes master-pieces of literature, art, and music; significant social writings; great experiments in science, and so on.

Textbook plays a secondary role; if used at all, it is used to provide background information.

C. *Instructional methods*

Critical interpretation, analysis, and evaluation of original works through discussion methods. In the laboratory sciences, also performance or demonstration of crucial experiments.

Lectures play a secondary role; if given at all, they are given to provide a background for the discussions to follow.

Emphasis throughout is upon practice in effective thinking and expression.

III. *EVALUATION*

A system of comprehensive examinations designed to evaluate progress toward the attainment of the objectives. The examinations emphasize demonstrated competence, and so make considerable use of *unfamiliar* as well as familiar materials. The examinations also emphasize the integration of experience, both within a field and across several fields, since this is an explicit aim of the program.

In addition, the college utilizes other procedures such as interviews, questionnaire surveys, and experiments to determine the effectiveness of the means for attaining the ends.

In summary, our primary purpose in reviewing this extended illustration is to see how philosophy functions in the choice of educational objectives and in the choice of means for attaining them. Our purpose is not to set up one type of general education as the ideal. We could, with profit, bring in illustrations from other schools or colleges to show how differences in philosophy lead to differences in objectives and practices. Suffice it to say that some schools and colleges emphasize a philosophy of individual development, others emphasize the social role of the institution in preparing young persons to take useful places in society, and still others blend a variety of considerations into their philosophy. What philosophy a school follows will determine, more or less, the objectives which it seeks to accomplish with its students.

17. Considerations other than the philosophical helped shape the Chicago plan of general education just presented. One of these was the very superior intellectual ability of the student body. Another was the nature of the society into which these students would eventually go. Identify those particulars in the Chicago statement which were based on a con-

ception of the nature of society rather than a conception of the good life or some similar philosophical focus.

18. Do you agree with the following statement? "It is just as important to delete possible aims from a list as it is to add them."

19. Should instructors in social studies or human relations courses try to alter the social attitudes of their students—for example, in the direction of greater liberalism and tolerance?

20. Can you think of an instance where two instructors teaching the same subject emphasized different aims because they embraced different educational or social philosophies?

21. Apart from serving as a screen for sorting out objectives, can philosophy also serve as an original source of ideas for objectives?

## Using the psychology of learning

The psychology of learning and human development can serve as the second screen for selecting and eliminating goals. What we need most of all are good answers to the following questions:

To what extent is growth toward the objective a function of general maturation or general intelligence rather than of instruction?

Can the objective be readily attained at the given level of maturity?

At what levels of maturity are particular objectives best attained?

What is the optimum growth which may be expected of different kinds of students with respect to the objectives?

What is the retention value of different types of outcomes? Are some more lasting than others?

What is the transfer value of different types of outcomes? Are some more widely transferable than others?

Does the attainment of the objective tend to correlate highly with that of other objectives?

At the present time, we do not have good answers to all of these questions. There are serious gaps in research. But we do have some significant findings upon which to base our choice of aims.

The first question is put at the top of the list because it is fundamental. It asks whether the kind of growth an instructor expects to bring about is really a *proper* educational goal; that is, something which *requires* deliberate cultivation and does not come about through general maturation. Though this may seem to be a farfetched question, there is some evidence to challenge commonly accepted notions about certain forms of school achievement. The researches of Courtis are especially challenging (4, 5).

In one study he traced the rate of growth of spelling ability, as illustrated in Figure 1.

As the figure shows, there is little difference in the growth curves for the two words, one of which was taught as a regular part of the spelling lessons and the other was not. On the basis of these and other data, Courtis contends that it is maturation, not teaching, which accounts for the simi-

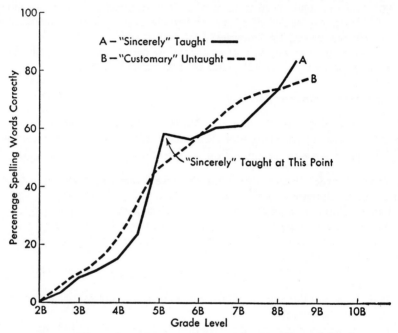

Fig. 1. Effect of teaching on the growth of spelling ability *

larity in the shape of growth curves for spelling, vocabulary, reading comprehension, and arithmetic. A few other investigators add corrobora-tive evidence (15, 16). Even earlier, T. L. Kelley found that whatever is measured by a general achievement test battery (covering the above mental functions) is pretty much what is measured by a general intelli-gence test (13).

Studies such as these compel us to re-examine our ideas about the development of *general comprehension and reasoning with language and*

* (Reproduced by permission of the Macmillan Company, from a redrawing in *Educational Psychology* by G. M. Blair and others.)

*number.* If, as the studies suggest, so much of this development represents the effects of maturation rather than the effects of teaching, then there is serious question about deliberately trying to stimulate such growth. This is not to deny the importance of educative experience. Experience with language and number is necessary before facility with them can develop. But the rate at which individuals develop and the levels which they ultimately attain in such general abilities appear to be genetically determined. If this is so, then programs of general education in late adolescence are especially open to criticism if they include among their objectives such highly general abilities.

A knowledge of psychological findings on the attainability of objectives is also quite helpful. It can help us distinguish goals that are reasonably attainable from those that are likely to take a very long time or be practically unattainable at the given maturity level. The nursery or primary school, for example, may well aim at desirable changes in personality structure since the latter is somewhat alterable at that age level. But the high school or college may find such an objective unrealistic. By late adolescence, so much of personality development has taken place that re-education becomes a very difficult task and unlikely to be attained through a normal school program. Social attitudes are also difficult to alter. Profound changes are not likely to occur in a few months.

A realistic concern for attainability of objectives can forestall a common error. This error is likely to happen when instructors and faculty committees try, for the first time, to formulate goals. What often happens is that they formulate many more than students can possibly attain in the time available. A sounder approach is to list a few well-chosen objectives than to try to do too much. Sometimes even a single objective, such as the ability to read and evaluate articles on scientific developments, when further analyzed, will embrace most of the other aims fundamental to a well-planned course of study (8, p. 297).

With respect to the placement of objectives at particular maturity levels, research has mapped out fairly well where different things should be taught. Research shows that it is unrealistic to try to place particular experiences at a single grade or maturity level. Better to think in terms of a range of grades or maturity levels.

Findings on the sequence of learning are likely to be more helpful than those on grade placement as such. Thus, although we may not be able to place certain objectives at given grade or maturity levels, we may be able to determine the *sequence* in which they should be attained. For example, objectives emphasizing careful interpretation and analysis of literary works must surely wait until students have developed a good vocabulary and sufficient skill in reading, as well as some interest in such activities.

On the question of optimum growth to be expected, we have precious little information to go by. Before-and-after studies of educational progress are relatively rare, and those that have been conducted offer little information on the *optimum growth* to be expected of *different kinds of students* with respect to given objectives. It is hoped that this deficiency will be corrected so that instructors can have a better understanding of what kinds of growth to expect of students at different aptitude levels.

Studies on the retention value of different outcomes are also scarce. However, the few which have been done are quite suggestive. Tyler's studies are outstanding (19, 20). They show that knowledge of specific information is not a very lasting outcome of instruction. In one study Tyler gave a zoology test to a college class at the start of the course, at the end of the course, and one year later during which they studied no zoology. The results in Table 1 show that the ability retained for the

### Table 1

### Retention of different outcomes of zoology
#### (after 20, p. 76)

| Type of Examination Exercise | Mean Score | | | Per Cent of Gain Which Was Later Lost |
|---|---|---|---|---|
| | START OF COURSE | END OF COURSE | ONE YEAR LATER | |
| 1. Naming animal structures pictured in diagrams | 22 | 62 | 31 | 77 |
| 2. Identifying technical terms | 20 | 83 | 67 | 26 |
| 3. Recalling information | | | | |
| a. Structures performing functions in type forms | 13 | 39 | 34 | 21 |
| b. Other facts | 21 | 63 | 54 | 21 |
| 4. Applying principles to new situations | 35 | 65 | 65 | 0 |
| 5. Interpreting new experiments | 30 | 57 | 64 | 25 [a] |
| Average for all exercises | 24 | 74 | 63 | 22 |

[a] The percentage set in italics was a permanent gain.

longest period of time was that to apply principles to new situations and to draw conclusions from new data. These findings suggest that the latter two types of ability, because of their more enduring value, are as much worth cultivating, or more so, as is the acquisition of information.

On the transfer value of different outcomes, our knowledge is unusually good. Here the psychology of learning has much to offer the instructor who seeks guidance on the choice of objectives. A vast amount of research spread out over several decades has rather fully clarified how transfer takes place and what kinds of learning transfer best. We know that, other things being equal, the more widely useful an outcome of instruction, the greater its transfer value. Hence, priority should generally be given to those facts, concepts, principles, skills, and attitudes which have the greatest transfer value. The mathematics teacher who emphasized the ability to factor complex algebraic expressions overlooked this consideration. On the other hand, the leaders of the general education movement have taken it quite seriously. They have given highest priority to objectives emphasizing generalized modes of thinking because they believe that these outcomes have wide application in all kinds of life situations.

Finally, the psychology of learning sheds light on the correlation of outcomes. Whenever we formulate a list of objectives, we imply that the distinctions drawn are valid. We assume that the several objectives really do represent somewhat different things. Otherwise, there would be no point in listing them separately. A list of objectives, for instance, may include the acquisition of information, the ability to apply this information to new situations, and the ability to draw inferences from new data. The question now is whether these are really different types of outcome or whether they really all belong together under the category of knowledge. Twenty-five years ago Tyler sought the answer to this question (22). In numerous courses at Ohio State University, he correlated tests supposed to measure different types of outcomes. He found rather low correlations between scores on information and scores on application, between scores on information and scores on inference, and between scores on application and scores on inference. Since students did not develop corresponding degrees of ability in these three types of outcome, Tyler concluded that, in courses of this kind at least, the three types of outcome are not the same thing. The educational implications of his findings are twofold:

1. It is necessary in teaching to aim explicitly at each of these major objectives, rather than to assume that the development of ability to think arises from the acquisition of information.

2. It is necessary in evaluation to develop tests for each of the important objectives in a course rather than to assume that an information test by itself will measure all important forms of intellectual ability.

An extensive study by the writer supports Tyler's findings and conclusions (11). However, there is evidence to the contrary and the issue may not yet be settled. Remmers and Gage review several of the pertinent studies that bear on this issue (17, pp. 28–31). They caution that the degree of correlation is not absolute but depends upon several important factors, such as the way a course was taught, the degree of similarity between the original learning situations and the test situations, the age or maturity of the learners, and the inaccuracy of the measuring instruments. Nonetheless, their conclusion is similar to the second point made above.

Every instructor and every school should also formulate and use a defensible theory of learning. The theory should consider the conditions under which learning best takes place, the role of student interests, some conception of the instructor's functions, and so on. The particular theory held will influence the choice of objectives. If one holds to the theory that group problem-solving represents an efficient form of learning experience, he will value highly such aims as cooperativeness, willingness to tolerate other people's ideas, ability to sense how others will react, and ability to fill various roles in small group activities. If one does not view group learning in this way, he will probably not place such aims high on his list.

22. A science teacher outlined the following objectives for a one-year general science course:

    a) Important functional knowledge and understandings.
    b) Useful work habits and study skills.
    c) Effective methods of thinking.
    d) Manipulative and motor skills useful in everyday life.
    e) Emotional appreciation and sensitivity.
    f) Wide range of significant interests.
    g) Desirable social and scientific attitudes.
    h) Better personal-social adjustment and a consistent philosophy of life.

Each of these he further subdivided into three or four important categories, e.g., c)—ability to interpret data; ability to use the scientific method in problem solving; ability to apply principles of science. How would his statement have differed had he based it on a knowledge of the psychology of learning?

23. Studies on learning have repeatedly shown that there may be a disjunction between knowledge or ability to think and the *disposition* to

apply these to everyday situations. What implications does this fact have for the formulation of educational goals?

24. Give a few illustrations of broad objectives that cut across two or more subject fields.

   a) To what extent should a school appraise the student's integration of learning (knowledge, abilities, attitudes, values, etc.) across subject fields?

   b) What implications would such an approach have for evaluation practices?

25. Formulate a list of general goals for a course or unit of instruction.

   a) Indicate what sources of evidence you took into account in deciding upon your list.

   b) Justify each goal on the basis of its importance for the intended group and subject.

   c) Indicate whether you believe the list to be comprehensive enough for the course or unit.

### Teacher-student planning and self-selection

The generalized procedure which has now been presented is a procedure for those who have responsibility for planning courses or curricula. It may seem that we have left the student and his purposes out of the process. This is not true, in one sense, since student needs and interests can be taken into account in curriculum planning.

Teacher-student planning is a further process by which instructor and students can work together to plan learning activities. The strategy is to capitalize on the students' immediate purposes, and at the same time to reach the broader objectives which the instructor seeks. This strategy is further supported by the fact that the same set of objectives can generally be attained through a variety of learning activities.

An instructor exercises least control over goal selection when the student selects activities and materials on his own. A process of self-selection takes place when the learner is free to use the resources of his environment in line with capacities, needs, and satisfactions that are self-defined. This principle seems to come out most clearly at the early ages, when biological growth forces markedly influence behavior. Thus, there is some evidence that children do tend to seek experiences in line with their individual growth needs (15). Studies of reading show that when children are allowed to choose their own reading materials and to consume them at their own rates, they do so in accordance with their own individual growth needs. The principle of self-selection can apply to higher age levels too, but the demands of society are likely to make its application more difficult there.

Teacher-student planning and self-selection thus bring us down to the concrete activities of the learner. It is at this level that the learner's purposes should come to the fore. There is no necessary conflict between these purposes and the broader objectives to which the instructor and school commit themselves.

## STATING THE OBJECTIVES IN GENERAL TERMS

### Illustrations of general objectives

As a result of following a systematic approach such as was outlined, an instructor or staff will normally come out with a small list of important objectives. Two examples of such a list of general objectives appear below. It must not be assumed that each list is ideal for the given course. Another instructor or another staff might well have formulated a somewhat different list for the same type of course.

#### American History

1. Knowledge of important facts in American history.
2. Ability to summarize trends and to make generalizations from American history.
3. Ability to judge relations between events, trends, and conditions in American history.
4. Skill in reading, analyzing, and evaluating discussions of social issues.
5. Ability to relate knowledge of American history to discussions of social issues.

#### First-year French

1. To acquire a good pronunciation.
2. To become acquainted with French expressions commonly used in English: on radio, in newspapers, magazines, and books.
3. To understand English expressions derived from, or related to, French.
4. To master the principles of grammar and the vocabulary necessary to read, write, speak, and understand the French taught in this course.
5. To recognize the contributions of the French people to world culture and especially to our democratic way of life.
6. To become an understanding and appreciative friend of the French people through a study of their geography, history, customs, spirit, ideals, and problems (28).

## Suggestions for stating objectives

1. *State the objectives clearly in terms of behavior*. Each statement of an objective should imply a particular kind of behavior on the part of the student. For, as we noted, an objective is not something the instructor does; nor is it an element of subject matter.

2. *State the objectives at the right level of generality*. Objectives should not be so general as to be vague, nor so specific as to be fragmentary. Moreover, the several objectives should be of the same level of generality.

3. *Be sure that the objectives in the list do not overlap*. That is, the several categories of behavior should be kept relatively independent. Group together those objectives which belong together.

26. Examine each of the following miscellaneous aims, indicating in what respects it is satisfactory or unsatisfactory as a statement of a general objective.

    a) To become a participating citizen in school and community. (H.s. social studies)

    b) To be able to explain or demonstrate different rhythmic patterns in music and to follow melodic patterns or tunes in music. (Elem. sch. music)

    c) To help students better recognize their abilities and capacities and to work as nearly as possible to maximum ability. (H.s. guidance program)

    d) To be able to understand maps. (Elem. sch. social studies)

    e) To be able to understand more fully today's problems from a study of the past; to profit from past experience. (Jr. h.s. core course—Amer. History and Institutions)

    f) To develop a better personality. (H.s. English)

    g) To have an appreciation of the importance of graphic representation in everyday life, and the ability to use the graphical method as a valuable mathematical tool. (H.s. algebra)

    h) To be able to understand nonliteral statements (metaphor, symbolism, irony, exaggeration) in work of literature. (College course in English literature)

27. How could this list of general goals for fifth-grade arithmetic be improved?

    1. To help pupils find the facts, question, and choose the correct operation in solving a problem.

    2. To develop attitude of respect for accuracy, good workmanship, and knowledge.

3. To provide practice, self-diagnosis, and remedial work required to make learning permanent.

4. To develop the ability to read for understanding.

5. To furnish knowledge of the development of numbers and of weights and measures as a basis for better understanding of civilization.

6. To develop the important concepts, vocabulary, skills, and relationships needed for success in problem solving.

7. To develop and increase skill in arithmetical computation.

8. To develop a sensitiveness to numbers in social situations and the habit of using numbers effectively in such situations.

9. To desire to learn more about arithmetic and its application.

## REFERENCES

1. Bloom, B. S., and Broder, L. J. *Problem-solving processes of college students: An exploratory investigation.* Chicago: Univer. of Chicago, 1950. Copyright 1950 by The University of Chicago.

2. Bloom, B. S., Engelhart, M. D., Furst, E. J., Hill, W. H., and Krathwohl, D. R. *Taxonomy of educational objectives, handbook I:* cognitive domain. New York: Longmans Green, 1956.

3. Buros, O. K. (Ed.) *The fourth mental measurements yearbook.* Highland Park, N. J.: Gryphon, 1953.

4. Courtis, S. A., Maturation as a factor in diagnosis. *Yearb.,* Nat. Soc. Stud. Educ., 1935, **34**, 169–198.

5. Courtis, S. A. The rate of growth makes a difference. *Phi delta kappan,* 1949, **30**, 316–323.

6. Diederich, P. B. An ethical basis for educational objectives. *Sch. Rev.,* 1951, **59**, 78–86.

7. Dressel, P. L. Information which should be provided by test publishers and testing agencies on the validity and use of their tests: achievement tests. In *Proc. 1949 Invit. Conf. on Test. Probs.* Princeton: Educ. Test. Serv., 1950.

8. Dressel, P. L. Are your objectives showing? *Nat. Educ. Ass. J.,* 1955, **44**, 297–298.

9. Flanagan, J. C. (Ed.). *The aviation psychology program in the Army Air Forces;* AAF Aviation Psychol. Prog. Res. Rep. No. 1. Washington: U. S. Govt. Print. Ofc., 1948.

10. Flanagan, J. C. Measuring research effectiveness. In *Proc. of the Conf. on Scient. Manpower,* 118th Meeting of the American Ass. for the Advancement of Science, Philadelphia, 1951. Washington: Ofc. of Naval Res., 1951. Pp. 74–80.

11. Furst, E. J. Effect of the organization of learning experiences upon the organization of learning outcomes. *J. exp. Educ.,* 1950, **18**, 215–228, 343–352.

12. Havighurst, R. J. *Developmental tasks and education.* Chicago: Univer. of Chicago, 1948. Copyright 1948 by the University of Chicago.
13. Kelley, T. L. *Interpretation of educational measurements.* Yonkers: World Book, 1927.
14. Lindberg, Lucile, and Orleans, J. S. *Lindberg-Orleans test of arithmetic understanding.* (Prelim. Ed.) To be published by Houghton Mifflin Company, New York.
15. Olson, W. C. *Child development.* Boston: Heath, 1949.
16. Olson, W. C., and Hughes, B. O. Concepts of growth: their significance to teachers. *Childh. Educ.,* 1944, **21**, 53–63.
17. Remmers, H. H., and Gage, N. L. *Educational measurement and evaluation* (Rev. Ed.). New York: Harper, 1955.
18. Schwab, J. J. Criteria for the evaluation of achievement tests: from the point of view of the subject-matter specialist. In *Proc. 1950 Invit. Conf. on Test. Probs.* Princeton: Educ. Test. Serv., 1951.
19. Tyler, R. W. What high school pupils forget. *Educ. Res. Bull.,* 1930, **9**, 490–492.
20. Tyler, R. W. Permanence of learning. *J. higher Educ.,* 1933, **4**, 203–204.
21. Tyler, R. W. Characteristics of a satisfactory diagnosis. *Yearb.,* Nat. Soc. Stud. Educ., 1935, **34**, 95–111.
22. Tyler, R. W. The relation between recall and higher mental processes. In Judd, C. H., and others. *Education as cultivation of the higher mental processes.* New York: Macmillan, 1936. Pp. 6–17.
23. Tyler, R. W. Basic assumptions which guide my work in educational measurement. In *Research on the foundations of American education,* Official report, Amer. Educ. Res. Ass. Washington: 1939. Pp. 139–140.
24. Tyler, R. W. *Basic principles of curriculum and instruction.* Chicago: Univer. of Chicago, 1950. Copyright 1950 by the University of Chicago.
25. Wrenn, C. G. *Manual of directions, Study-Habits inventory.* Stanford Univer.: Stanford Univer., 1941.
26. *Announcements: the College.* Chicago: Univer. of Chicago, 1952. Copyright 1952 by the University of Chicago.
27. *Critical requirements for research personnel.* Pittsburgh: Amer. Inst. for Res., 1949.
28. *Foreign languages in the Atlanta community high school.* Atlanta Board of Education. (Mimeo.)
29. *The idea and practice of general education:* an account of the College of the University of Chicago. By faculty of the College. Chicago: Univer. of Chicago, 1950. Copyright 1950 by the University of Chicago.

## FURTHER READINGS

Bloom, B. S., and others. *Taxonomy of educational objectives, handbook I:* cognitive domain. New York: Longmans Green, 1956.

Dressel, P. L., and Mayhew, L. B. Selected chapters. *General education:* explorations in evaluation. Washington: Amer. Coun. on Educ., 1954.

Lindquist, E. F. The selection of objectives. In E. F. Lindquist (Ed.), *Educational measurement.* Washington: Amer. Coun. on Educ., 1951. Pp. 121–141.

Smith, Huston. The aims of liberal education. *The purposes of higher education.* New York: Harper, 1955. Pp. 149–205.

Travers, R. M. W. Rational hypotheses in the construction of tests. *Educ. Psychol. Measmt.,* 1951, 11, 128–137.

# Defining the Behavior

Thus far, we have tackled the problem of determining what
to evaluate. Since efforts to meet this problem will normally result
in rather abstract formulations, such as a statement of educational objectives, it is necessary to consider a closely related problem. This is the
problem of defining in behavioral terms whatever objectives or qualities
we want to evaluate.

To bring out the distinction between the problem treated in this chapter
and that in the preceding, let us note the requirements which a useful
definition should meet. A clear set of specifications to satisfy these
requirements:

1. *Should include all the more important aspects of behavior related to the problem of evaluation.*
2. *Should specify the kinds of responses that may be accepted as evidence of these
   aspects of behavior.*
3. *Should specify the limiting conditions under which these responses are likely to
   take place.*

**57**

If we have followed procedures like those outlined in Chapter 2, then probably we have already met the first of these requirements. We may, in fact, have carried our analysis further than that, perhaps to the point of listing specific types of responses under the broader headings. If this is so, we may also have met the second requirement. Note that this was done in the study on problem-solving and also in the study on scientific work.

The point is that when we begin to determine what to evaluate, we have then begun this process of definition. *But determining what to evaluate is more than mere definition, since it involves isolating the critical aspects of behavior.*

If our analysis has not carried us much beyond the first requirement above, then we have more work to do. This chapter treats ways of meeting the second and third requirements. In addition, it considers some other decisions that must often be made before the actual development and administration of an evaluation instrument.

To readers who approach this book with a specific interest in test development as such, not all of these further decisions may seem important or even relevant at this stage. However, it should be clear that what information a test yields will depend as much upon the conditions under which it is given and upon the criteria adopted for scoring or summarizing the evidence, as upon the test materials themselves. Also, it should be clear that we are discussing problems common to a broad range of techniques, not just to paper-and-pencil tests, and that some of these considerations are more critical for other techniques, such as direct observation.

## SPECIFYING THE KINDS OF RESPONSES

### How far to carry the analysis

It is common in many courses to state a general aim of this sort: "Knowledge and understanding of basic principles. . . ." To some persons, this statement may perhaps seem clear enough; to others, not at all. Much ambiguity would reside in the term "understanding." This term can be, and is, stretched to include just about any kind of intelligent act from the simplest to the most complex. Although the word "understanding" occurs frequently in statements of objectives, it does not convey any clear-cut, uniform meaning.

Almost any statement of a general aim suffers from some ambiguity, so that further analysis is both necessary and desirable. Consider the general aim, "Knowledge and understanding of principles of mental hygiene." How should this be further defined so that we may have a clearer conception of what is involved? This is how one instructor preferred to define it for his course (a principle is given for illustration):

1. Knowledge and understanding of principles of mental hygiene (e.g.: Opportunities should be provided for individuals to release their emotional tensions harmlessly rather than hold them in.)—
   1.1 To be able to state in one's own words the important principles.
   1.2 To be able to tell in one's own words what each principle means and to give an illustration of each.
   1.3 To be able to tell why the principle is considered important and sound by mental hygiene specialists.
   1.4 To recognize that each principle is a tentative generalization, subject to modification as fresh evidence comes in.

Evidently for this instructor, knowledge and understanding means more than verbatim recall. For him it must involve some restatement on the part of the student, some illustration drawn from personal experience, and some explanation of the significance and soundness of a principle. Had he stopped his analysis at 1.1, or even 1.2, there would be serious question as to whether it included all the more important ways a student should demonstrate his understanding. As it is, the analysis could have been extended to include specifics involving application of principles to concrete situations. But these additional types of response could be covered as well under a separate general aim.

One important consideration, then, is that such an analysis be reasonably comprehensive. It should include specifics that are sufficiently representative of the intended general area of behavior.

Another important consideration is that the specifics be clear-cut. Wherever possible, they must refer to identifiable behaviors. In this illustration, the behaviors for the most part involve stating or telling, and hence they would be readily identifiable. The analysis does not make clear whether the student is to express himself orally or in writing. Perhaps it is assumed that the mode of response would ordinarily be written. Trivial as this point may seem, at some educational levels mode of response may make a significant difference in individual cases. There are some individuals who could only demonstrate their grasp of a principle by being allowed to express themselves orally rather than in writing. At those levels, the definition should make clear the mode(s) of response.

It is possible to increase clarity by continuing one's analysis with more and more specifics. As valuable as this seems, it has limits. Some of the additional specifics may be only minor variations of others already on the list. This merely increases the verbiage without really adding to clarity. But more important, too detailed an analysis may give the impression that the specific aspects of behavior are highly independent when in reality they may not be.

A pertinent example of overanalysis is to break reading comprehension down into many specific abilities, somewhat as follows:

Ability to follow directions
 "  " note details
 "  " find antecedents of words and phrases
 "  " follow the organization or sequence of ideas
 "  " see a relationship
 "  " infer a relationship
 "  " determine the writer's point of view
 "  " determine the writer's purpose
And so on.

While the listing of specifics such as these may be helpful for suggesting specific test questions—e.g., "What point of view does the author take on protective tariffs?"—it creates the impression that reading comprehension is a composite of many independent skills. This does not seem to be the case. There is good evidence that it is a highly generalized ability, manifesting itself rather uniformly through a variety of specific operations such as those detailed above (7, 12). Unfamiliar or technical subject matter, however, does cut down on the generalization of this ability, a point on which we will have more to say. For the moment, let us extend the idea brought out just previously: some abilities and traits are so generalized that it is *un*necessary to try to list all of the important ways or situations in which they can occur.

Too detailed an analysis also runs the risk of leading to a fragmented kind of evaluation, that is, to the testing of highly specific reactions rather than of some larger and more important complex. Such a complex is skill in reading, analyzing, and evaluating discussions of social issues. One major aspect of this complex involves ability to evaluate evidence or authority for conclusions. This, in turn, can be broken down into a number of specifics such as ability to distinguish between verifiable and unverifiable data. Value judgments and opinions, for instance, are usually unverifiable, whereas material of a factual nature is capable of proof or disproof. Now given such a breakdown of specifics, it is possible to frame a series of items each of which tests for one of these specifics but does so in isolation from the others, without reference to any common body of background material. While there may be occasions for which such isolated testing of specifics is useful, something of the wholeness of the original complex task (general objective above) is here lost.

Nevertheless, there are occasions when a detailed analysis of objectives is important. This is especially true of diagnostic studies of arithmetic, reading (including perceptual aspects), written composition, and other processes. The usual purpose of such studies is to locate specific difficulties that students are having. Because the difficulties may stem from many sources, the diagnosis has to be correspondingly comprehensive and detailed. Hence, it is important to analyze the larger complex into simpler part processes.

In summary, the answer to the question—How far to carry the analysis?—will depend mainly upon the following considerations:

1. *The importance of certain specific types of response,* as educational outcomes in their own right or as component parts highly indicative of success or failure in a larger complex activity. The specifics should be sufficiently representative so as to give a comprehensive picture of the general area of behavior under study.

2. *The vagueness or generality of the original statement.* Much more analysis is necessary for those statements of objectives which are highly general to begin with. To communicate the right meaning to other persons, such as students or colleagues, the analysis should be carried to the point where they will know what specific behaviors to accept as evidence of the larger attribute.

3. *Practicability.* There is little point in making a detailed analysis of some behavior unless one will also have the means to collect evidence of it. Since a detailed appraisal is often so time-consuming or so expensive in equipment and resources, a detailed analysis may be uncalled for.

> 1. What else needs specification in the statement, "Knowledge and understanding of principles of mental hygiene"?

## How to define the behavior

We have had an inkling now of what it means to define an educational objective or similar characteristic in behavioral terms. This is necessary because most terms or short phrases are too general to convey any precise meaning.

Many terms that we use refer to covert processes, that is, to reactions that take place inside the skin. Feelings of confidence or inferiority, feelings of frustration, a strong desire to take part in some activity, satisfaction in a job well done—these are reactions that we cannot see. Yet we can recognize signs of them. And we know they occur in others because we've experienced them ourselves. So too with acts of comprehension. None of these are directly observable, but we can infer them from their *effects*—related reactions, such as a down-in-the-mouth look; or products, such as a written answer to a thought question. Inside-the-skin reactions, especially feelings, are important for educational purposes. We should make an effort to define them. In most cases it is possible to list other responses that are good signs of the subjective feelings or the thought processes. This has been done in the example below. The authors list overt acts and verbal responses which they will accept as evidence of "appreciation of literature" (11, p. 251).

1. Satisfaction in the thing appreciated
    1.1 He reads aloud to others, or simply to himself, passages which he finds unusually interesting.
    1.2 He reads straight through without stopping, or with a minimum of interruption.
    1.3 He reads for considerable periods of time.
2. Desire for more of the thing appreciated
    2.1 He asks other people to recommend reading which is more or less similar to the thing appreciated.
    2.2 He commences this reading of similar things as soon after reading the first as possible.
    2.3 He reads subsequently several books, plays, or poems by the same author.
3. Desire to know more about the thing appreciated
    3.1 He asks other people for information or sources of information about what he has read.
    3.2 He reads supplementary materials, such as biography, history, criticism, etc.
    3.3 He attends literary meetings devoted to reviews, criticism, discussions, etc.[1]

(The list continues with four other types of behavior, which are omitted here.)

This outline illustrates a common procedure for defining educational goals or characteristics of behavior. We list the kinds of responses which we are willing to accept as evidence of the particular characteristic. The list then functions as a set of signs, or indicators. Each sign points to, and

[1] By permission from *Appraising and Recording Student Progress*, by E. R. Smith, R. W. Tyler, and others. Copyright, 1942. McGraw-Hill Book Company, Inc.

helps define, the larger attribute that concerns us. It should be possible to define any educational goal or psychological characteristic in this way. If we cannot do this, then for practical purposes the goal or characteristic is meaningless. We then do not know what evidence to look for, nor do we know what responses to cultivate in students.

Another way is to write out an analysis of the behavior. This is also very common. To illustrate, let us again turn to the volume by Tyler and others (11, pp. 38–41). Here the authors discuss how a committee analyzed the objective "interpretation of data." The committee recognized that this goal was complex, and then singled out two aspects for analysis: (1) the ability to perceive relationships in data, and (2) the ability to recognize the limitations of data. Their description of this goal runs into several pages, but we will only quote a paragraph on the first ability mentioned above (11, p. 38):

> The first of these involves the ability to make comparisons, to see elements common to several items of the data, and to recognize prevailing tendencies or trends in the data. These behaviors are dependent on the ability to read the given data, to make simple computations, and to understand the symbolism used. It became apparent that these operations vary for different types of data. Thus in the case of graphic presentation the student must be able to locate specific points on the graph, relate these to the base lines, recognize variations in length of bars or slope of graph line, and so on. In many cases, students must understand simple statistical terms (e.g., "average"), the units used, and the conventional methods of presentation of different forms of data.[2]

This paragraph illustrates another point too. It suggests a distinction between those behaviors that are *critical* in doing a task, and those that are necessary but ordinarily not critical. (Compare this with the critical requirements approach outlined in the preceding chapter.) Thus, the authors imply that the ability to make comparisons, to see common elements, and to recognize trends are critical behaviors in interpreting data; but that the ability to read the data as such, to make simple computations, and to understand the symbolism, are not. We might call the latter "enabling behaviors."[3] They enable a person to take at least the first steps in interpreting data, but they are not sufficient for making the interpretations themselves. Normally, we would assume that all members of the group taking the test had already acquired these enabling behaviors. These abilities should be *common* to all members of the group and thus

[2] *Ibid.*

[3] A term I owe to Chester W. Harris, now of the University of Wisconsin.

would not account for individual differences in interpreting data. Of course, if the test directions were couched in difficult language or if the symbolism was unfamiliar, then the ability to handle these preliminary tasks would become critical. We would then be testing these abilities along with ability on the larger task. In our definitions, we should generally emphasize only those responses that are *critical* for our purposes. At the same time, we should recognize that most tasks are so complex that they involve many kinds of responses, not just those we happen to be aiming at.

Recently, Flanagan outlined a promising method of defining precisely what is to be tested (4). He calls this the method of *rationales*. (This is a sophisticated term, but the details of the method will serve to define it.) The method begins with a list of critical behaviors to be sampled or predicted. The purpose is to develop a series of sets of specifications for writing test items that will give good estimates of each behavior on the list. Each *rationale,* or set of specifications, consists of three parts: (1) description of the behavior, (2) analysis of the behavior, and (3) formulation of item specifications.

1. *Description of the behavior* involves the definition and illustration of the types of responses included. For example, the critical behavior, "performed a series of simple computations without error," is described as follows:

> This behavior consists of doing a series of simple arithmetic problems with no errors. Calculations may be done either entirely "in one's head" or with the aid of paper and pencil. By "simple arithmetic" is meant addition, subtraction, multiplication, division, percentage, and fractions. Speed is of little concern here— accuracy throughout an extended series of calculations is the important factor. In many instances, the individual has plenty of time to perform the necessary arithmetic computations which are a part of his job. In spite of this, however, some individuals make errors even though they are trying to be very careful. A flight engineer would be considered ineffective if his computation on gas consumption was erroneous because he said $43 - 11 = 22$. Effective behavior, on the other hand, would be illustrated by a navigator whose computations while making a round-the-world training flight were found both by himself and by others who checked his work periodically, to contain not a single error (4, p. 153).

2. *Analysis of the behavior* involves classifying it with respect to other behaviors and making inferences about its nature. This should result in the formulation of one or more hypotheses regarding its generality and predictability. The analysis for the previous example might run as follows:

The performing of simple computations is probably influenced by both basic aptitude and long-established training or habits. Individuals effective in this regard do
not have to make a conscious effort to avoid errors; their computations are "just
naturally" correct. Individuals lacking the fundamental characteristics may also turn
in errorless work but their effectiveness is due to the fact that they very carefully
checked and rechecked their work so that all errors were eliminated. Actually, it
may be that the person who is given credit for possessing the fundamental ability
has an "automatic" checking system of which he is not consciously aware and
which operates simultaneously during the making of the actual computations. In
any event, his computations come out accurately the first time without undue
effort or concern on his part (**4**, p. 154).

3. *Formulation of item specification* carries the procedure a step
farther. Here one would describe a specific type of test item or situation
that *seems* likely to give a good estimate of the behavior in question. This
step would consist mainly of deductions and practical suggestions. For
the previous example, the formulation might run as follows:

For measuring computational behavior, the test should consist of a large number
of relatively simple problems involving addition, subtraction, multiplication, division, fractions, and percentages. They should not include any particularly difficult
or any "trick" problems. The examinee would be instructed to work at his own
rate but not to spend more time on any problem than is necessary to get *an* answer
(**4**, pp. 154–155).

The entire procedure thus goes beyond the definition of behavior as
such. It includes definition, but also other types of analysis. It shows
clearly how one can relate definition and analysis of behavior to the
formulation of item specifications. All in all, it lays the groundwork for
a very systematic and rational approach to item writing and test development.

Although we have emphasized the definition and analysis of behavior
in this section, we have had broad hints that there are other things to
specify also. Specifying the kinds of responses is not all there is to definition. We also need to know the nature of the conditions under which these
responses are to take place. In specifying these conditions, we recognize
that *behavior cannot be understood independently of the conditions that
produced it.*

   **2.** Define each of the following in terms of behavior.
      a) Ability to choose educational aims wisely
      b) An understanding of the interdependence of peoples
      c) Scientific attitude

3. For a course or unit of instruction for which you have stated general aims, define these in terms of behavior.

4. One level of understanding is for the student to be able to avoid crude errors and to reject gross misconceptions of basic principles. Are these abilities ever useful as specifics in defining achievement? Can you cite instances where they have been used as evidence of achievement?

## SPECIFYING THE LIMITING CONDITIONS

In general, we may think of limiting conditions as aspects of the situation that help determine the response. The concept of situation is crucial in studying behavior. It helps us understand why particular responses take place. And it must be reckoned with if we plan to evoke particular responses in order to generalize about particular attributes.

Like most psychological terms, situation is used with different intended meanings. Usually it refers to a stimulus pattern to which the individual responds. This may be illustrated as follows:

$$S \rightarrow I \rightarrow R$$

Thus, a situation (or stimulus pattern) leads to an interpretation which, in turn, leads to a response. S refers to that part of the total environment to which the individual responds. I refers to the individual's interpretation of the total situation. R, of course, refers to the response the individual makes.[4]

The concept of situation just outlined is basic in psychology, and several important implications follow. Typically, the situation or stimulus pattern is complex and patterned, rather than simple and atomistic. It is the total state of affairs acting upon, and being acted upon, the individual at any moment. Conceivably, this state of affairs might include all the universe at the moment, but for ordinary purposes we may disregard those features of the universe which have no appreciable effect on the person. The situation is thus defined by interaction between the individual and his immediate environment. In this sense, S is necessarily personal and momentary; the individual is an integral part of the psychological situation. This implies that there are other features of the external environment to which the individual does not respond at the moment. It is

---

[4] This scheme seems helpful for purposes of testing, but it should not be viewed here as suggesting a stimulus-response theory of behavior. A comprehensive theory of behavior seems to call for a consideration of other factors.

this notion of external environment that introduces a second usage of the term.

The second important usage of the term "situation" refers to the conditions or elements external to the individual, whether or not they are perceived by him at the moment. Such external conditions or elements, however, must be potentially accessible to the individual so that he may interact with them (if he is able to perceive them at the time). Psychologists talk of setting up test situations to evoke particular kinds of responses; instructors do likewise, and in addition talk of setting up situations for stimulating learning. In these instances, the discussion is in terms of planned, external conditions in the hope that these will become psychological situations of a certain kind—situations that will call forth the desired forms of response.

There are many kinds of external, or environmental, conditions that influence the person's response. Not all of them influence the person at the conscious level, nor are they all psychological. Some are physical in nature, such as the amount of lighting and the degree of temperature, and affect the person's physiological processes. We will consider some of the important conditions under the following headings: (1) nature of the objects, or stimuli, (2) special psychological conditions, and (3) social and physical settings.

### Nature of the objects or stimuli

A further step in the definition of an educational objective or other characteristic is to specify the nature of the objects to which the person must relate his efforts. In the first step, our concern was with the question: *How* is the person to react? In this next step, our concern is with a complementary question: *What* is he to react to?

As a very broad classification of objects, the following list seems to cover the scope of possibilities:

Physical objects—materials, tools, apparatus, instruments, etc.
Plant or animal objects—as in biological work.
Human objects—examiner, interviewer, coworkers or peers, superiors, clientele, etc.
Symbols—oral or written words or concepts, pictures, ink blots, or other representations. Also, areas of symbolic reference such a topics of discourse and knowledge.

In effect, these various objects become possible stimuli to which individuals can react.

For many types of appraisal, specifying the kinds of objects or materials with which the person is to work amounts to an *analysis of content*. This is particularly true of ability tests, i.e., tests of achievement, intelligence, and aptitude. The content indicates the kinds of materials through which the responses are to be expressed.

To take a simple example, let us assume that we want to test vocabularv or really, knowledge of word meanings. In behavioral terms, this might take one of several forms: given a word, to supply its meaning; given a word, to recognize a synonym from among several offered; given a word, to recognize a definition from among several offered. This merely illustrates different ways of reacting to a given word. The other main variable is the sample of words on which the person is to demonstrate his knowledge. At one level, we can view sampling in terms of the *particular* words chosen. This decision, of course, has always to be made. At another level, we can view the sampling problem in terms of the *range* or *variety* of words to be included—whether they should all deal with general vocåbulary, whether they should be drawn from several subject matter fields, etc. Thus, there is a prior decision to be made about the range of variety of content to be sampled before one comes to the decision of particular content. It is generally necessary to make some decision about the range of content or situations that may be expected to bring forth the desired responses. This problem is illustrated further in the accompanying chart.

Since the chart is more or less self-explanatory, we might confine our comments to a few subtle points. Notice that, opposite the first characteristic, the word "possibly" qualifies the heading. This suggests that one might think of per cent problems as varying in the type of calculation demanded, as well as in the area of life in which the problem falls. However, a sounder argument might be that the type of calculation really represents a variation in the type of reaction called for, and hence belongs in the behavioral analysis and not here. This illustrates the difficulty of trying to separate behavior and content in such analyses, especially in the field of mathematics. Content and process are so interwoven that their separation is indeed difficult. In reality, of course, it is impossible to separate content and process: they occur simultaneously. There can be no content unless a person responds to it, and there can be psychological process unless there is also some content to which to respond.

Why, then, is it necessary to make the distinction at all? Because it is useful for purposes of stating educational objectives and for purposes of sampling outcomes. If we specify objectives in terms of content alone, we fail to do justice in the many ways in which students can react to (or

| Behavior or Characteristic | What to consider in specifying the Range of Situations |
|---|---|
| Skill in computing and using per cents | Possibly two major considerations:<br>1. Type of calculation, e.g.,<br>   given two numbers, to find the per cent one is of the other;<br>   given one number and a per cent, to find that per cent of the number.<br>   to determine a gain or loss, and to express it as a per cent.<br>2. Area of application, e.g.,<br>   business transactions—interest on loans, per cent saved on a sale price, per cent profit;<br>   home economics—shrinkage in fabrics, per cent of budget allowed for different items. |
| Ability to interpret data in various forms | This is so broad that one would have to pin down both the *form* in which the data are to occur, such as graph, table, chart, report of experiment, etc., and the *subject matter or area of life* with which the data are to deal. |
| Appreciation of good music | Types of music, opera, folk songs, symphony, etc., which would be appropriate for calling forth reactions of appreciation. |
| Constructive attitudes toward current social problems | Toward what social problems—public vs. private power, migrant labor, control of monopoly, divorce, juvenile delinquency, etc.—is the student to show "constructive social attitudes?" |

use) that content. The tendency then is to emphasize factual outcomes and to neglect intellectual skills and abilities. There is also a tendency to forget that content differs in its relative value. Some kinds of content are useful for purposes of illustration, while others are important in their own right. Much of the content that a student encounters is of temporary value. It enables him to acquire certain skills, understandings, and the like, but it is not important enough to be permanently retained. Other content, however, is important enough to be singled out for retention. Important generalizations and understandings are of this character.

For some types of appraisal, we may not need a detailed analysis of content. Particular content may be relatively unimportant. This is true of many arts and skills. In these outcomes, content serves as a medium of expression. What counts most is *how* the individual uses his skill, rather than his knowledge of the particular content he happens to be working with. Note how this applies to such skills as reading, interpretation of data, public speaking, and typing. We wouldn't want to push this point too far because it is necessary to specify at least the *type* of materials or situations with which the student is to cope.

But why is it necessary to specify the *range* of situations as we have emphasized before? The main reason is psychological: there are limits to the generalization of behavior. We cannot expect a person to be completely consistent in his reactions from one type of situation to another. Thus we cannot assume that the student who can calculate straight per cents can also handle the trickier problems involving per cent of a gain or loss; or that the student can apply a principle equally well through its many variations in specific situations; or that the student who shows a constructive attitude toward the solution of the public versus private power problem will show a similarly constructive attitude toward the migrant labor problem; or that the student who understands and enjoys folk songs will do the same for opera and symphonies. In most individuals, behavior is rarely so highly generalized.

Yet sometimes the experimental evidence indicates the contrary, and it is then not necessary to sample so widely as first believed. A case in point is the measurement of literary comprehension. To get a broadly representative measure of this ability, it would seem necessary to include selections from literary works that differ in form, style, topics treated, and purpose. This would mean using works of prose, poetry, essay, narrative, and drama as the objects to be comprehended. The assumption behind such sampling is that the comprehension of any one type would present a somewhat different task from the comprehension of another type. According to this assumption, the comprehension of poetry would constitute a somewhat different task than the comprehension of prose. Some English teachers undoubtedly base their teaching procedures on this assumption, believing that the two types of material demand somewhat different abilities. Harris tested this assumption and found it refuted by his data (7). The evidence suggested that various literary selections, differing in the characteristics above, test essentially the same ability. Hence, from the standpoint of sampling, it would not be necessary to include selections from all major types of literature in order to get a representative measure of comprehension.

The notion of sampling has wormed its way into our discussion at a number of points, so that we might let it come out into the open now. There is an intimate connection between the problem of sampling and the problem of specifying the range of situations. Briefly, it is this: *the purpose of specifying the range of situations is to provide for representative sampling.* If we want to get a sample of behavior that will be truly indicative of what the person can do, or of what he habitually does, we must plan for this by defining the range of situations to be observed or presented to him.

5. For each outcome below, indicate why it would be desirable to specify the range of situations in which such behavior could be expressed.

   a) effective written composition
   b) ability to explain everyday natural phenomena on the basis of scientific principles
   c) concern for the welfare of others
   d) sensitiveness to the use of numbers (quantitative ideas) in social situations

6. Consider the objective for a first-year French course—"To become acquainted with French expressions commonly used in English: on radio, in newspapers, magazines, and books."

   a) Give several examples of such expressions.
   b) Which needs more elaborate specification here, the behavioral or the content aspect?
   c) Do you think it is important here to specify the variety of situations in which the student should be able to recognize such expressions?
   d) Would there be any value in pretesting students for such knowledge? Why or why not?

### Special psychological conditions

#### Motivation

The questions to ask at this point are: How is the person to be motivated, and to what degree? The first question deals with the source of motivation. Does it come primarily from within or from without? If we are interested in the person's *typical behavior*—how he reacts when artificial incentives and pressures are not present—then we should clearly indicate that these are not to be present when the observations are made. On the other hand, if we wish to study performance under artificial incentives, then we should specify precisely what these conditions are to be.

The second question deals with the extent of motivation: To what degree shall the person be motivated? If we wish to study performance at its maximum, when a person does his very best, then we have to see that he is highly motivated. This would undoubtedly call for some pressure from without, in the form of a special request, encouragement, or incentive. Most ability tests are conducted on this basis.

Many appraisal procedures are weak at this point. They neglect performance under everyday conditions, when the artificial pressures are absent. For example, the usual achievement test measures the student's ability, but not his *disposition,* to put that ability to use in everyday life. The disposition to put an ability to use, to be logical in one's thinking, and so on, depends greatly upon one's motivation. To obtain evidence of this disposition, it is necessary to observe the person in everyday situations—or to resort to some indirect technique which can be shown to give results which correlate highly with the everyday behavior.

### Freedom of response

This is important whenever we want to find out how the person does on his own, how he performs when there are few restrictions upon his behavior. When we indicate that the behavior is to take place under such conditions, we mean that the person is to be more or less responsible for defining what he is to do, how he is to do it, and setting the standards that his performance, or its results, should meet.

Such freedom permits, even compels, the person to impose his own individuality on whatever he does. It is thus very helpful in personality study, and in studies of creativity where we want to give the person plenty of chance to show his stuff.

The extent to which we allow freedom of response will thus depend upon our purposes, and upon the ability of the person to take responsibility for his own acts.

### Work methods

It is often necessary to specify, and to try to control, the work method that individuals are to use in carrying out a task. A work method is any learned way of performing a particular task. It may range from a broad and habitual method of attack, such as in problem-solving, to a rather narrow and temporary mental set to be adopted for the task at hand. It may be a habit or set of which the person is quite conscious, or it may be one of which he is quite unconscious.

It is especially important to control work methods if we wish to measure individual differences in ability. For such purposes, scores should reflect individual differences in performance when all persons have used *similar* work methods; otherwise scores will hardly be comparable. Sometimes instructions may control the work method, but often this is not the case. As one writer comments:

In measuring individual differences it is not sufficient to control the instructions or working situation, for the observer's previous incidental background may lead him to adopt very different work methods than those expected. It follows that "control" limited to ordinary instructions and demonstrations is incomplete, and that other unnoticed factors operate to modify the work method actually adopted (10, p. 123).

For diagnostic purposes, it is usually desirable *not* to try to control the particular work methods to be used. This procedure was followed in the study of problem-solving cited in the previous chapter. Under such conditions we are more likely to evoke the individual's own habitual work methods rather than some artificial methods that are not his very own. It is these habitual methods, of course, that should be the logical starting points for any remedial work. How the individual scores in terms of number right, time taken, number of units of work, and similar *product* measures may be of less interest than the actual *processes* he uses.

Therefore, the very fact that we do not try to control work methods may be an indication of the importance we attach to them. The emphasis upon work methods, or manner of performance, is by no means new. Athletic coaches have long emphasized form both in teaching and in their appraisals of skill; so have teachers of other skills. But there is apparently an urgent need for paying more attention to manner of performance in appraising physical or mental skills (1, 2, 3). It is quite possible for individuals to achieve the same over-all score but actually differ in certain key elements of performance. This has been shown, for example, in wartime studies of airplane piloting (1). Studying performance only in terms of achieving a given result, such as making a proper turn, covered up important differences in manner of performance. Such differences were important because they were found to be correlated with differences in ability to perform under adverse conditions and in retention of the skill.

### Pressure for speed or accuracy

If speed is an important component of an activity or of a trait under observation, then it should be specified as one of the limiting conditions. In such cases, the task would have to be carried out under timed conditions. This would be true for many skills, such as typing, filing correspondence, reading, and others.

If speed is unimportant, then we should specify that the task is to be carried out under untimed, or work-limit, conditions. This is desirable when we are mainly interested in the level at which a person can perform, rather than in the rate at which he works. In this case our question is: Can the person solve these problems or do this task if given enough time? Many current ability tests operate on this principle; hence, they allow ample time for nearly everyone to finish.

However, time limits are often set for the sake of administrative convenience, even when speed is recognized as a relatively unimportant factor.

In the past, both standardized and informal tests have probably placed too much emphasis upon speed as an index of accomplishment. One authority on the teaching of arithmetic believes this to be true of that field (8). He argues that speed is only a symptom and not a guarantee of mastery in arithmetic. Then, too, there are those pupils who have mastered a process but never show much speed because they tend to be deliberate in everything they do. Furthermore, the emphasis upon speed runs counter to the contemporary emphasis on teaching pupils to be thoughtful about what they do—for instance, to estimate answers in advance and to judge after finishing a problem whether or not the answer makes sense, all of which takes time.

It is often important to specify the degree of accuracy that the person should set for his work. This is essential for mathematical work where the calculations can be carried out to several decimal places. Here we would indicate to how many decimals, if any, the calculations should be carried. For typing, we would probably want to specify the level of accuracy that the typewritten copy should meet. For many kinds of precision work, such as that found in the industrial arts and skilled trades, we would have to specify the tolerance or degree of error to be allowed. To the extent that we specify accuracy as a condition and convey it to the subjects by means of directions, do we put a further pressure on performance.

Some activities call for both speed and accuracy. Usually this is demanded for typing, reading, and certain precision skills. If such is the case, then we have to specify both of these conditions. However, this is not so easy as it sounds. Telling the subject to "work as rapidly and accurately as you can" does not convey a clear-cut meaning. In fact, it represents a logical fallacy—the double superlative. Strictly speaking, a person cannot *simultaneously* work toward two superlatives such as maximum speed and maximum accuracy. He works either toward one or the other, or a compromise of the two. This is what happens in actual practice. Some people emphasize speed in their performance; others, accuracy; most of them work out a compromise to directions such as the above. Our specifications, and the corresponding directions to the subjects, should indicate in enough detail how this compromise is to be worked out.

## Stress

Normally, we do not go out of our way to observe or test people under conditions of stress. If anything, we try to provide conditions free from undue stress. Although the usual ability test puts some pressure on the person, this can hardly be severe unless unusual rewards and punishments are connected with the results.

Yet there are purposes for which it is desirable to observe people under stress. This is justifiable in personnel selection and training when, as a normal part of a job, individuals must perform stably in the face·of unusual obstacles, distractions and confusions, criticism, frustrations from conflicting demands, and physical dangers. Systematic attempts to set up such conditions include the Observational Stress Technique of the Air Forces, used to estimate the ability of aviation trainees to resist distraction and confusion (6); a stress interview given to prospective police officers (5); and the wartime assessment program of the Office of Strategic Services (9). In addition, experimental and clinical studies of personality have used such conditions. How an individual controls his emotions evidently gives considerable insight into his personality.

### Social and physical settings

It is probably not too important for the usual test to specify the nature of the social setting in which behavior is to take place. At least, most group tests aim at some aspect of individual competence, and the social setting is assumed to be more or less incidental. This assumption may or may not' be sound. Certainly the presence of others can often be a source of distraction, and artificial incentives, such as intergroup competition, can markedly affect performance. And, in an individual examination, the personality of the examiner can have quite an effect on the rapport he establishes with the subject and the confidence he inspires in him.

For those skills that do have an important social component, however, some attention must be paid to social factors. A social trait, such as leadership, can hardly be discussed in the abstract. More specific questions remain: What kinds of activities is the person to direct? What kinds and numbers of people is the person to lead? How much responsibility will be given? How is performance to be evaluated and by what observers? Questions such as these relate to factors in the social setting likely to influence the behavior under study. The characteristic under study can have no real meaning apart from specification of such social factors.

To the extent that physical factors set important conditions under which performance is to be carried out, they too should be specified. Though probably not important in many educational situations, they clearly are in certain kinds of industrial and military jobs. Unusual or adverse conditions of temperature, light, and ventilation are common examples.

## SPECIFYING OTHER FACTORS

### Nature of the group

Rarely are evaluation instruments developed for use with but a single person. They are almost always intended for use with some defined group. Since an instrument may be appropriate for one group but not for another, it is necessary to specify the nature of the group for which the instrument is intended.

This is very important in testing any kind of ability, for we must be sure that the test items and directions are appropriate. By knowing the nature of the group, we can make the items of the appropriate level and range of difficulty.

### Range of time

In studies of typical behavior, it is often necessary to define the range of time over which behavior is to be observed. This is necessary because behavior shows cycles and trends. People often have ups and downs in mood, as from the somber to the lighthearted and gay. Over a period of several days, a student may be quite gloomy, so that we might consider this to be typical of him. Over a longer period, however, it might prove only a temporary condition, caused by disturbances at home and not at all typical.

Abilities do not seem to show cycles as personality traits sometimes do, although they too are influenced by changes in mood, energy level, and motivation. They are more likely to show longtime trends of growth or decline. At any time, however, they are stable enough so that we can accept them as typical of the person. Hence, in testing abilities it is generally not necessary to specify the range of time.

Of course, if we want to study growth or stability of some function or characteristic, then we have to carry out our observations over a period of time. It is then necessary to make at least two observations, spaced some time apart.

### Criteria for judgment

Up to this point, we have emphasized the importance of defining the behavior and indicating the limiting conditions under which it is to take place. We have also gone beyond these specifications to consider the nature of the group and the range of time over which we are to observe. These specifications should enable us to suggest the right kinds of situations from which we might get evidence.

However, there is a further problem. We have to specify the *criteria* to be used for judging that behavior or its effects. It is not enough for us to describe and analyze the behavior, and to indicate the limiting conditions. An act of judgment is usually called for.

To illustrate, suppose we want to appraise skill in typing. We define what we mean by typing and the conditions under which it is to be done. However, we still have to answer the question: What do we mean by *skill* in typing? Usually, a person is said to have skill in typing if she types so many words a minute, if her work is accurate, and if it is neat. In other words, we have laid down three criteria—speed, accuracy, and neatness. These are the properties or attributes that we must appraise to arrive at a further judgment about *skill* in typing.

Again, suppose we wish to get evidence of a person's generosity. Generosity is, of course, a property of a person's behavior. The ultimate referents are certain acts of giving. We might indicate our concern with one class of those acts—giving to charitable organizations. The question now arises: What criteria should we use to determine whether a person's acts of giving show "generosity?" We probably would agree on the following criteria against which to judge his behavior: whether the money or goods or services are given of his own free will, whether they are frequently given, and whether they are large in proportion to his resources. So here too we must have standards of some sort before we can make any summary statement about a person's generosity.

With most ability tests, the usual standard or criterion of judgment is accuracy. One's performance is judged to be good if it is accurate. A person has ability in the task if he is generally able to do it correctly. On a test with many items, this means getting most of the answers right. The act of judgment is that of comparing the person's answers against the key, that is, the answers previously judged to be right, and comparing his over-all results against some over-all standard of goodness. There are other, and often better, ways of summarizing performance on ability tests. The methods and standards one chooses will depend upon what characteristics he wants to generalize about.

In general, if our statement of purposes does not make clear what characteristics we wish to study or what criteria we will use to judge the presence of those characteristics, then this is a good time to specify these. It is probably better to be clear on these points before making observations or tests than after the data have been collected.

The limit to specification is the operational definition. When we specify clearly the responses we will look for and when we specify the conditions under which these responses are to take place, we have taken some big steps in the right direction. When we specify further what situations we will use to evoke these responses, what methods we will use to observe and record them, and what methods we will use to evaluate the results, we have just about defined the characteristic as completely as possible. In the end, the characteristic is defined by whatever operations are necessary to obtain and evaluate evidence of its presence.

REFERENCES

1. Bartlett, F. C. The measurement of human skill. *Occup. Psychol.*, 1948, **22**, 30–38, 83–91.
2. Bloom, B. S., and Broder, L. J. *Problem-solving processes of college students: an exploratory investigation.* Chicago: Univer. of Chicago, 1950. Copyright 1950 by the University of Chicago.
3. Brownell, W. A. Rate, accuracy, and process in learning. *J. educ. Psychol.*, 1944, **35**, 321–337.
4. Flanagan, J. C. The use of comprehensive rationales in test development. *Educ. psychol. Measmt.*, 1951, **11**, 151–155.
5. Freeman, G. L., and others. The stress interview. *J. abnorm. soc. Psychol.*, 1942, **37**, 427–447.
6. Guilford, J. P. (Ed.). *Printed classification tests.* AAF Aviation Psychol. Prog. Res. Rep. No. 5 Washington: Govt Printing Ofc, 1947.
7. Harris, C. W. Measurement of comprehension of literature: II. Studies of measures of comprehension. *Sch. Rev.*, 1948, **56**, 332–342.

8. Morton, R. L. *Teaching arithmetic:* what research says to the teacher. Washington: Nat. Educ. Ass., 1953.
9. OSS Assessment Staff. *Assessment of men.* New York: Rinehart, 1948.
10. Seashore, R. H. Work methods: an often neglected factor underlying individual differences. *Psychol. Rev.,* 1939, **46**, 123–141.
11. Smith, E. R., Tyler, R. W., and others. *Appraising and recording student progress.* New York: McGraw-Hill, 1942.
12. Thurstone, L. L. Note on a reanalysis of Davis' reading tests. *Psychometrika,* 1946, **11**, 185–188.

## FURTHER READINGS

Dressel, P. L., and Mayhew, L. B. Selected chapters. *General education: explorations in evaluation.* Washington: Amer. Coun. on Educ., 1954.
Smith, E. R., Tyler, R. W., and others. Selected chapters. *Appraising and recording student progress.* New York: McGraw-Hill, 1942.

# CHAPTER 4

# Selecting Appropriate Situations

GETTING IDEAS FOR SITUATIONS

The Specifications as a Source of Ideas
Tapping Other Sources
Learning situations. Written work and other learner products. The learners themselves. Instructional materials. Current tests and related materials. Further sources of content.

TYPES OF SITUATIONS

Classification by Medium
Printed or paper-and-pencil materials. Motion pictures. Sound. Apparatus or performance tasks. People.
Classification by Objective
Classification by Other Characteristics

DIRECT AND INDIRECT APPROACHES

Natural versus Test Situations
Direct observation of behavior in natural situations. Tests as substitutes for the "real thing." Tests as improvements over natural situations.
Illustrations of Direct and Indirect Approaches

QUALITIES TO BE SOUGHT IN EVALUATION SITUATIONS

Appropriateness or Relevance
General considerations. Fulfilling special conditions.
Control of Irrelevant Factors
Complex or ambiguous directions. Unintentional clues. Familiar or unfamiliar content. Response sets. Desire for social approval. Chance errors.
Practicability
Reliability
A problem of samplng. Estimating size of sample needed.
Appropriateness from other standpoints

If the problem of definition has been well met, we should now have some rather clear specifications to guide us. Logically, the next step is to select or devise situations that will permit the expression of the right behavior and that will also give us a chance to get a record of it. This step will now be our concern.

## GETTING IDEAS FOR SITUATIONS

### The specifications as a source of ideas

One of the important uses of a statement of educational objectives, and of specifications in general, is to provide a starting point for suggesting evaluation situations. Given a clear statement, it is usually a relatively easy step to begin to think of situations in which students can show their attainment of the objective.

For example: What are the types of situations in which we could get evidence of ability to detect political propaganda? There are many possibilities here, depending both upon the medium one chooses and upon the area of public affairs in which the propaganda is to operate. Thinking just in terms of the medium, one can suggest a natural situation in which the subjects would actually see and hear (say, on television) some speaker known to be biased in his speechmaking, after which they would be instructed to analyze the speech for the presence or absence of propaganda, and the devices, if any, used to achieve that affect. The instructions both for hearing the speech and for analyzing it afterward could be varied somewhat, depending upon the degree to which the purposes of the exercise were to be disclosed. Alternatively, one could use a sound recording of the speech or just a reprint. Note that these three types of situations differ amongst themselves. The first presents the most cues, having both visual and oral elements, in addition to the actual ideas in the speech. It also involves problems of aural comprehension and of distortions because of forgetting or selective remembering of parts of the speech. These latter problems would also tend to be present in the second type of situation, which would lack the visual cues. The third type of situation, involving the reading of the speech, would lack both the visual and oral cues. Within the medium of the printed word, of course, one could think of other common situations, such as newspaper editorials, magazine articles, and political pamphlets. When we add to these variations in type of stimulus material the different ways of asking questions and of recording responses, we see how numerous indeed are the types of situations in which such an ability might be expressed.

Another example: What are the types of situations in which we could get evidence of reading interests? By reading interest is meant a liking or preference for reading certain kinds of materials when a free choice is given. The obvious situation that comes to mind is one in which the person is confronted with a variety of reading matter and in which he has a free hand to choose whatever he wants. It is then only necessary to note the actual choices he makes and to characterize these in some useful way. This approach has been used very effectively in research studies.

One more situation is one in which the person is presented with an annotated list of books and magazine articles, on which he checks the items that he would especially like to read. The contrast between these two types of situations is that between the direct observation of reading interests and the verbal report of the person.

Such is the approach with which we can profitably begin. It is easier, of course, than the further step of locating or devising *specific* situations for actual use. Yet this step would seem no less essential. It can get us off on the right track, and it may very often lead to creative test invention. But if glossed over or ignored entirely, it might lead to the choice of the wrong situations.

The further step of getting ideas for *specific* situations also calls for the free play of imagination. But of course the requirements are more specific, and in a way the demands upon our ingenuity are greater than when we try to think only of appropriate *types* of situations. In test development, this is the problem of getting item ideas. More commonly, such ideas come from specific sources such as we are about to review.

1. For a list of general aims that you have formulated, suggest types of situations suitable for collecting evidence thereon.

### Tapping other sources

When we suggest types of situations in the way just illustrated, we establish certain mental sets that help guide us in our further search for ideas, for the translation of those ideas into evaluation situations, and for specific materials. If we are resourceful, our search should carry us to certain other sources which are well worth canvassing, namely, actual learning or job situations, written work and other learner products, the learners themselves, instructional materials, current tests and related materials, and many everyday sources of content.

### Learning situations

Actual learning situations provide a good source of ideas for evaluation situations. It would be more accurate to say that they provide at least two good sources, for we can single out both the particular learning tasks and the teaching process itself.

When a second-grade teacher wants to find out how well Susie can read, she gives Susie some printed materials to read. When a fourth-grade teacher wants to find out how well Johnny can multiply, she gives Johnny some multiplication problems to work. When a public-speaking teacher wants to find out whether Sally has learned to make a good impromptu speech, he has Sally get up before the class and make an impromptu speech. In all these instances, the teacher uses situations that *reproduce* the essentials of the original learning task. There is no more fundamental way than this for the evaluation of learning.

As obvious as this approach seems, it needs to be exploited more fully. There is still too common a tendency to fall back upon convenient but artificial approaches, to use situations that do not give a genuine opportunity to demonstrate the attainment of particular aims.

The alert instructor, and particularly the instructor who adopts an evaluation point of view, will pick up many leads from classroom discussion. It is here that many of the learners' difficulties and misconceptions are brought to light. It is here too that unsettled problems, and questions regarding the application of practices to life situations, are raised. With a little ingenuity, these can often be converted into evaluation exercises.

Hugh Wood, author of the *Behavior Preference Record,* reports that his inspiration for this device came originally from a classroom discussion. This happened in the late 1930's when he was visiting an eighth-grade social studies class. The pupils were developing a unit on democracy, and had gotten to the point of listing behaviors that would characterize the pupil who lived democratically. The discussion then moved to the question: How can we measure these characteristics in individuals? This brought forth many suggestions of everyday situations in which the presence or absence of these characteristics would be shown. Out of this discussion, and from critical incidents described in writing by these pupils, came the first set of problem situations. The following are examples (**28**, p. 38):

Jack is reading a library book and you see him accidentally tear a page. Later he tells the teacher he didn't tear it, but that you did. What would you do?

A committee is being chosen. You have some good ideas and want to be chairman. Instead, Betty is chosen chairman, but you are on the committee. What would you do?

You are playing baseball on a vacant lot with the neighborhood gang. Your mother asks you to take your little sister along while she goes to town. You know the gang will laugh. What would you do?

Subsequently, Wood built the various forms of this device around verbal problem situations of this sort. In many preliminary tryouts, pupils were asked to write out what they would do in such situations (or had done previously in similar situations), and to give their reasons for choosing a particular course of action. These tryouts gave Wood the most frequent pupil responses, which he then incorporated in the final forms.

### Written work and other learner products

Such specimens provide a very fruitful source of ideas. Most of these products will be in the form of written work, such as themes, term papers, essay examination papers, and the like; but almost any kind of learner product has possibilities.

One approach is to collect samples of work and then to cull these for misconceptions, common difficulties, faulty technique, or differing stands on controversial issues. The next step is to convert these into suitable questions or exercises.

Another approach is to collect samples of work and to use these in their entirety—or at least the essential features thereof. What kinds of samples are most useful? In general, those that illustrate either particularly good or particularly bad technique, that represent different ways of achieving the same effect, or that represent different stands on certain issues. It is an easy matter to duplicate copies of a theme, term paper, or other piece of writing; also to make photographs of drawings, paintings, and other objects. When the latter is not feasible, it may be possible to put the specimen on display in a classroom, laboratory, or shop to have students examine it individually as part of an evaluation exercise.

The next step in this second approach is to build an exercise around a particular specimen, or around two contrasting specimens if one wants to evoke comparison and contrast. We might duplicate a poor theme, for example, and instruct each member of a class to revise it. The success with which a student revises such a theme should indicate his understanding of principles of language and written composition, and perhaps even his ability to write. A less direct method would make use of multiple-choice questions requiring the student to recognize specific features of the theme that were faulty. In a social studies course, we might duplicate a student's paper in which he proposes a plan to reduce juvenile delinquency, and frame a series of questions calling for critical analysis and evaluation of the proposed plan.

Such specimens are relatively easy to obtain and lend themselves to teaching as well. However, they fit only certain testing needs—chiefly exercises in critical interpretation, analysis, and evaluation. When we use them for such purposes, we assume that a student demonstrates his grasp of principles when he applies them in the critical study of another person's work. Thus, the student who knows principles of language and written composition should be able to recognize the presence or absence of these in another person's composition. But the further assumption that skill in analysis is *highly* indicative of skill in composition seems unwarranted.

### The learners themselves

"Would you like to make your own test in social studies, or would you rather have the teacher make up a test for you?" Such was the question one enterprising teacher put before a seventh-grade class at the end of a unit of instruction (11). How did the class react? At first they were rather amazed at such a proposal; but soon interest grew and they enthusiastically accepted the idea of making their own test. In this case, the teacher had laid the groundwork by pointing out the need for evaluation. For this project, he divided the class into four groups on the basis of their ability. Group I, the most able, was to compose multiple-choice questions because these were believed to be the hardest to write; Group II, matching; Group III, completion; and Group IV, the least able, to prepare true-false questions. The pupils in each group spent considerable time consulting any notes, books, current materials, and maps that had been made or used in class. Each group then met in committee to discuss, evaluate, and select their questions for the test. These activities provided an excellent experience in selecting, interpreting, and evaluating materials, as well as a good review. The entire project took three hours of class time; the taking and scoring of the test, an additional two hours.

This is an illustration of what a group of seventh-graders was able to do when given the opportunity. There is no good reason to believe that younger children should not be able to take a hand in the evaluation process; and certainly no good reason why older children and adolescents could not.

Canvassing the learners in this way taps an important source of ideas. It has further advantages. It draws the learners into the evaluation process and thus gives them responsibility and needed experience; it helps them to clarify in their own minds the objectives of instruction; and in some courses it gives a good indication of their understanding of the important ideas.

### Instructional materials

In the area of achievement testing, instructional materials have traditionally furnished the greatest source of ideas. They probably still do, since so much of formal instruction is tied in with them. The usual procedure is for one to go through textbooks, student manuals, syllabi, and course of study outlines to glean ideas, then to convert these into suitable questions.

Up to a point, instructional materials are a necessary source of ideas. They certainly are basic to a content analysis of a course or subject, for they contain the particular facts, terms, concepts, and principles to be mastered. But if an instructor wants to get evidence of understandings, he must normally seek situations other than those discussed in the instructional materials. He may find sample exercises at the end of chapters, or even interspersed in the discussion; these often contain good leads. He might use some of these directly or alter them slightly to fit his needs; well and good if he can. However, it would seem generally desirable for him to turn to additional sources for leads: to the learning situation, to the learners, and to the sources discussed below.

### Current tests and related materials

Tests and other instruments of evaluation are worth inspecting for ideas. Often they provide good models for us to imitate. There seems to be no harm in studying the work of experts; in fact, it would seem desirable to try to imitate the good points in their technique.

Collections of problems and questions comprise another important type of source. Increasingly, textbook publishers are issuing instructors' manuals which include such collections. Educational Testing Service is sponsoring a series of folios of test items which should bring excellent materials within the reach of instructors.

Books and articles on testing and evaluation comprise another important type of source. These are so numerous that it is not possible to list even the most generally significant.

Some of these sources carry their own tags of excellence but others are of unknown quality. Hence, it is necessary to use caution when inspecting the latter. But in no case should one "lift" items which have no close connection with instructional aims.

### Further sources of content

Extensive as the foregoing sources may seem, they do not exhaust all of the possibilities. The possible sources that we may canvass for ideas, and for actual content, are virtually as broad as life itself.

Consider, for a moment, the wealth of materials upon which to draw for evaluation situations: books, magazines, scholarly journals, newspapers, government bulletins, business reports, laws, and other printed matter; cartoons, drawings, art objects, and printed copies thereof; both still and motion pictures; musical compositions and recordings; recordings of speeches and other forms of oral presentation; tools, apparatus, machinery, and the like. To these, we should add our own firsthand observations of everyday life and the reflections we make upon these observations.

In short, sources such as these provide good content for evaluation as well as for teaching purposes. One can, of course, get good leads from occasionally browsing through such materials, without planning to use that content in a specific exercise.

## TYPES OF SITUATIONS

Let us pause temporarily to review the types of situations useful for evaluation. This review should help us, first, to recognize the wide range of potentially useful situations, not just those of the paper-and-pencil variety; second, to recognize that there are many ways of classifying test situations and that some useful distinctions can be made; and, third, to become sensitive to the directness with which situations approach or reproduce the real thing.

Any discussion of types of situations presupposes various systems of classification. While there are many possibilities here, it is only necessary to concentrate on a relatively few. Needless to say, none of these systems yields clear-cut categories.

### Classification by medium

A very meaningful classification is that based upon the medium through which the stimuli present themselves. Five important media are: printed or paper-and-pencil materials, motion pictures, sound, apparatus or other objects to be manipulated, and people.

#### Printed or paper-and-pencil materials

These represent by far the most common medium. Paper-and-pencil situations may be further classified according to the nature of the stimulus materials: language, number, geometric figures, pictures, drawings, maps, other representations, and various combinations of these. The essence of this medium is that it presents a series of static, visual stimuli.

Without a doubt, paper-and-pencil tests owe their wide use to the ease with which they can be administered and, in the case of most of them, to the ease with which they can be scored. These advantages have stimulated testers to try to extend these techniques to uses for which they have heretofore been considered inappropriate. Not all of these efforts will prove fruitful, but many will.

For better or worse, paper-and-pencil situations are often used as substitutes for real-life situations. A common technique is to describe a problem situation and then to ask the person to tell what he would do in that situation, or to choose the course of action that he would consider best. As an example of this technique, let us review an exercise devised by a seventh-grade teacher for use with a literature class. It might help to reproduce here also the statement of objectives which guided this teacher:

*Statement of Objectives:*
A. Development of the ability to participate in group thinking through discussion.
    1. Considers with fairness the opinion of others;
    2. Bears in mind the interests of the group rather than of himself or of any one person;
    3. Cooperates with the group in maintaining an orderly discussion.
B. Development of social techniques which will assist the individual in finding happiness in the group situation.

*     *     *     *     *     *

*Problem Situation:* In a literature class, after reading *A Christmas Carol,* one of the members, John Jones, says, "Charles Dickens is not as good a writer as some of the writers whose stories I have read in magazines at home." One of John's classmates, Tom Brown, disagrees with John, and finally says, "John probably didn't even read *A Christmas Carol.*" Tom, however, knows that John has read the story.

1. If you were John, which one of the following would be best for you to do?
   a) Tell him that you have read *A Christmas Carol.*
   b) Give further reasons for your remarks.
   c) Ignore Tom's remark and say nothing further on the point.
   d) Ask the class how many of them agree with you.

2. As a member of the class (being neither Tom nor John), which one of the following would you do if you believed that John was right?
   a) Say, "I think Tom ought to tell John he's sorry."
   b) Say nothing and let the teacher take care of the situation.
   c) Tell John after class that you agree with him.
   d) Say, "I think John has a point," and tell why.

3. Now suppose you agree with Tom that Dickens' writing is superior. Which of the following would be best to do?
   a) Say nothing and wait for the teacher to take care of the matter.
   b) Ask the teacher what she feels is the right viewpoint.
   c) Mention neither Tom nor John but give reasons why Dickens is superior.
   d) Say, "John may have a point, but I agree with Tom."

4. Now pretend that you are the teacher. No one has said anything after Tom's remark. Which of the following would it be best to do first?
   a) Ask John to give further reasons for his opinion.
   b) Demand that Tom tell John he's very sorry.
   c) Change the subject to something else.
   d) Offer your own opinion on the matter.

While such a verbal situation is a far cry from the "real thing," it does at least reproduce the intellectual components that one would face in the life situation. This sort of technique seems very promising for many educational outcomes, and we will undoubtedly see more use made of it.

Another paper-and-pencil technique that seems very promising is the pictorial, or graphical, type of situation. The material may be in the form of a photograph, drawing, diagram, map, or graph. One of the main advantages of pictorial forms is that they can present complex situations or materials with few, if any, words. In this connection, note Figure 2. Think of the number of words one would have to use to present this problem without the use of the drawings, and of the language burden

48.  Which is the best method of suspending a
     splice in spiral four cable?

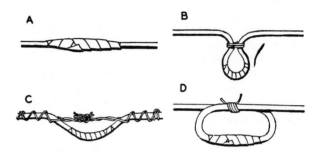

Fig. 2. Picture test item showing right and wrong procedures. (From Department
of the Army bulletin [31]. Reproduced by permission of the Secretary of the
Army.)

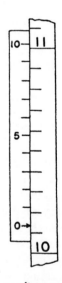

50.  What is the reading on the vernier
     shown in the drawing at the right?
     A)  10.03
     B)  10.13
     C)  10.14
     D)  11.04

Fig. 3. Picture test items may measure skill in using instruments, reading maps,
etc. (From Department of the Army Bulletin [31]. Reproduced by permission of
the Secretary of the Army.)

placed upon the person who is used to working with his hands. A further advantage of pictorial forms is that they can sometimes be used to measure a skill directly, as shown in Figure 3.

### Motion pictures

Although most of us associate motion pictures with entertainment or instruction, this medium is now proving useful for testing purposes. During World War II the Army Air Forces made extensive use of motion picture tests, and now civilian agencies are turning to this medium for similar purposes.

Motion pictures have certain unique advantages, the most obvious of which is the introduction of movement into the stimulus field. This makes it possible to test such abilities as perception of rate of movement, direction of movement, objects in flight, and the like. Thus, the AAF developed an aircraft-recognition test that was pieced together from shots of planes in actual flight against a natural background of sky, clouds, land, or distant horizon (12, 100 ff.). The film included shots of American, British, German, and Japanese planes. The exposure interval of each plane was from two to five seconds, and the interval allowed for recording one's answer, seven seconds. This illustrates a second important advantage of the motion picture: it allows us to control both the length of time for presenting the stimulus and that for the subject's response. A further advantage ·is the realism that can be attained. By using motion pictures with sound, it may be possible to present situations that come close to the real thing. Finally, if instructions and illustrative exercises are incorporated in the film and sound track, motion picture tests can just about eliminate variations in those aspects of test administration, and hence often surpass printed tests in standardization of procedure.

Clearly, the development of motion pictures, whether for purposes of instruction or evaluation, is beyond the reach of most schools. This is a costly operation and one that requires considerable technical skill. Today, most schools borrow films that are produced elsewhere and distributed on a state, regional, or national basis. Many of these films lend themselves nicely to evaluation purposes. A common procedure is to show a film and follow this with a series of questions to test comprehension. Another way is to repeat the film, stop it at various critical points, and then ask questions at each of those points. The alert instructor will find some motion pictures ideal for purposes of evaluation.

## Sound

Of the formal techniques utilizing sound as the stimulus, the traditional oral examination is no doubt the best known. Once the favored approach in determining the student's accomplishments, the oral quiz or recitation is now quite out of favor. Technical, as well as educational, weaknesses have relegated it to a minor role in modern education, at least in the United States.

And yet the oral examination does serve certain special purposes well. It permits the examiner to be very flexible in his procedure—adapting questions to fit the individual's unique background, probing for meanings behind vague or incomplete statements, posing new questions during the course of the examination itself, and so on. Such flexibility is desirable in individual intelligence tests and in orals given Ph.D. candidates. The oral examination is also the preferred medium for testing children and others who are limited in their reading comprehension.

Oral questioning, as a part of instruction, is of course very much with us today. It is both a good instructional technique and a valuable informal means of appraising student progress.

For testing auditory comprehension, sound is the obvious and necessary medium. The sound itself may be an actual presentation or the playback of a recording. The latter is more common for large-scale testing purposes. Sound recordings are being used to test skill in taking dictation by means of shorthand, in comprehending a foreign language, in critically judging works in music appreciation courses, and in interpreting radio code. They are also used in the well-known Seashore battery (RCA) to measure sensitivity to pitch, loudness, time interval, timbre or tone quality, rhythm, and tonal memory.

Recently, teachers of English and communications skills have stressed the importance of oral comprehension. They argue, and with some validity, that ability to comprehend materials presented orally is an important skill and one that most of us need to cultivate more fully. To obtain evidence of this skill, some staffs have developed tests of listening comprehension. They first select materials of a kind that represent common listening situations—for instance, textual materials such as might form the content of a lecture or an argumentative speech. They then frame a series of questions, either in short essay or multiple-choice form. Typically the questions deal with two aspects of listening comprehension: the accu-

rate reception of details contained in the materials; and thoughtful re-
flection on the details, such as interrelating or evaluating ideas. The procedure then is to read each selection aloud before the class. During this
reading, students listen but are not allowed to take any notes. Immediately
afterward, they answer the questions—which, by the way, are usually
presented orally too.

### Apparatus or performance tasks

A fourth medium is represented by those tasks that require the manipulation of apparatus, mechanical equipment, or other physical objects. The
term "performance test" refers to tasks of this kind when they are administered as tests. A term that places more emphasis upon the medium
itself, and that might therefore be better, is "apparatus test" (24, p. 43).
Either term covers those tasks, or situations, in which the motor aspect
of the subject's response is central.

The various types of apparatus cover the whole range of complexity.
Among the simplest are form boards that require the subject to fit blocks
of different shapes into the proper spaces, pegboards that require one to
place small pegs in a series of holes as fast as possible, and just an
ordinary pencil and piece of paper on which a pupil has to demonstrate
his handwriting. Beyond these very simple types, one finds all sorts of
apparatus or equipment that set tasks for human beings: typewriter,
sewing machine, shop machines of various kinds, musical instruments,
slide rules, and so on. Some complex types have been developed specifically
for training and testing purposes: the Link Trainer, a device that reproduces for the student pilot all the characteristics of flying a plane by
instruments; and the Celestial Navi-trainer, a device that presents the
student navigator with a continuous view of the sky and stars as they
would appear to him in a plane flying over a given route at a specified
time (24, p. 43). Such devices come very close to reproducing the actual
job itself.

### People

Much of any person's life is spent in relations with others. Through
other persons we develop our personalities, and learn to understand ourselves and others, to satisfy basic needs, and to contribute to the social
good. That human relations are crucial in any person's life, and in the
workings of any society, hardly needs emphasis.

Face to face interaction provides the best situations for bringing into play such varied behavior as the following:

cooperativeness
mastery of the social graces
understanding of child and adolescent behavior
effective participation in group discussions
skill in leading small groups
skill in teaching
skill in personal counseling or interviewing

While everyday life provides natural situations for the expression of such behavior, it is often necessary in teaching and evaluation to create special situations. Some investigators and instructors have shown remarkable ingenuity along those lines.

A promising approach of recent origin is that of role-playing, or sociodrama. This is a form of spontaneous dramatization in which an individual or small group acts out certain predesignated roles. In teacher education, for instance, it is a good experience for students to play the role of parent or teacher in hypothetical (but nonetheless true to life) parent-teacher conferences. One such situation might be this:

*Teacher's role*—You are a primary-grades teacher about to have a conference with the mother of one of your pupils. You know that the child has not been making normal progress, as judged by grade standards, but that the progress shown is consistent with the child's general maturation.
*Parent's role*—You are the mother of a child in the primary grades who has not progressed to your satisfaction in tool subjects like arithmetic and reading. You feel that in large part this stems from the school's overemphasis upon group projects, which take away valuable time from the regular subjects.

Student teachers can take turns playing the respective roles of teacher and parent (in different situations of course). A third individual can serve as an observer and critic of interviewing technique. In this way the student teacher gets a firsthand evaluation of her technique, in addition to the reality practice itself.

Role-playing is also an effective teaching and evaluation technique for children and adolescent groups. One variation, the problem-story approach, appears especially useful for helping children and youth "to understand themselves and others, to develop social skills and attitudes, to think critically, and to be concerned with the welfare of others" (19, p. 6).

This approach involves reading aloud to a group an open-ended story, usually built around a developmental task,[1] and then encouraging the group to finish the story in role-playing sessions.

2. From an evaluation standpoint, what advantages would role-playing of parent-teacher or pupil-teacher conferences have over paper-and-pencil situations?
3. How could the problem situation on page 89 be adapted to role-playing?
4. It was stated that through interaction in social situations an individual may learn to understand himself better. Explain how this might come about. Give a possible illustration.

### Classification by objective

This is the classification that would probably be most useful in education. It would indeed be most helpful if there were available some system of classification such that existing tests and similar materials were classified on the basis of educational objective. And it would be "out of this world" if there were available some central library of such materials from which teachers all over the country could draw!

No doubt such a classification could work tolerably well throughout a good part of the range of educational objectives, but especially the cognitive, for these can be pinned down to specific paper-and-pencil test situations. As a matter of fact, the *Taxonomy* (2) really amounts to a classification of test situations as well, but with this reservation, that one must know or assume something about the nature of the students' prior experiences before one can classify a test item in a particular category. Thus, while on the surface a test item may seem to deal with the *application* of a principle, in the actual situation one could not be sure unless one knew whether the situation was in fact *new* to the students or whether it had been discussed previously. To consider the item as an application situation, one would have to assume that it was new to the students; otherwise it would fall in the recall-of-information category.

Although classification by objective has possibilities, there are two serious limitations. One is that the classification of any situation is not fixed but is relative to the nature of instruction. The other is that most situations involve more than one type of behavior, so that classification is relative to the behavior considered critical in the situation.

[1] See p. 33 for a definition of this concept.

### Classification by other characteristics

Occasionally it is helpful to judge situations on the basis of some other quality, such as complexity, abstractness, novelty, or difficulty. Later in this chapter we will discuss how situations can differ in these characteristics, and how such differences have a bearing on the appropriateness of the situations for given purposes.

Another basis of classification is the *directness* with which situations sample the defined behavior. This is a problem of such significance that we must highlight it in the next main section.

## DIRECT AND INDIRECT APPROACHES

### Natural versus test situations

#### Direct observation of behavior in natural situations

Earlier we noted types of situations suitable for collecting evidence of ability to detect political propaganda and reading interests. For each example, we were able to suggest more than one type. This is quite common with educational outcomes, for often there are several good possibilities. But among those suggested for each outcome, some discrimination would be possible. Thus, in each example, the first type of situation represented a rather natural way for a person to express the behavior in question, whereas the remaining types represented more formal and test-like situations.

Natural situations often have the advantage of revealing directly the behavior in question, and so are to be preferred to less direct approaches. By preserving the real-life complexity of the situation, they are less likely to distort the behavior under observation and hence are more likely to get at the real thing.

Of course, some forms of behavior cannot be directly *observed*, no matter how natural the situation. This would be true of ability to detect propaganda, which consists for the most part of covert thought processes. It would also be true of other thought processes, of feelings, and of certain physiological responses. Such acts are not open to direct observation. In such instances, we do the next best thing—we directly observe effects of the underlying behavior as it occurs under natural conditions. And we draw inferences about the underlying behavior and its properties from these effects. This is not direct evidence. But, if it is ultimately based upon behavior under natural conditions, it is as good evidence as we can get and as direct an approach as we can make.

Even when direct observation of natural behavior is possible, it is not often practical or desirable. Natural behavior is often inaccessible. It may occur outside the school or away from a formal setting. Recreational activities and health habits are of this nature. Then, too, many forms of behavior do not occur until long after schooling, so that we cannot get direct evidence of them in school. This would be true of voting behavior, and of vocational and marital adjustment. Still other acts occur so infrequently that we wouldn't know just when to be on the spot to observe them as they did occur. Acts of unusual originality are probably of this nature. Another obstacle is the lack of comparability in the behavior samples of different individuals (16, pp. 143–44). For example, to get evidence of spelling ability, we could make a running count of the errors pupils make in their own writings over a semester. But these samples are probably not comparable. A poor speller can confine his writing to simple topics and avoid hard words, while a good speller may show up no better because he has tackled more difficult topics and used harder words. A further obstacle to direct observation is that it is often too costly in effort and resources.

### Tests as substitutes for the real thing

For a variety of practical reasons, therefore, we often resort to less direct methods of collecting evidence. We rely upon test situations as substitutes for the real thing. Instead of directly observing behavior as it takes place in the natural run of events, or directly observing the effects of that behavior, we *set up* special situations to evoke the desired behavior. This is the strategy behind most tests—*to control the situation in such a way that we can stimulate the desired behavior at will.*

Whenever we use test situations as substitutes, we have an added responsibility. We have to determine whether the test results are good evidence of the real thing—criterion behavior, as this is called technically. Often it involves correlating test results against direct observations.

### Tests as improvements over natural situations

Although test situations are often poor substitutes for natural situations, they can be decided improvements too, for the usual practical reasons. Often test situations can isolate the appropriate behaviors more readily and, furthermore, can control the conditions under which they take place.

Consider how directly a good one-hour test of general intelligence samples a person's ability to do abstract thinking. In the uncontrolled activities of everyday life, we might not get any really good evidence of this ability. Like the pupil who avoids words that are hard to spell, a person might avoid tasks that demand abstract thinking.

### Illustrations of direct and indirect approaches

A good way to bring out the distinction between direct and indirect approaches is to turn to some vivid illustrations. Table 2 contains a summary of several.

Each illustration there contains a brief statement of some behavior or characteristic to be appraised; a description of a direct or fairly direct way of collecting evidence; a description of a supposedly less direct or indirect way of collecting evidence; and finally, a brief summary of the relationships reported in an actual study.

The last item of information is especially crucial, since it throws light on the appropriateness of the indirect approach. These findings help answer the question: To what degree do the results obtained by the less direct method correlate with the results obtained by the direct, and presumably more relevant, method?

To interpret the findings, which are reported for the most part in terms of correlation coefficients, one needs some explanation of this statistic. A correlation coefficient is a summary index expressing the degree of relationship between two sets of scores on the same individuals. The coefficient may take any value between $+1$ and $-1$, depending on the actual correspondence between the scores. A coefficient of $+1$ indicates a perfect positive correlation. In this case, the standing of each person on the one test corresponds exactly to his standing on the other, the person standing highest on the one test also standing highest on the other, the person standing next highest also standing next highest on the other, and so on right down the line. When a correlation of $+1$ results, we can predict any person's standing on either test, knowing his standing on the other. Such correlations rarely occur. Instead, as will be evident in our data, the coefficients generally fall short of a perfect correlation. A coefficient of o indicates no predictable pattern of relationships between the two sets of scores. Negative coefficients indicate inverse relationships: individuals tend to stand high on one test but low on the other. A coefficient of $-1$ indicates a perfect inverse relationship, and for purposes of prediction it is just as useful as a coefficient of $+1$.

Each illustration deserves careful study in its own right, both for the specific findings reported and for the methodology. Most of these experiments are in the nature of "classics." In each case, the technical problem is highly significant, for it throws light on the soundness of a practice that is, or might become, widespread. Moreover, the methodology shows how we can check, and indeed why we *must* check, the validity of approaches intended as substitutes for more direct approaches. Furthermore, the findings in each case are likely to be representative, even though a single experiment cannot establish a generalization.

There are some highly significant points tucked away in Table 2. Since these are somewhat subtle, we shall make them explicit.

First, in most of these illustrations the direct approach is taken as the standard, or criterion. Strictly speaking, we compare the *results* obtained by the supposedly indirect approach with the *results* obtained by the direct approach. This process of checking the indirect method against the direct method is technically known as validation. It is a process of determining the validity of a test or method of appraisal for some specific purpose—that is, the extent to which the test results measure, or otherwise indicate, a specific characteristic.

Second, in one illustration and partly in another, the direct approach was really not taken as the criterion. Thus, in the third illustration, the results of the direct approach, as well as those of the indirect approach, were independently correlated with an external criterion, i.e., grades in later mathematics courses. This also represents a process of validation, but a procedure much more common in aptitude testing. Primarily, the question here was whether the multiple-choice test was a good indicator of later achievement in mathematics courses; and only secondarily, whether it measured the same sorts of things that the free-response test did. To check this second question—which is an entirely different question—the investigators could have (and probably did) correlate scores on the multiple-choice test with scores on the free-response test. This correlation would simply tell whether or not the tests were measuring the same abilities, without any reference to their predictive value for some other specific purpose. But the fact that each form showed substantially similar correlations with an outside criterion was indirect evidence that they were measuring about the same things.

In the last illustration, this problem comes out again but in a somewhat different guise. When we correlate students' inventory responses with their verbal formulations of personal philosophy, we use the latter re-

## Table 2

### Illustrations of direct and indirect approaches

| *Behavior or characteristic* | *A direct approach to appraisal* |
|---|---|
| Knowledge of vocabulary in beginning German | Context recall. A short passage of the usual elementary-reader type, with certain words and phrases underlined. These were listed at the right of the passage, where the student was to *write in* the English translation that best fit the context. |
| Skill in pronouncing French | Phonographic recording of the student's pronunciation as he read test passages aloud. These were later judged independently by three competent judges, with a high degree of agreement. |
| Proficiency in mathematics considered necessary for college entrance | A traditional kind of test sampling mathematics achievement in algebra and other areas. Students worked out their solutions to the problems. |
| Ability to formulate for oneself a reasonable generalization from specific experimental data (in botany and zoology). | Students were presented with a number of sets of specific experimental data *which were new to them*. Beneath each, they wrote the generalization that they thought could be most reasonably made from the data given. |

## Table 2 (Continued)

### Illustrations of direct and indirect approaches

| *Less direct, or indirect, approach* | *Relationships reported* |
|---|---|
| Best-answer recognition. The same German words were listed, but without the passage, each followed by 5 English words. The student was to *choose* the English word that correctly translated the corresponding German word and to write the number in a blank to the left. | The recall and recognition exercises measure essentially the same ability. (Uncorrected correlation = .91.) ". . . the lucky guessers on the recognition test are also the fortunate recallers on the recall test." Recall was more difficult than recognition, a fact which the authors regard as established for other types of achievement also (21). |
| The student was given a sheet listing a series of 4 items. Each such set contained either 4 words or 4 word groups that were similar but not identical in sound. Upon hearing one of them pronounced by a competent reader, the student indicated which of the four he had heard. | Recognition exercise yielded results that correlated highly with actual pronunciation—correlations as high as .84 (23). |
| The same problems as those in the traditional free-response version were now cast in multiple-choice form. Students were to work the problems and choose the answer from the alternatives presented. | The multiple-choice form correlated with grades in later mathematics about as well as did the free-response form (29). |
| The same data were repeated, but this time with 5 suggested generalizations for each exercise. Students were asked to check the best generalization of each five. | The multiple-response test could *not* be used in place of the original test which required students to formulate their own generalizations. Coefficient of correlation = .38 (26). |
| The same data were repeated, but this time the 5 alternatives were drawn from generalizations actually proposed by students on the original free-response test. Students were now asked to check the *best* and the *poorest* of each five. | The scores on this test correlated highly (.85) with scores on the original free-response version (26). |

Table 2 (Continued)

Illustrations of direct and indirect approaches

| Behavior or characteristic | A direct approach to appraisal |
|---|---|
| Ability to plan experiments to determine the truth or falsity of certain hypotheses (in botany and zoology). | Students were presented with various hypotheses *which were new to them.* Beneath each, they described an experiment which could be used to test it. |
| Skill as a gunner (naval training center) | Observation of performance as a member of a gun crew, and rating of performance by instructors. |
| Attitude toward cheating on examinations | Students in a college psychology class were given a course examination each Friday. These were collected and secretly scored by the instructor. On Monday, papers were returned to their owners to be graded in class. There was ample opportunity to change answers during this scoring. Cheating was measured by comparing the score after class correction with that recorded secretly by the instructor. |
| Students' general goals in life, or philosophy of living | Have the students write an essay describing their philosophies of life, with special reference to some of the main goals they wish to pursue. This could be supplemented by interview material obtained under conditions of good rapport. |

## Table 2 (Continued)

### Illustrations of direct and indirect approaches

| Less direct, or indirect, approach | Relationships reported |
|---|---|
| The same hypotheses were repeated, followed in each case by a description of five possible experiments originally proposed by students. Students were asked to check the *best* and the *poorest* for each hypothesis. | The scores on this test gave somewhat similar results (correlation = .63) to those obtained by the original test but not close enough for one to be used entirely in place of the other (26). |
| The same hypotheses were repeated, followed again by a description of five possible experiments originally proposed by students. But students were now asked to *rank* the five in order of goodness. | The scores on this test gave results still closer to those obtained by the original test (correlation = .79). This is a high relationship but a still better one could be sought (26). |
| A verbal test was built to sample knowledge about parts of the gun, duties of the crew, appearance of tracers when the gun was properly aimed, etc. | Results correlated .62 with instructors' marks, and the test was therefore not a good substitute for the performance ratings (32). |
| A pictorial test was built to sample exactly the same knowledge as the verbal test did, but with pictures rather than words alone. | Results correlated .90 with instructors' marks, and the pictorial form was therefore a good substitute for the performance ratings (32). |
| The students were given a 50-statement attitude questionnaire on cheating. They marked each statement according to a code indicating degree of agreement or disagreement. Both signed and unsigned questionnaires were obtained on each student. The latter were identified through secret marks and used for deriving scores because of their inherently greater validity (truthfulness). | The verbal opinions regarding cheating on examinations were found to be unrelated to actual cheating practices. A correlation of practically zero was obtained between the questionnaire results and those based on class correction (4). |
| Administer an instrument such as the inventory, *General Goals of Life* (30). This inventory contains 20 common goals such as self-development, living for the pleasure of the moment, serving God, etc., each of which is paired against all the others. The student checks the goal in each possible pair that he values more. | Evidence from one large-scale study indicates that results derived from the inventory are a valid equivalent of the *verbal* statements (10, 37 ff.).<br><br>There remains, of course, the further question of how close the verbal statements or inventory results agree with actual conduct. (They need not be perfectly consistent.) |

sponses as our criterion. In doing this, we assume that what a student *professes* as his philosophy of living may be of some significance in its own right. However, we then implicitly assume that what a person says he does or says he will do is a good indication of what he *will* do. This assumption may be wholly unsound, for a person may say one thing and do another. Opinion and action are not always highly consistent. This leaves us with a choice: shall we take a person's verbal statements or his actions as the criterion of his philosophy of living? Most of us would agree that the latter is the *ultimate* criterion, although one that is not too accessible to us. If we accept a person's actions as the best criterion of his personal philosophy, then we are obliged to check both his verbal formulations and his inventory responses against this criterion. When we do this, we resort to an external criterion.

Third, in most of the illustrations, the direct approach makes use of situations that approximate the real thing. This makes sense, for behavior in natural situations should furnish the ultimate criterion for any kind of test which purports to sample or to predict that behavior. In the first sentence above, the word "approximate" was used deliberately; for, in these illustrations, the direct approach does not always correspond to the observation of behavior in natural situations. But it is true that the direct approaches listed do not differ appreciably from the real thing. In our illustrations they tend toward *free-response* methods of collecting evidence.

Finally, methods which purport to yield indirect evidence do not always work. If they do not work, then we have no right to call them indirect approaches. Only if they do yield results that correlate highly with those obtained by direct methods can we call them indirect methods for appraising the same characteristics. When Table 2 was prepared, an effort was made to get illustrations of negative instances. The reasons: to sound a caution and to dramatize the need for validation.

5. An English test for foreign students contains some items designed to measure pronounciation (14, 15). One such item appears below:
   1. I spoke slowly and he underst____d.
   2. He brought more w____d for the fire.
   3. We ate the f____d comfortably.
   The student's task is to decide whether he pronounces the sounds represented by the hyphens the same or not. He records his choice on a separate answer sheet, as follows:
   1&2(×)    1&3(  )    2&3(  )    1&2&3(  )    none (  )
   a) In what sense does this type of situation represent a direct approach?
   b) In what sense does it not?
   c) How could one validate this technique?

6. It has been suggested that children's everyday writing is a good indicator of word knowledge. Do you think that the systematic collection of written work and the tabulation of word frequency counts provides a more direct approach than does a word knowledge test?

7. A leading authority on testing has recently made the statement that "our most valid tests [of aptitude and achievement] are essentially work samples of their criteria" (7, p. 32). What is meant by the expression, "work samples of their criteria"? If possible, give an illustration for each of the two domains of behavior mentioned.

8. If you are interested in some promising technical developments in the testing of problem-solving processes, read the accounts of Glaser, Damrin, and Gardner (13) and Rimoldi (18). These investigators have developed similar, but not identical, techniques for recording the sequence of a subject's decisions as he attempts to solve a given problem. An important feature of each technique is that the subject gets a feedback after each decision through information provided on the back of a card or tab, the front side of which indicates a question to ask or an operation to perform next. The back side tells him what he would find out. Through the use of this card or tab device, each technique approaches more directly the thought processes of the subject.

## QUALITIES TO BE SOUGHT IN EVALUATION SITUATIONS

In various ways we have come to grips with the problem of choosing or devising situations. We have also arrived at certain basic concepts and principles. It now remains for us to push our thinking to higher levels of generalization. In this last section, therefore, we will systematically consider four major qualities which *any* sample of evaluation situations should possess.

### Appropriateness or relevance

#### General considerations

The single most important quality to be sought in evaluation situations is appropriateness—in technical language, *relevance*. A technique must surely present, or sample, the *right situations* if it is to evoke the *right behavior*.

*An evaluation situation is relevant to the degree that it gives each individual an opportunity to show the attainment or nonattainment of an educational objective.* Thus, not only should a situation permit the student to show desirable behavior, but also undesirable behavior associated with lack of attainment of the objective. If students have misconceptions about certain health practices and it is the instructor's aim to eliminate these false ideas, then the evaluation situations should permit students to show the *specific* misconceptions which they still hold. This latter condition may seem easy to fulfill, but actually in framing test items, such as multiple-choice, instructors often fail to include *the specific misconceptions prevalent in the student group.* (This problem comes in for detailed treatment in Chapter 8.)

In general, a situation will be relevant to the degree that it meets the conditions laid down in the specifications. This means that *it should either sample directly the defined behavior or sample reactions that provide good indirect indexes of this behavior.*

There is really nothing profound about the concept of relevance. The situations we use should be of the right kind. But time and again one can inspect situations, particularly those of the paper-and-pencil variety, and find them sorely lacking in this requirement. True-false items are used to sample a variety of outcomes, for only some of which they are appropriate; content thoroughly discussed in class is used as a basis for assessing the student's progress in application, when in reality all one can get from this is an indication of how well the content was remembered; and questionnaire items are used to elicit expressions of attitudes under conditions in which truthful responses seem unlikely. The pressure to use an economical technique undoubtedly accounts for many such practices.

9. Our discussion has emphasized choice of the right situations. Show how, in the case of achievement tests, this includes sampling the right *content*. Illustrate from your own field or activity.

10. Name a few important outcomes of instruction, preferably from your own field, for which paper-and-pencil situations would not be appropriate.

11. On open-book examinations, textbooks and other references are permitted. Name one important outcome of instruction for which this condition would improve the relevance of the evaluation procedure and explain how it would.

### Fulfilling special conditions

The notion of relevance does cover a lot of ground, for situations must usually be appropriate in a number of respects if they are to be useful for a given purpose. Some special conditions which deserve discussion here include those of complexity, abstractness, novelty, structure, difficulty, and power to motivate.

*Degree of complexity.* Complexity is a property of a situation that refers to the breadth of elements or relations with which the individual must cope. It varies with the number of significant elements required for a satisfactory response, and with the pattern of their interrelationships.

Ready illustrations of this property come from the field of mathematics. In this connection, contrast the two problems below which have some similar elements, yet differ in complexity. Try working them yourself so as to be able to pinpoint the differences. (For this purpose you will need to know that the formula for the circumference is $\pi\, d$, where $\pi$ is approximately equal to $\frac{22}{7}$, or 3.1416, and $d$ is the diameter. It is not necessary to carry out computations in either problem.)

*Which problem is more complex? Why?*

1. A circle has a circumference of 2000 feet. If the circumference is increased by 6 feet, what will be the approximate increase in the diameter?
2. The Coliseum at Rome is encircled with 2000 feet of rope which fits tightly. If the length of the rope is increased by 6 feet, how many men, if any, could stand between the rope and the building?

   a) no man        b) six men        c) 100 men        d) 1000 men

The need for complexity is most evident for tests of thinking. If complex thinking is the intended process, the situations used must be sufficiently complex to stimulate it. Many achievement tests fail at this point; they present problems much too simple to evoke other than the simplest of responses.

12. Select several problems or questions from your field so as to represent a range of complexity. Then analyze each in detail to identify features that contribute to its complexity.
13. If one includes a variety of questions on the same topic, is one sure to attain complexity?

*Degree of abstractness.* Abstractness refers to the degree to which situations depart from concrete reality. Highly abstract situations tend to include materials expressed in symbolic form, such as number, language, geometric figures, formulas, and the like. Some examples appear below.

In the following division problem, each letter stands for a digit. What is the numerical value of $X$?

$$
\begin{array}{r}
DEFX\phantom{00} \\
AB\overline{)BCDBX} \\
AB\phantom{0000} \\
\overline{HID}\phantom{00} \\
HDX\phantom{0} \\
\overline{ADB}\phantom{} \\
ADB\phantom{} \\
\hline
\end{array}
$$

The four problem figures below make a series.[2] Select the one figure from among the answer figures which belongs next in the series (after 1).

Problem figures                               Answer figures

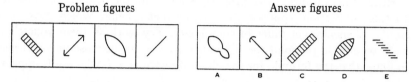

Abstract situations are inherent in such subjects as mathematics, logic, philosophy, and the sciences. They are also common in standardized tests of general intelligence.

14. Why do you suppose tests of general intelligence make heavy use of abstract, artificial materials?
15. What advantage would a test utilizing abstract materials as above have for measuring the general reasoning ability of individuals who have reading or other language deficiencies?
16. If a school were interested in measuring the progress of its students toward the broad objective of effective thinking, would the use of abstract situations as the above be the most appropriate?

*Degree of novelty.* Situations may vary from the familiar to the relatively unfamiliar or novel, depending on the individual's background of experience. Novelty is especially important to obtain evidence of understanding or intellectual skills and abilities of any kind. Familiar situations, those in which the student needs only to remember solutions, simply will not do for such purposes.

Novelty can be introduced in different ways. The usual way is to include materials that are somewhat new but that do not involve different relations from those previously studied. Such materials may be purely fictional or hypothetical. Another way is to include materials like those studied, but that also include some new relations or elements.

There are limits to novelty, however. Situations can be too much divorced from the individual's schooling or general experience. In that case, they really amount to puzzle situations and are unfair.

17. Examine the *Taxonomy,* especially the section on application, for illustrations of ways in which novelty can be introduced into problem situations.

*Degree of structure.* Situations may also vary in a characteristic known as structure. A situation is structured to the degree that it conveys a

[2] Reproduced by permission of the Psychological Corporation, New York.

definite meaning to all individuals concerned. Most situations in everyday life, because of their familiar features, tend to be highly structured. Objective test situations also tend to be highly structured. By presenting a specific problem or question, and fixed alternatives, they restrict the variety of ways in which a person can react.

In contrast, unstructured situations are inherently ambiguous. They convey no definite meaning of what is wanted or required. For some purposes of appraisal, notably personality study, this condition is an advantage. It encourages, indeed compels, the individual to impose his own peculiar interpretation and method of performance.

Ambiguity or lack of structure can be introduced into test situations in two main ways. One way is to use stimulus materials that are bizarre or otherwise ambiguous: inkblots, pictures, drawings, incomplete sentences, and the like. All of these materials permit varying interpretation by the person. The other main way is to keep the directions for the task quite general, if not downright vague: "Tell me what you see in this picture," "You may do anything you like with these materials." As a result the person does not get a clear idea of one's purposes nor of the inferences to be drawn from the recorded test behavior. In practice, ambiguity is likely to be fostered by a combination of ambiguous materials and directions.

18. Occasionally examination questions take this form: "Discuss juvenile delinquency," "Discuss America's entry into the First World War," etc. Are these highly structured situations? Explain.

19. For which of the following attributes would it be desirable to use relatively unstructured evaluation situations?
   a) willingness to take responsibility
   b) reading interests
   c) knowledge of the basic terminology of a course
   d) ability to evaluate a work of art such as a painting on the basis of criteria considered appropriate

*Appropriate difficulty.* The difficulty of any task or situation depends largely upon its complexity, abstractness, novelty, and structure. Situations should be neither too easy nor too hard for the intended group. Those which are too easy do not fully reveal individual differences nor do those which are too hard because they either fail to bring out any response or they encourage random activity such as sheer guessing. It may be possible to estimate the difficulty of a situation but actual tryout is the surest way to determine difficulty.

*Potency or power to motivate.* Not only must situations be appropriate in most of the foregoing respects but they must also be capable of motivating the desired behavior. *It is not enough just to give the person an opportunity to express the right behavior: he must want to express it.*

This is obviously quite crucial for so many of our efforts to appraise behavior depend upon our getting the person's full cooperation. If the results are to be valid, individuals must be motivated to do their best on the usual intelligence, or achievement, test; they must want to be honest in situations calling for a self-report of their interests, attitudes, personal problems, or habits; and they must want to act naturally in situations calling for an expression of their typical behavior.

Perhaps the most common approach for building potency is to make the situations intrinsically interesting for the intended group. Problems and materials chosen for tests and other evaluation situations should be of such a kind that students genuinely want to find the answers to the questions raised.

As individuals become increasingly mature, it seems important to emphasize the *cooperative* nature of appraisal and the individual's stake in the process. When the student sees that he will benefit directly from an evaluation, he is more likely to put forth his best effort or to be frank in his responses. This places responsibility on the instructor or counselor too, for he must assure that the situations deal with significant outcomes and that there will be follow-up in the form of a report of results, or counseling, or modifications in instruction. If these latter conditions are not met, one can hardly expect a student to approach the situations with a high degree of intrinsic motivation.

### Control of irrelevant factors

The second major quality to be sought in evaluation situations is the control of irrelevant factors. These are unwanted factors that seriously influence behavior and thus distort the results. Probably every technique is open to these distortions. Indirect approaches, which tend to introduce artificial conditions, seem especially susceptible.

Some irrelevant factors arise from defects in the test situations; the problem here is to see that the situations are free of such defects, or to take steps to eliminate them beforehand. But some factors are difficult to eliminate entirely; they must be controlled either by experimental or statistical means, or by some combination of these two. Guessing on objective-type tests is such a factor. Usually testers try to control this through a combination of appropriate directions for taking the test and a correction formula applied to the scores.

In the following sections we shall consider common irrelevant factors, under these headings: (1) complex or ambiguous directions, (2) unintentional clues, (3) familiar or unfamiliar content, (4) response sets, (5) desire for social approval, (6) chance errors.

### Complex or ambiguous directions

Situations that contain an element of language—and certainly this is true of most test situations—often introduce variables apart from the intended task. Take the case of objective-type questions. Various secondary features often change the nature of the task or throw the emphasis where it was not intended. While the examiner may assume that the question alone sets the task and determines its difficulty, this may not be the case. External considerations, such as confusing directions, poor format or arrangement of data, or a complicated method of recording answers, may distort the entire problem.

As an illustration, try working the following problem (3, p. 48):

Each of the following items consists of a STATEMENT, followed by three COMMENTS on the statement. You are to judge which one is the *best* comment. The best comment is the one which shows most understanding of the subject discussed in the statement. *Blacken* the answer space corresponding to the number of the one best comment.

88. If one means by education the matter of going to school, there is equality of education in America.

  1. There are some slight exceptions to this statement, but it is essentially true to the facts. School attendance is now compulsory in all the states.
  2. Differences in quality of schooling provided are important in spite of virtual equality of opportunity to attend school.
  3. Differences in income between individuals and between communities affect both the length and the kind of schools available to most children.[3]

Now try to review your thinking. Were the directions clear enough so that you knew what was wanted? Did such expressions as "best comment" and "most understanding" convey a clear-cut meaning to you? If your answer is yes to these two questions, you are an exception. Most students would probably find such an item confusing.

In an actual tryout of this item, the directions were found to be rather confusing (3, p. 48). The confusion centered on the terms "best comment" and "most understanding." Some students tried to find the comment that agreed most with the original statement. Others looked for the comment

[3] Reproduced by permission of the University of Chicago Press.

that showed the most connection to the statement but had difficulty determining what type of connection was wanted. Still others chose the comment they believed to be the most true and complete irrespective of the original statement. And some chose the comment that "throws the most light on the statement." Thus, what was intended to be a clear-cut problem became a confusing one and a different problem for each student.

Such features as confusing directions may become the primary source of difficulty, and the intended problem or question only secondary. A careful job of editing will uncover and eliminate some undesirable features; but experimental methods are necessary to control or eliminate others. Having a small but carefully selected sample of students think out loud while solving problems is a good way to detect such undesirable features. This may be done as a pretesting operation, before using the situations on a larger scale.

### Unintentional clues

Occasionally clues find their way into test situations. Perhaps the most notorious examples are "specific determiners." These are telltale words or phrases that tend to give away the correct answer. They are especially common on true-false items. It has been found that statements containing absolute terms such as "all," "always," "certainly," "entirely," and the like are much more likely to be false than true. On the other hand, words or phrases that qualify the statement, such as "generally," "sometimes," "as a rule," "may," and the like, are much more likely to be true than false. Also, the longer the statement, the more likely it is to be true.

20. Irrelevant clues are common in other items such as multiple-choice. Recall instances in which the framing of items or their arrangement gave a clue to the right answer.
21. How do such clues reward the testwise student? How can they be eliminated?

### Familiar or unfamiliar content

Tests aiming at critical judgment or interpretation often fall short because they include familiar content. One widely used reading test contained a passage on the topic Rubber, followed by a number of questions testing comprehension of the passage. Yet a well-informed pupil could answer many of the questions without having read the passage. If the exercise is to test reading *comprehension* and not knowledge about the subject of the passage, then it should include content that is relatively new to the group for which intended.

22. If a course aims at the development of skills in interpretation and application, as well as a fund of informaton, would it be desirable to separate the evaluation of these? Explain.

23. Does the following item from a standard intelligence test involve content that is likely to be familiar to most elementary school children (8)?

A symphony is to a composer as a book is to what?

( ) paper    ( ) sculptor    ( ) author    ( ) man    ( ) musician

## Response sets

A response set may be defined as "any tendency causing a person consistently to make different responses to test items than he would have made *had the same content been presented in a different form*" (5, p. 491).[4] We have already mentioned such tendencies in our discussion of unintentional clues. Since response sets do affect the person's reactions and his ultimate score, and since they very often are extraneous variables, we must reckon with them.

So far, six types of response sets have been indentified (5):

1. Tendency to gamble; caution versus incaution. This tendency occurs on objective tests when students are allowed to omit items. Under such conditions, some students consistently omit more items than others who have equal knowledge. It also occurs as a kind of evasiveness on interest, attitude, and personality inventories that contain a neutral category (e.g., "like-indifferent-dislike," "yes- ?-no").

2. Definition of terms. Individuals differ in the meanings consistently given to certain response categories in questionnaires and inventories: "like," "indifferent," "agree," "uncertain," "frequently," and so on. This means that two individuals with similar interests or beliefs might receive different scores because of their different habits of responding.

3. Tendency to give many responses, when the subject is to list or check as many statements as he wishes. This occurs in such essay questions as "Point out differences between—" or "List the causes of—." One student may give an extensive list of points, another only a short selected list. Which receives the better score depends on the system of scoring, but the score may reflect the set in answering as well as ability. The same possibility occurs in some objective tests and attitude inventories.

4. Bias, in which the subject tends to give one particular answer when

[4] Italics are mine.

in doubt. This set tends to occur whenever two alternatives are offered: true-false, yes-no, like-dislike, agree-disagree, and so on. It has been shown, for example, that on true-false tests a majority of students tend to say true when in doubt (6, p. 50). Acquiescence thus tends to make false items more valid, and true items less valid.

5. Speed versus accuracy. This is important on timed tests. A person's score often depends on which set he adopts: to work rapidly or to work accurately.

6. Style of answer on essay examinations. There are probably as many sets here as there are styles of composition: coherent and organized, "shotgun" approach, "bare bones" outline, and so on. Unless the task is clearly defined, choice of style will depend on the student's set and his idea of what is wanted. Differences in grades received will tend to reflect differences in style of answer as well as in knowledge or ability.

Response sets have the greatest influence in ambiguous or unstructured situations.

. . . If a situation is structured for the student so that he knows the answer required, he responds directly to the content of the item, and response sets probably are unimportant. If he does not know the answer, his response is determined by caution, acquiescence, or other sets. Acquiescence appears on difficult true-false items; bias on difficult pitch judgments; and evasiveness on attitude judgments where the student has no strong opinion. Ambiguity may be increased by the test situation or by directions which leave the student to judge whether guessing is penalized, whether speed is more rewarding than carefulness, how many statements should be checked, or what is meant by "indifferent."

. . . No "objective" test is truly objective, so long as any part of the stimulus situation is sufficiently unstructured to permit individual interpretation. Degree of structuration varies from the item where the response is obvious for the group tested, to the one where the student has no idea what is wanted (5, pp. 483–84).

Hence, the best way to control response sets is to eliminate the ambiguity or lack of structure from test situations. This can be done in various ways: use the multiple-choice form, which seems free of response sets, when possible and otherwise desirable; make choices less ambiguous, by reducing the number of alternatives for a judgment and eliminating the neutral response; increase the testwiseness of the student by an explanation regarding his response sets (5, pp. 487–91).

24. Under what general conditions might it be undesirable or unnecessary to try to control a response set?

### Desire for social approval

In the appraisal of abilities, the usual purpose is to find out *how well* the individual does. In the study of interests, attitudes, and other personal characteristics, however, the usual purpose is to find out something about the individual's *habits*. It should be clear that in the former case control lies in the task and thus with the examiner, for it is the task that defines the requirements of a good response and that channels thinking accordingly. It should be clear too that in the latter case, when we rely upon the individual for a report, control generally lies with him, for it is he who knows his habits well and he alone who can decide what to tell.

In any situation calling for a self-report, whether interview or questionnaire, it is thus quite important that the subject give a truthful report. This is often difficult to get, especially if the subject wants to make a good impression or describe himself in terms that are valued by his fellows or superiors. In a community with conservative political views, for example, a liberally inclined student might feel some hesitancy about disclosing his own views on social issues, at least to the extent of playing them down on an attitude questionnaire. In a school which places great value upon enjoyment of music and other cultural activities, a student might feel some pressure, however subtle, to report these as his own preferences when in fact they may not be. Modern society, and especially American society, places a heavy premium upon conformity; hence, it is no wonder that this pressure to conform often distorts a person's description of himself. After all, who wants to be "different"?

The pressure to conform or to please others is thus a subtle irrelevant factor in self-report situations, and also in situations where the person knows his personal characteristics are under observation. Establishing good rapport with the subject, especially by making him feel free to accept himself as he is, seems to be the soundest way to control this factor.

### Chance errors

Chance errors of measurement, which are difficult to eliminate entirely, are a further class of irrelevant factors. These errors stem from two main sources: inadequate sampling of situations so that we do not get a representative picture of the person's behavior: and minor variations in reacting to a given situation—"lucky guesses," misreading directions, recording an answer in the wrong space, and the like. These errors are discussed more fully under Reliability (p. 117 ff.).

25. Table 2 contains a brief description of an indirect technique for measuring pronunciation of a foreign language. What possible irrelevant factors might such a technique introduce?

26. Under what conditions is speed of handwriting likely to be an irrelevant factor in a written examination?

27. In the item below, would it be possible for a student to arrive at the correct answer through a process other than the intended (and other than guessing)?

The formula $C = \frac{5}{9}(F - 32)$ relates the thermometer readings on the centigrade scale C and the Fahrenheit scale F. The readings on the centigrade and Fahrenheit thermometer will be the same when $C = F =$

a) $-40$      b) 0      c) 32      d) 100      e) 212

## Practicability

The third major quality to seek in evaluation situations is practicability from the standpoints of time, effort, and facilities required. Not only must situations evoke the right behavior and control irrelevant factors, but they must also be practicable.

For various practical reasons as we noted earlier, it may not be possible to rely upon natural situations for sampling behavior. The alternative is to set up a controlled situation in which the *opportunity* for the defined behavior or correlated behavior may be offered at will. This is an efficient approach, for the evaluation can now be made much more quickly than otherwise. But a major problem here is to control the situation without introducing irrelevant factors.

Pressures of time and cost also force us to rely more and more upon group situations. When large numbers of people are to be examined or surveyed for their opinions, it is much more economical to do this on a group basis than individually. There is no harm in doing this, provided the group situation yields sufficiently valid results.

Situations that require expensive equipment or facilities also pose practical problems. While it is often desirable to get sound recordings of classroom discussions, or of utterances during a problem-solving session, or of pronunciation of a foreign language, it becomes quite costly to do this on a large scale, i.e., for several classes in a school. Equipment itself is only one factor here: special rooms with soundproofing may be required; clerical costs must be allowed for if the record is to be transcribed; and much effort must often be devoted to interpretation or scoring.

Practicability thus looms as an important factor. Cost compels us to choose the simpler of two techniques, *if* it gives results substantially equivalent to those yielded by the more direct or complex technique.

The search for simpler, yet adequate, techniques is the main way to meet this problem of practicability. But there is another good way to achieve practicability—a way that does not aim at simplification of the technique but rather at group procedures for evaluation. If essays, English compositions, and term papers represent worth-while learning experiences, as they most probably do, and if the job of reading and evaluating these is too much for the instructor, why can't this job be shared with students? After all, this gives the student an enlarged responsibility and a valuable experience in itself. That such a procedure can work is vouched for in recent experiments making use of group evaluations (20, 27). The pattern in such experiments was either to make each student individually responsible for grading five or so of his classmates' papers, or to have him work jointly with a subgroup of the class on an equal number of papers. In this kind of setup, the instructor may serve merely as a guide or consultant, or he may reserve for himself the right to review the student evaluations. It would seem that this approach is basically sound and deserves wider use.

28. "In any learning situation the individual is learning more than one type of response." What implications for evaluation do you see in this generalization?

### Reliability

#### A problem of sampling

The fourth major quality to seek in any sample of evaluation situations is reliability. This refers to the adequacy with which a test, or any instrument or series of observations, samples the defined behavior. The series of situations should sample the defined behavior in such a way that the conclusions drawn from this sample are dependable. This means (1) *sampling the range of situations* in which the behavior may be expressed and (2) *including a large enough number of these situations* so that the behavior noted is typical of the individuals concerned. Note that it is first necessary to sample widely, so that the sample of behavior will be representative rather than too narrow, and then to insure enough repetition of the situations so that the results will be reasonably stable.

Too limited a range of situations may give a wholly misleading picture. In the writing of English compositions, for instance, the kind of topic has quite an effect on the quality of students' compositions. The topic, "Should We Break Up Our Big Cities?" may stimulate a student to produce a copious flow of ideas and to organize them well. He may write "way over his head" simply because he has strong convictions about the topic and a good fund of information. Another topic, "How Can We Control Juvenile Delinquency?" may leave him flat—so flat, that his writing may seem mediocre compared with the first effort. Because of such variations in the stimulus value of topics and in a student's background of information, it is necessary to have him write on a variety of topics before we can truly generalize about his skill. Usually, too, it is necessary to vary the task so as to sample different types of writing—exposition, argument, description, and so on. Whether or not one varies the task itself would depend upon the narrowness or breadth with which one defines this skill.

Why is it necessary to include a large enough number of situations? Simply because an individual may not respond consistently from situation to situation, nor from one occasion to another even when the situations are similar. For evidence of this, let us turn to a study by Traxler and Anderson (25). These investigators had students write a pair of two-hour essays a few days apart. They took great pains to make the tasks comparable from student to student and on the two exercises. This was done by assigning two highly similar topics, "The Discovery of Gold in California" and "The Pony Express"; by distributing a set of instructions for writing each essay, an outline giving the four main divisions of the paper, and a set of unorganized notes on each division written in the form of incomplete sentences; and by requiring that the entire paper be written from the notes supplied. The investigators found that competent readers agreed very closely in the grades given to each set of essays, so that variation in grades between the two sets of essays could not be attributed to the readers. Yet despite such careful grading and the comparability of the writing assignments, grades on the two sets of essays correlated only .6o. This suggests that writing is somewhat variable from one occasion to another and that more than one essay is needed before dependable conclusions can be drawn about a student's skill.

So even when situations are comparable we find variation in behavior. Much of this source of variation comes from the person himself—from variations in mood, energy, speed of reaction, accuracy, memory, attention, and other characteristics from one occasion to the next. The remaining variation not caused by differences in the situations comes from many minor chance influences such as lucky guesses, recording an answer in the wrong space, and the like.

Because human behavior is not perfectly consistent from one situation to another nor from one occasion to another, single situations are no-toriously unreliable. So, too, are other small samples of behavior.

If single situations and small samples are generally unreliable, then how many situations should one include for a given evaluation? This is the question to which we now turn.

### Estimating size of sample needed

We cannot answer the preceding question in the abstract except to say "as many situations as are needed to give the degree of reliability desired." The number of situations to include depends ultimately upon the degree of reliability we want the results to have. This in turn goes back to the specific uses we want to make of the results. While high relia-bility is generally desirable, there are some purposes for which it is un-necessary.

High reliability may be desirable for a given purpose, but practical considerations may stand in the way. It may be possible to increase the reliability of our results by including more items in a test or by extending the number of observations, but the added cost in terms of time and effort may rule this out. It is also true, as in most sampling problems, that we tend to reach a point of diminishing returns beyond which further observations add nothing to the dependability of the results.

It is possible too that some forms of behavior are so highly variable, and hence inconsistent, that a high degree of reliability is out of the question whether we like it or not. This is true of characteristics which are undergoing rapid change as a result of maturation or learning, as, for example, sensorimotor abilities in the one-year-old child (tapped by some infant intelligence tests); social behavior of young children, when they are making their first adjustments to other children and strange adults; attitudes toward the opposite sex in the early stages of adolescence; a student's pattern of life goals, which may be undergoing disturbing re-organization in late adolescence. It is also true of characteristics that reflect personality disorganization or hopeless confusion in attitudes. In all these instances, the instrument we use or the observations we make cannot do the impossible—reveal consistency where none is present. At best, they can show that certain individuals are consistently inconsistent.

Granted that the desired level of reliability is possible, the size of the sample needed will depend mainly upon the variability of the defined behavior. If the behavior in question is highly consistent from situation to situation, then it takes only a relatively small sample to yield reliable results. Such could be the case with skills in arithmetic computation or with information on American history. On the other hand, if the behavior in question tends not to be highly consistent, then it takes a relatively large sample. This is very likely so for traits such as cooperativeness, kindness, and originality.

Ordinarily, it is not possible to know how variable a given kind of behavior will be. For this reason, it is not possible to know in advance exactly how large a sample of situations will be needed. Nor is it possible to estimate accurately the degree of reliability a *given* number of test items or observations will yield. However, past experience sometimes allows us to make a reasonably good guess.

The upshot of all this is that *reliability really cannot be estimated until after a measuring instrument has been tried out, or after a series of observations has been made.* A tryout is necessary because reliability always pertains to the *results* of a test or series of observations. We speak very loosely of *the* reliability of a test or of some other procedure, as though reliability inheres in it as a fixed property. But it is more proper to recognize that reliability is a characteristic of certain specific results obtained on a specific group or individual with a specific instrument or procedure; and furthermore that the estimate of reliability is itself a function of the particular method of estimation, of which there are several.

The common methods of estimation yield a coefficient of correlation, or reliability coefficient. In general, a reliability coefficient gives us an indication of whether a sample of situations is adequate. If the coefficient is relatively low, this usually means that the sample is too small for one to draw dependable conclusions about the characteristic. In the case of a test, it is then necessary to increase its length by adding more items; in the case of observations of behavior, to increase the number and range of situations—at least until no further appreciable changes in reliability take place.

**29.** Per unit of time, objective tests yield more dependable results than do essay.

   a) What explanation will account for this?
   b) On technical grounds, is this a sufficient basis for preferring the objective type?
   c) What generalization can you make on this point (b) which will apply to any technique of evaluation?

## Appropriateness from other standpoints

The preceding four qualities are largely technical. They are good as far as they go, but in education we must often take other things into account. It is very difficult, if not fundamentally unsound, to choose or develop situations without regard to other than purely technical considerations.

One frequently neglected consideration is the effect of the evaluation procedure upon the person's physical well-being. Unnecessarily long tests and tests of poor typography should not be allowed to find their way into school programs. Eyesight is much too precious to spend on such

Another consideration is the effect of the evaluation procedure upon mental health. The sample of situations and the way in which they are used should promote rather than endanger the mental health of those concerned. Situations that unduly threaten the student's feelings of adequacy and security, or that encourage a morbid introspection and preoccupation with the self, should generally be avoided.

A third consideration is the effect of the situations on human relations, such as those between students and those between students and instructor. Test situations should promote good human relations rather than disrupt them. Situations that overemphasize competition among students or that set the instructor up as watchdog or taskmaster have no place in modern education.

A fourth consideration is the extent to which the situations foster desirable learning. This consideration comes to the fore in arguments over the relative merits of essay and objective examinations. Some instructors prefer the essay, not on technical grounds but on grounds that it stimulates students to organize their thinking not only in writing the examination but also in studying the course. There is some evidence for this point of view (9, 17, 22). Other things being equal, those test situations are to be preferred which provide an excellent opportunity to practice the behavior at which instruction is aimed. Good learning situations are potentially good evaluation situations, and vice versa.

A final consideration, and one that hardly needs mentioning, relates to the area of ethical standards. Evaluation procedures should not violate the integrity and rights of the individual. They should not embarrass the person before others, nor force him to disclose attitudes and facts about himself that he prefers to keep private or confidential.

**30.** Some situations can give the individual an on-the-spot feedback, or report, on the adequacy of his responses. This may even be true of paper-and-pencil situations (see p. 149 for a discussion of the self-scorer).

a) To what extent should this process of feedback be a criterion for a satisfactory evaluation procedure?
b) Is this more than a "technical consideration"? Explain.

## REFERENCES

1. Bennett, G. K., and others. *Differential aptitude tests:* Abstract reasoning, form A. New York: Psych. Corp., 1947.
2. Bloom, B. S., and others. *Taxonomy of educational objectives, handbook I:* cognitive domain. New York: Longmans Green, 1956.
3. Bloom, B. S., and Broder, L. J. *Problem-solving processes of college students:* an exploratory investigation. Chicago: Univer. of Chicago, 1950. Copyright 1950 by the University of Chicago.
4. Corey, S. M. Professed attitudes and actual behavior. *J. educ. Psychol.*, 1937, **28**, 271–280.
5. Cronbach, L. J. Response sets and test validity. *Educ. psychol. Measmt*, 1946, **6**, 475–494.
6. Cronbach, L. J. *Essentials of psychological testing*. New York: Harper, 1949.
7. Cronbach, L. J. New light on test strategy from decision theory. In *Proc. 1954 Invit. Conf. on Test Probs.* Princeton: Educ. Test. Serv., 1954.
8. Davis, A. Education for conservation of human resources. *Progr. Educ.*, 1950, **27**, 221–226.
9. Douglass, H. R., and Tallmadge, Margaret. How university students prepare for new types of examinations. *Sch. & Soc.*, 1934, **39**, 318–320.
10. Dunkel, H. B. *General education in the humanities*. Washington: Amer. Coun. on Educ., 1947.
11. Early, L. J. A pupil-made test in social science. *Elem. Sch. J.*, 1942, **43**, 29–32.
12. Gibson, J. J. (Ed.) *Motion picture testing and research;* AAF Aviation Psychol. Prog. Res. Rep. No. 7. Washington: U. S. Govt Print Ofc., 1947.
13. Glaser, R., and others. The tab item: a technique for the measurement of proficiency in diagnostic problem solving tasks. *Educ. psychol. Measmt*, 1954, **14**, 283–293.
14. Lado, R. *English language test for foreign students*. Ann Arbor: Geo. Wahr, 1951.
15. Lado, R. Phonemics and pronunciation tests. *Modern Lang. J.*, 1951, **35**, 531, 542.
16. Lindquist, E. F. (Ed)., *Educational measurement*. Washington: Amer. Coun. on Educ., 1951.
17. Meyer, G. An experimental study of the old and new types of examination. *J. educ. Psychol.*, 1934, **25**, 641–661; and 1935, **26**, 30–40.

18. Rimoldi, H. J. A. A technique for the study of problem solving. *Educ. psychol. Measmt*, 1955, **15**, 450–461.
19. Shaftel, George, and Fannie R. *Role playing the problem story:* an approach to human relations in the classroom. New York: Natl. Conf. of Christians and Jews, 1952.
20. Simpson, R. H. Patterns for rating learning products. *Educ. psychol. Measmt*, 1953, **13**, 614–619.
21. Stalnaker, J. M., and Kurath, W. A comparison of two types of foreign language vocabulary test. *J. educ. Psychol.*, 1935, **26**, 435–442.
22. Terry, P. W. How students review for objective and essay tests. *Elem. Sch. J.*, 1933, **33**, 592–603.
23. Tharp, J. B. A modern language test. *J. higher Educ.*, 1935, **6**, 103–104.
24. Thorndike, R. L. *Personnel selection:* test and measurement techniques. New York: John Wiley, 1949.
25. Traxler, A. E., and Anderson, H. A. The reliability of an essay test in English. *Sch. Rev.*, 1935, **43**, 534–539.
26. Tyler, R. W. Ability to use scientific method. *Educ. Res. Bull.*, 1932, **11**, 1–9.
27. Walcott, F. G. Experiments in composition. *Sch. Educ. Bull*, 1949, vol. **20**, 65–68. Ann Arbor: Univer. of Michigan.
28. Wood, H. B. *Curriculum bulletin:* improving student evaluation. Eugene: Univer. of Oregon, 1952, No. 118.
29. College Entrance Examination Board. 46th annual report of the executive secretary. New York: CEEB, 1946.
30. Educational Testing Service. *General goals of life inventory.* Princeton: Educ. Test. Serv., 1950.
31. How to Make the Picture Test Item. (DA AGO PRT-873) Washington: Dep. of the Army, 1948.
32. Training Aids Section. Ninth Naval District Headquarters, Great Lakes, Ill. A comparative study of verbalized and projected pictorial tests in gunnery. Unpublished, 1945. Cited in reference 6, pp. 277–278.

## FURTHER READINGS

Bloom, B. S., and others. *Taxonomy of educational objectives, handbook I:* cognitive domain. New York: Longmans Green, 1956.
Cronbach, L. J. The meanings of problems. In Buswell, G. T. (Ed.), *Arithmetic 1948. Suppl. educ. Monogr.*, 1948, No. 66, 32–43.
Lindquist, E. F. Basic approaches in educational measurement. In E. F. Lindquist (Ed.), *Educational measurement.* Washington: Amer. Coun. on Educ., 1951. Pp. 141–157.

# Getting a Record

In the previous chapter we considered the problem of selecting appropriate situations, but we did so without paying much attention to the companion problem of getting a record. Yet no matter how good a situation may be for bringing out the right kind of behavior, it is of little value unless we can also get a record of that behavior. The decision to use a particular type of situation may thus hinge as much upon the possibility of getting a good record as upon considerations of relevance.

This suggests one way in which these two basic problems are related. There is yet another and more intimate way, true only of certain techniques. Some techniques actually combine the specific situations *and* the recording device into a single instrument. The usual printed test booklet, complete with questions, response options, and answer spaces, illustrates this combination well. The heart of any evaluation technique consists of a combination of these two features, so that the respective problems of choosing appropriate situations and devising a record must usually be treated together.

For our purposes, however, there is some advantage in separating these two problems. In this way, we can as before bring a single problem into sharp focus and give it rather close study. A word of caution is in order: remember that in this chapter we will be discussing types of records and *not* types of situations. If the reader is not careful, he may carry over a mental set from the previous chapter and not make the necessary distinction. For example, in the previous chapter we discussed motion pictures as a testing medium, but in this chapter we will consider them only as a *way of recording* behavior.

Our first purpose in this chapter is to acquaint the reader with a variety of records and with their main uses, advantages, and limitations. This will give a background for accomplishing the second purpose, which is to develop an understanding of the qualities a good record should possess.

## TYPES OF RECORDS

### Records made by an independent observer

#### Written accounts

One of the simplest ways of getting a record of behavior is to write an account of it. This may be done on the spot, shortly thereafter, or in some cases even several weeks later if the event itself stands out boldly in one's memory.

On theoretical grounds, it is clear that a complete account of any behavior is out of the question. There are too many things going on for an observer to note more than a few of them. He must of necessity concentrate on those reactions that are especially significant for his purpose, ignoring those that are insignificant or irrelevant.

Fairly complete accounts are rare, but they are sometimes made. In research on group dynamics and in group development projects, it is common practice to have two members of a group serve as detached observers of the group's functioning. One observer concentrates on the *processes* taking place as the interaction proceeds: the way the leader functions, the ways in which different members contribute to the discussion, the extent of participation, the dead spots in group discussion, and so on. His job is to get a record that will be helpful in analyzing the group's functioning and in suggesting ways it can improve its efficiency. The other observer concentrates on the *content* of the interaction: the major issues discussed by the group with the pros and cons indicated, the major agreements reached, the decisions made, and the recommendations for action agreed upon.

In contrast to such extended accounts, brief reports of single incidents are more common. The critical incidents on page 23 are of this kind. "Anecdote," or "anecdotal record," are terms frequently used to refer to such brief reports. An anecdotal record is simply a statement telling what an individual said or did in a concrete situation. Here is a sample series of such notes on an eleven-year-old boy (after 19, pp. 1–2):

2/8/56   Before class period when children were all talking in small groups, B stood alone.

2/14/56  Did not take part in discussion on what we would look for at the museum. Sat quietly.

2/15/56  Wrote about trip to museum but crumpled up his paper and threw it into basket.

2/17/56  Only child who did not volunteer to do something for the Mexican play which the children decided to produce.

2/23/56  In the yard at lunch time, asked B what he liked to do best outside of school. He replied, "Play the violin. My mother is going to help me become a violinist." Said he had no friends because his mother does not allow him to play with the boys on the street. Asked him if he would play his violin at assembly. He accepted with a smile, agreed to rehearsal in class tomorrow.

2/24/56  Brought his violin and played well. Children applauded and congratulated him. He smiled and offered to play any time we wished. Then he said he knew some Mexican songs for the play. (This is the first time he has volunteered anything.)

It is customary in writing anecdotes to describe exactly what happened and to avoid recording interpretations or value judgments of the behavior. If the observer wants to record interpretations along with the facts, he should set them off in parentheses or brackets. Keeping the records factual enhances their value. We can then accept each anecdote as a specific bit of behavior, search for patterns running through the anecdotes, and study each item in relation to other information on the person.

1. What generalizations can be drawn from the notes on the eleven-year-old boy?

2. Assuming that you would only study a few representative individuals, what aspects of student progress in your field could you study by means of anecdotal records?

### Check lists and schedules

Instead of writing an account, one may use a special recording form. This has advantages. By directing attention to certain observable acts, it tends to standardize the observations and to make them more objective. It also saves time in recording, since all one has to do is to check off items, mark tallies, write in numbers or short symbols, or draw lines. Finally, it lends itself more readily to summarization, as in the counting and classification of responses.

But special recording forms have their limitations too. They are obviously not as flexible as a written account. By setting up a fixed list of items or categories, they tend to lump many acts together, acts that may be only superficially alike. Furthermore, by compressing observations into fixed categories, they may cause the observer to overlook meaningful behavior which is not on the list. Finally, they do not include details on the circumstances surrounding an act, nor on the interrelations of acts, details that may be quite helpful in understanding the behavior.

The decision to use a special recording form will depend, first, on its appropriateness for the job, and second, on whether the advantages outweigh the limitations. Check lists and schedules do serve diagnostic purposes well, as shown in the following two examples.

The first example (Table 3) shows a list of common errors in addition. As the pupil works a standard sample of problems, the teacher checks each faulty habit observed. The complete test also includes problems on subtraction, multiplication, and addition, for which similar lists of errors are available.

The second example (Table 4) shows a form for recording a student's actions in finding an object under the microscope (18). Unlike many diagnostic check lists, this list includes both good and bad practices. Since the sequence of actions is important here, the record should provide for this. The observer accomplishes this by numbering the actions as they occur. Hence, the record shows what actions the student made and the order in which he made them. It also includes other items of information on the student's behavior and his mount. The record shown is that of a student who was very deficient in microscope skill.

Special recording forms are helpful also in studies of typical behavior. A pertinent example is the work of Anderson and associates, who were interested in teachers' classroom personalities—more specifically, in the effects of teachers' dominative and integrative contacts on children's class-

## Table 3
### Teacher's diagnostic chart for individual difficulties:
### Fundamental processes in arithmetic

Teacher's Diagnosis
for pupil _____

Name_____ School_____ Grade_____ Age_____ IQ_____

Date of Diagnosis:_____ Add.___; Subt.___; Mult.___; Div.___

Teacher's preliminary diagnosis _____

ADDITION: (Place a check before each habit observed in the pupil's work)

| | | |
|---|---|---|
| _____ | a1 | Errors in combinations |
| _____ | a2 | Counting |
| _____ | a3 | Added carried number last |
| _____ | a4 | Forgot to add carried number |
| _____ | a5 | Repeated work after partly done |
| _____ | a6 | Added carried number irregularly |
| _____ | a7 | Wrote number to be carried |
| _____ | a8 | Irregular procedure in column |
| _____ | a9 | Carried wrong number |
| _____ | a10 | Grouped two or more numbers |
| _____ | a11 | Splits numbers into parts |
| _____ | a12 | Used wrong fundamental operation |
| _____ | a13 | Lost place in column |
| _____ | a14 | Depended on visualization |
| _____ | a15 | Disregarded column position |
| _____ | a16 | Omitted one or more digits |
| _____ | a17 | Errors in reading numbers |
| _____ | a18 | Dropped back one or more tens |
| _____ | a19 | Derived unknown combination from familiar one |
| _____ | a20 | Disregarded one column |
| _____ | a21 | Error in writing answer |
| _____ | a22 | Skipped one or more decades |
| _____ | a23 | Carrying when there was nothing to carry |
| _____ | a24 | Used scratch paper |
| _____ | a25 | Added in pairs, giving last sum as answer |
| _____ | a26 | Added same digit in two columns |
| _____ | a27 | Wrote carried number in answer |
| _____ | a28 | Added same number twice |

Habits not listed above _____

(G. T. Buswell and Lenore John, 1925. By permission of the Public School Publishing
Co., Bloomington, Ill.)

room behavior. To obtain evidence of both teacher and pupil behavior, these men devised an observation blank "for recording in certain defined categories the behavior of one child at a time and simultaneously all the

## Table 4

### Check list of student reactions in finding an object under the microscope

| STUDENT'S ACTIONS | Sequence of Actions | STUDENT'S ACTIONS (Continued) | Sequence of Actions |
|---|---|---|---|
| a. Takes slide | ....1... | ah. Turns up fine adjustment screw a great distance | ........ |
| b. Wipes slide with lens paper | ....2... | ai. Turns fine adjustment screw a few turns | |
| c. Wipes slide with cloth | ........ | aj. Removes slide from stage | ...16... |
| d. Wipes slide with finger | ........ | ak. Wipes objective with lens paper | ........ |
| e. Moves bottle of culture along the table | ........ | al. Wipes objective with cloth | ........ |
| f. Places drop or two of culture on slide | ....3... | am. Wipes objective with finger | ...17... |
| g. Adds more culture | ........ | an. Wipes eyepiece with lens paper | ........ |
| h. Adds few drops of water | ........ | ao. Wipes eyepiece with cloth | ........ |
| i. Hunts for cover glasses | ....4... | ap. Wipes eyepiece with finger | ...18... |
| j. Wipes cover glass with lens paper | ....5... | aq. Makes another mount | ........ |
| k. Wipes cover with cloth | ........ | ar. Takes another microscope | ........ |
| l. Wipes cover with finger | ........ | as. Finds object | ........ |
| m. Adjusts cover with finger | ........ | at. Pauses for an interval | ........ |
| n. Wipes off surplus fluid | ........ | au. Asks, "What do you want me to do?" | ........ |
| o. Places slide on stage | ....6... | av. Asks whether to use high power | ........ |
| p. Looks through eyepiece with right eye | ........ | aw. Says, "I'm satisfied" | ........ |
| q. Looks through eyepiece with left eye | ....7... | ax. Says that the mount is all right for his eye | ........ |
| r. Turns to objective of lowest power | ....9... | ay. Says he cannot do it | ..19, 24.. |
| s. Turns to low-power objective | ...21... | az. Told to start new mount | ........ |
| t. Turns to high-power objective | ........ | aaa. Directed to find object under low power | ...20... |
| u. Holds one eye closed | ....8... | aab. Directed to find object under high power | ........ |
| v. Looks for light | ........ | | |
| w. Adjusts concave mirror | ........ | NOTICEABLE CHARACTERISTICS OF STUDENT'S BEHAVIOR | |
| x. Adjusts plane mirror | ........ | | |
| y. Adjusts diaphragm | ........ | a. Awkward in movements | ........ |
| z. Does not touch diaphragm | ...10... | b. Obviously dexterous in movements | ........ |
| aa. With eye at eyepiece turns down coarse adjustment | ...11... | c. Slow and deliberate | ...√... |
| ab. Breaks cover glass | ...12... | d. Very rapid | ........ |
| ac. Breaks slide | ........ | e. Fingers tremble | ........ |
| ad. With eye away from eyepiece turns down coarse adjustment | ........ | f. Obviously perturbed | ........ |
| ae. Turns up coarse adjustment a great distance | ..13, 22.. | g. Obviously angry | ........ |
| | | h. Does not take work seriously | ........ |
| af. With eye at eyepiece turns down fine adjustment a great distance | ..14, 23.. | i. Unable to work without specific directions | ...√... |
| ag. With eye away from eyepiece turns down fine adjustment a great distance | ...15... | j. Obviously satisfied with his unsuccessful efforts | ...√... |

| SKILLS IN WHICH STUDENT NEEDS FURTHER TRAINING | Sequence of Actions | CHARACTERIZATION OF THE STUDENT'S MOUNT | Sequence of Actions |
|---|---|---|---|
| a. In cleaning objective | ...√... | a. Poor light | ...√... |
| b. In cleaning eyepiece | ...√... | b. Poor focus | ........ |
| c. In focusing low power | ...√... | c. Excellent mount | ........ |
| d. In focusing high power | ...√... | d. Good mount | ........ |
| e. In adjusting mirror | ...√... | e. Fair mount | ........ |
| f. In using diaphragm | ...√... | f. Poor mount | ........ |
| g. In keeping both eyes open | | g. Very poor mount | ........ |
| h. In protecting slide and objective from breaking by careless focusing | ...√... | h. Nothing in view but a thread in his eyepiece | ........ |
| | | i. Something on objective | ........ |
| | | j. Smeared lens | ...√... |
| | | k. Unable to find object | ...√... |

dominative and social integrative contacts of the teacher which were directed toward that child either as an individual or as a member of a group" (1, p. 34). Each observer tallied the frequency with which certain acts occurred, using such categories and subcategories as the following for teacher behavior (1):

DC      Domination with evidence of conflict
DC-1    Determines a detail of activity in conflict (e.g., telling a troublesome pupil to sit still)
DC-5    Disapproval, blame, or shame directed toward the child as a person
DN      Domination with no evidence of conflict
DT      Domination in working together
IT      Integration with evidence of working together
IT-14   Helps child to define or advance a problem

The categories for pupil behavior were of course different from these. Experienced observers, making simultaneous but independent records of over six hundred incidents, agreed closely in their reports (1, pp. 43 ff.). Thus, in the hands of experienced observers, the blank provided a simple but adequate record of both teacher and pupil behavior.

3. Suppose you were to develop a check list or schedule which an observer might use to characterize an instructor's technique in leading class discussions.

    a) Explain how you could use the critical incident technique to help you get specifics for the recording form.
    b) Discuss the advantages and limitations of such a form as compared with a written account of an instructor's technique.

### Records made by mechanical devices

For many purposes, mechanical recording devices can replace the human observer. Not only that, they can very often improve upon him as well. In particular, they can minimize many of the errors that an observer is likely to make; they can "see" more than he can; and they can "stay on the job" for long periods of time without impairing their efficiency. Their greatest limitations are their cost and the fact that they cannot make the sorts of judgments that a human observer can.

Outside of big-time college football, the use of motion pictures for *recording* performance is rare in educational circles. Expense and other practical considerations virtually eliminate this medium for all but liberally supported research projects in human relations.

Through a process known as time-lapse photography, however, it is possible to obtain records that serve almost as well as motion pictures. This process requires the taking of still pictures at short intervals, either at will or automatically.

Photography has been put to a variety of uses. Perhaps the earliest to which it has been put is the recording of eye movements and fixations during reading. At first, photographs were used to record such phenomena, but since 1917 motion pictures have become the standard method. Time-lapse photography itself has been used to study the behavior of children in various group settings, such as the playroom or classroom. The armed services have also made effective use of photography for purposes of recording. One technique was to synchronize cameras with gun triggers used by aerial gunners (12). As each shot was fired, the camera recorded the point of aim. The film could be used for getting an accuracy score and for analyzing causes of misses.

## Sound recording

The mass production of efficient tape and wire recorders has put sound recording within the reach of the classroom teacher—indeed, in some schools, within the reach of individual students. Already we can point to many significant uses of these instruments, and the applications are growing steadily.

Sound recordings play a prominent part in the evaluation of speech and language habits. Recordings can be made of speeches delivered before public-speaking classes; these can be analyzed later by the class or the individual privately. Instructors can also profit from such recordings and analysis of their speech. Students in foreign language courses can make good use of recorders by reading aloud passages and then playing back the recording. This procedure gives the student a chance to evaluate his own pronunciation immediately after he speaks.

As illustrated in Chapter 2, some recent studies of problem-solving have used automatic recorders. The basic technique is to get the student to think out loud and not to worry too much about getting the answer. With practice, some students are able to do this sort of thing by themselves, merely by going through each problem in turn and speaking their thoughts into the recording machine. If it should happen that many students can operate in this way, the procedure could be applied in the schools on a very large scale.

In the training of counselors and interviewers, recordings are now pretty much standard practice. Not only does a sound recording capture words and their ideational content; it captures other content that a written record would miss: inflections, tone of voice, hesitation—qualities that especially reveal feelings and attitudinal content. Automatic recording has the added advantage of eliminating the need for an observer, whose presence might distract both counselor and client, and thus distort the interaction.

Recent studies of teaching and learning have made effective use of sound recording. At one level, the recordings may lead to a study of an individual instructor's discussion technique. From the utterances recorded and transcribed, it is possible to classify and study the instructor's activities, the participation of certain students, and the ways in which the discussion moved in the treatment of a topic (20). At another and deeper level, it is possible to study the conscious thought processes of individual students. This is done by using the method of "stimulated recall" (4). As before, sound recordings are made of an entire class period. Then later—usually within forty-eight hours after the original recording— these are played back to individual students. As the recording is played back, the experimenter stops it at certain critical points and asks the student to report the thoughts he had in the original situation at that point. The method thus gives a way of reviving thoughts that were not expressed orally in the classroom situation. Such data have led to many interesting findings on the relative merits of lecture and discussion methods of teaching (5), and on the effects of certain personality factors on learning (10).

Sound recording also accounts in no small way for the rapid strides made in the study of group dynamics. This is a frontier field that concerns itself with the dynamics of small, face-to-face groups—committees, conference groups, school boards, and so on. Transcriptions of the recordings are especially helpful in studying the group's problem-solving processes.

4. Airlines are now making use of recordings of dialogues between clerks and customers (20).

   a) If clerks are aware that their conversations with customers are now being recorded, how does this change the definition of the skills and traits being recorded?

   b) How could such recordings be most profitably used for in-service training?

5. What advantages would a sound recording of problem-solving utterances have over the subject's description (in retrospect) of the way he went about solving a problem?

6. List advantages and limitations of sound recordings as compared with a human observer for each of these purposes:

    a) A speech instructor wishes to judge his students' ability in public speaking.

    b) An instructor wishes to study the effectiveness with which he lectures.

### Graphic records of performance skills

In the execution of a skill, performance is often so rapid and so complex that an observer cannot record the significant actions. Even a motion picture recording might leave something to be desired. For such skills, graphic records might prove helpful, provided the performer's actions could in some way be registered by a mechanical device.

An excellent example of such a device is the apparatus devised by Lindahl for recording disk-cutter operation (13). This is shown schematically in Figure 4. In operating the machine, the worker presses a pedal to drive the cutting wheel and then releases it for the next cut. These actions are carried through the recording apparatus and yield records such as that shown in Figure 5. This series of records shows the degree of skill at various stages of practice. The record at the top shows lack of skill: long pauses between strokes (horizontal lines), uneven speed dur-

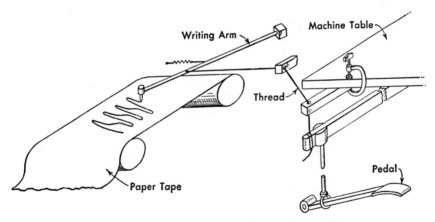

**Fig. 4. Device for recording disk-cutter operation (13).**

(Reproduced by permission from a redrawing in Cronbach [8].)

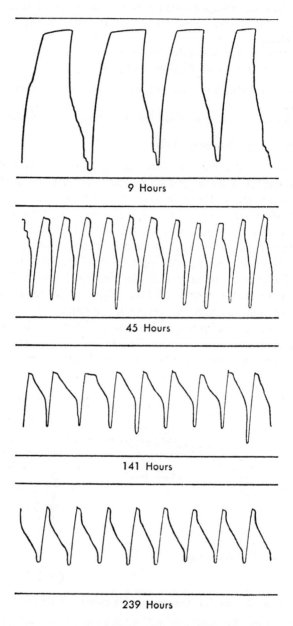

9 Hours

45 Hours

141 Hours

239 Hours

Fig. 5. Improvement in the foot-action pattern of a trainee (13).

ing the cutting operation (downstroke), jerky foot action toward the end of each stroke, and a rather deliberate release of the pedal (upstroke). The final record shows skillful operation.

Such graphic records are valuable for teaching purposes in that they show the trainee what errors he is making and they help him recognize the "feel" of the machine when he performs the operation correctly.

### Other devices

For the sake of completeness, we should note another large class of mechanical recording devices. These are the various devices used to obtain measures of physiological reactions and sensory discrimination, of which the following are good examples: the chronoscope, for recording reaction time; the psychogalvanic reflex apparatus, for measuring changes in electrical resistance associated with muscular and nervous activity; and more recently, an electronic device for recording body sway while the subject stands blindfolded or with his eyes closed. Accounts of such devices may be found in standard books on experimental psychology and in some references on personality assessment.

## Records made by the subject himself

As a person goes through a school program, indeed as he goes through life in general, he produces many records himself. Some of these are simply self-reports, in which the person describes or appraises his own behavior and characteristics; others are not reports as such, but personal products that arise out of his daily activities and that serve well as records of his past behavior.

### Self-reports

Imagine, for a moment, that you have been given the task of describing another person's philosophy of life. You have ample time and opportunity to associate with this person and to observe him or her in everyday life. Undoubtedly, from such contacts, you could piece together many bits of evidence that would faithfully portray this person's philosophy of life. But think of the cost in time and effort! And think too of the many thoughts, feelings, and actions of this person that you could not possibly observe, for reasons of inaccessibility and privacy.

It is for such practical reasons that self-report procedures have come into prominence in recent years. Instead of following a person around to get evidence of his behavior, we try to enlist him as an observer. We assume that no one is in a better position to observe his activities than he.

This last statement must be taken with some reservation. Clearly, a person cannot give full attention to some task and at the same time serve as an observer of himself. To a degree, he should be able to remember how he went about the task or solved a particular problem, and to give a reasonably adequate report of this. Where this kind of follow-up report is called for, the person must make it as soon after the activity as possible to avoid errors in remembering.

Most self-reports deal with *typical* behavior rather than with any specific task or event. They call for statements or judgments about one's habitual ways of reacting, whether in the realm of thinking, feeling, or acting. It is now common practice to ask students or other subjects to report upon a wide variety of personal habits: leisure-time activities, reading interests, study methods, health practices, buying habits, social attitudes, modes of adjustment, feelings about self, activity preferences, and others.

Self-reports do not necessarily have to deal with past behavior only. They may deal with present, future, or hypothetical situations, as shown in the following examples: "Name two other students with whom you would like to work on a course project"; "How many hours a week are you going to study during the next term?"; "If you had $2,000 and a month of leisure, how would you spend them?"

Self-reports may be simple written accounts. The most obvious examples that come to mind are diaries and logs, in which the person records events almost as soon as they occur. In education, diaries are rarely used to gather intimate details of a person's life, although this kind of material has proved valuable in studies of personality development and acculturation processes. They may deal, however, with emotion-laden material, such as things or people that bother the student, or the way he feels about certain events. More commonly they deal with interests both inside and outside the school, and with progress reports in studies and school projects. Because the diary or log places responsibility upon the student for recording significant events and for evaluating his own progress, this technique would seem to deserve wider use than it now enjoys.

Generally, self-reports are made on special recording forms. These forms also contain the necessary questions or statements to which the person responds. As with tests, the choices may be recorded on the booklet or on a special answer sheet. The effect is the same: a record of judgments which, in most instances, are not the behaviors in question but indicators of them, either assumed or demonstrated to be so. We shall have more to say about this distinction shortly. But for the moment, let us note some of the common ways in which individuals record their judgments on self-report devices.

1. Simple check list. Given a list of items, the subject checks off those that apply to him. Instructions vary: sometimes they ask him to check all that apply to him; other times, only the five or so most important. The items may be leisure-time activities, personal problems common to youth, attitude statements, motives for choosing a given occupation, reactions that the student made in carrying out some task or solving some problems, and so on. Sometimes too the record blank may list after each item two or more options, one of which the subject is to check.

2. L-I-D (Like-Indifferent-Dislike). This form is common on interest inventories. The subject encircles the one symbol that expresses his feelings about the activity. Note that this gives a kind of "absolute" judgment—i.e., each activity is judged on its own merits without comparing it to one or more other activities.

3. Marking a preference. The subject chooses which of two items he prefers, the best- and least-liked of three, and so on. The Kuder Preference Record[1] illustrates this form:

|  |  | *Most* | *Least* |
|---|---|---|---|
| P. | Visit an art gallery ................................. | P | |
| Q. | Browse in a library ................................ | Q | |
| R. | Visit a museum ..................................... | R | |

In contrast to the L-I-D form, this one records a relative judgment. Note too that the marking of the most- and least-liked activities automatically yields three preferences.

4. Yes-No-?. This is a common form on many questionnaires and inventories. The subject encircles the appropriate symbol. Some questionnaires drop the "uncertain" category, and thus reduce the judgment to a forced choice (*cf.* the previous illustration in this respect).

5. A-U-D (Agree-Uncertain-Disagree). This pattern is common on attitude inventories. This may be expanded by adding two extreme categories, Strongly Agree and Strongly Disagree.

There are of course other types of such recording forms in use, some of them more complicated than what we have shown here. But all of them illustrate how the design of the form itself permits a record of the appropriate behaviors or judgments.

If self-reports are to be valid, they must fulfill two main conditions: (1) the person must know himself and his behavior well enough to be

---

[1] Reproduced by permisison of Science Research Associates, Chicago.

able to report the truth, and (2) he must be willing to tell the truth rather than distort it.

How well the first condition will be met depends somewhat upon the type of report called for. If the report deals with a specific event or activity in the immediate past, the chances are good that the person will be able to remember details. But the more remote the event, the less chance is there of an accurate report. As time passes, selective remembering tends to operate—the person tending to remember features that struck his fancy or were unusually pleasant, and so on. Rarely should such reports go back more than a few days, unless they deal with events that are likely to stand out boldly in memory, as is the case with highly pleasant or unpleasant, and highly successful or unsuccessful, incidents. But even so there will be individual differences in ability to remember. If the report deals not with a *specific event* but with a *generalization* about the person's typical behavior, then it sets a far more difficult task. The task is not that of reporting a single incident, but of generalizing about many incidents, few of which the subject can actually recall. When asked a question such as: "Do you tend to daydream when you study?" a student naturally begins to go over his past experiences to arrive at a generalization. Again, individuals will differ in their ability to recall such experiences, and to weigh them properly. But most students would probably want to qualify any judgments they made, answering, "Yes and no," "It depends," or "Sometimes I do; sometimes I don't." These are perfectly reasonable replies; they illustrate well the difficulty of the task and the inadequacies of the record so obtained.

How well the second condition will be met depends upon a variety of factors. One factor is the kind of information sought. If the report deals with behavior that arouses anxiety in the person, it may lead to distortion or concealment. This could be the case with conduct of which the person is ashamed or which differs in some way from conventional norms. (The influence of direct or indirect social pressures to conform has already been discussed in the preceding chapter.) Another factor is the possibility that rewards and punishments will be connected with the use of the information. They need not be, certainly not in most school situations. In such situations, the subject must feel free to express himself, knowing that whatever information he discloses will be used for his benefit or for that of his group. However, if the student believes that he will get a low mark for expressing his true attitudes, interests, and the like—or if this actually will be the case—then one cannot expect full cooperation. Similarly, if the results are to be used for determining fitness for admission to a school or for a job, then there is an incentive for the person to make a favorable impression and to suppress any damaging information. In such circumstances, full cooperation is more difficult to get and self-reports must be taken with a grain of salt unless controls are used to prevent or detect distortion.

7. How might language factors interfere with the making of an accurate self-report?

8. Discuss the advantages and limitations of self-reports as compared with the collection of anecdotal records and the use of interviews, respectively.

9. Devise a simple self-report questionnaire for a course you teach, asking students to comment on special interests which they may have developed, special learning difficulties connected with the course, and so on.

### Personal products

Test papers constitute perhaps the largest class of such records. When a person writes out his answers to essay questions, when he works out on paper his solutions to problems, when he marks his answers on a test booklet, or when he records them on a special answer sheet, *he is in effect making the record himself.* This procedure is immensely practical; not only does it do away with the need for an independent observer and recorder, but it also allows us to present many types of test situations on a group basis.

Test papers differ, as one might expect, in the type of data they record. Essay examinations, and papers including solutions to problems, include data on the student's thought processes, as well as the actual judgments or answers that followed from these processes. On the other hand, special answer sheets and marked booklets contain only the student's *choices* of certain response options; they contain little data on the thinking that led to the choices. Yet all test papers are essentially records in a *product* sense; that is, they record the products of thought rather than the thought processes themselves. Some tell more than others, but even the essay examination cannot include all the thinking that preceded the act of writing (happily, for the student would just as soon not have false starts, fantasies, and "doodling" appear on the record!).

Samples of work comprise another large class of personal products. At all levels, the schools abound with such products: various kinds of written composition, from the usual themes, reports, and term papers, to creative writing and postgraduate dissertations; specimens of handwriting, shorthand, and typewritten copy; products of the shop, sewing room, laboratory, and drawing board; musical compositions and photographic work. Outside the schools, the variety of such products is greater yet.

As a form of record, the work product has definite advantages. In a real sense, the product *is* the ultimate test of a person's ability. If he can produce a fine piece of work and do that consistently, then we must credit him with ability. The product of his efforts thus gives proof of his accomplishments. Furthermore, samples of work have analytic value in their own right. They may indicate strong and weak points in technique, and such personal habits as neatness, accuracy, style of expression, and methods of thinking. If they represent the outcomes of sustained creative effort, as many of them do, such products provide the only sure basis for judging a person's originality. Finally, those that can be filed or saved provide a valuable record for later interpretation by others as well as ourselves. Thus, a whole series of personal products gives us a basis for judging progress in the learning of a skill or in the development of some other characteristic.

10. Ideally, in appraising a skill, one would want both a record of performance in process, as well as any product or record of end-result. For each skill below, discuss the comparative advantages and limitations of process and product records.

a) Operating a typewriter
b) Making a water-color painting of a landscape
c) Mounting an object and finding it under a microscope.

## QUALITIES TO BE SOUGHT IN A RECORD

There are two main qualities that a satisfactory record of behavior should have: validity and practicability. Of the two, validity is by far the more important. Validity is necessary in a record, while practicability is highly desirable.

### Validity

#### Meaning and implications

By validity of a record is meant the degree to which it accurately records the significant reactions that actually took place.

On the basis of such standards, a valid record should indicate significant *behavior*, either by directly recording it or by accurately describing it. These are rigorous standards, and they rule out certain kinds of data that are essentially interpretations. Now, interpretations have a place, but they are not records of behavior. They are records of somebody's *judgments* about behavior.

There are cogent reasons for preferring a record of behavior to that of interpretations. In the first place, a record of behavior is relatively objective. Records of behavior deal more directly with the phenomena in question than do interpretations, which are a step farther removed and hence open to more distortion. Second, records of behavior can be cumulated over a period of time, so that the value of any single bit of evidence is greatly enhanced when it is studied in relation to other bits of evidence. Finally, records of behavior can be interpreted afterward by an indefinite number of judges, at their own convenience. This permits us to check the soundness of their interpretations and to find out how well different judges agree—checks that would not be possible had we recorded only our interpretations.

Some forms of behavior yield products which may serve well as indirect records of behavior. Such products indeed may often provide a more useful record than a recording or description of performance.

At times it is impractical to get a record of behavior or a product resulting from that behavior. This may happen in situations of the following sorts: a music tournament in which the performance of individuals, bands, and orchestras must be judged on the spot; the performance of a complex sequence of actions, as in flying an airplane or doing a gymnastic exercise; social interactions, in which abilities like leadership and the art of debate can only be demonstrated. In such situations, it may be necessary to make a summary interpretation on the spot, usually a rating of performance. A rating of any kind represents an act of judgment, a judgment that seeks to answer either one or both of the following questions: *To what degree* was the particular characteristic shown? *How good* was the performance?

Such judgments are really interpretations of behavior, and so do not logically fall within the scope of this chapter. They represent a step beyond that of simply recording behavior, and hence we reserve their treatment for the next chapter. For the same reason, we have made almost no mention of rating scales in this chapter. It is true that rating scales do represent a form of record, but the crucial question is, record of what? Upon close examination, most rating scales and many inventories turn out to be records of *summary* judgments or interpretations, rather than records of specific acts that a person did.

It is well to distinguish sharply between these two distinct problems: that of obtaining a record of behavior or its products, and that of summarizing or interpreting such evidence. One should also become sensitive to the nature of the data contained in particular records, distinguishing between behavior, product, and interpretation.

### Ways of enhancing validity

Granted that validity is essential in a record, how do we provide for it? We seem to have two main ways of enhancing the validity of a record. One is to control errors and biases likely to creep in. The other is to get more information on the record. These are the approaches in general; now let us look at some specific ways.

*Controlling errors and biases.* In the direct observation of behavior, the following practices seem highly desirable:

1. *Train the observer to record specific acts, not his interpretations of those acts.*

| *Comment recorded by an instructor after a class discussion* | *Comment as it should have been made* |
|---|---|
| "Joyce was extremely resourceful and energetic today. It is a pleasure to have her in class." | "When the class expressed an interest in learning what problems newcomers face, Joyce proposed that it interview a number of new families in the community." |
| *Comment recorded by an adviser after a conference with student* | *Comment as it should have been made* |
| "Henry shows the same indifference to the liberal arts as most technical students; he is hopelessly biased against any but 'practical' courses." | "When asked whether he would like to enroll in History of Western Civilization, Henry replied that he didn't believe this course would help him prepare for his vocation." |

2. *If a special recording form is to be used, see that it describes the behavior to be observed in specific terms* rather than in a series of highly general trait names or terms. Tables 3 and 4 (pp. 128–29) represent good technique in this respect.

3. *Use mechanical recording devices to replace the human observer whenever practicable.*

On tests in which the subject must record his answers, and on certain self-report forms, it is often desirable to do the following:

1. *Keep the recording form and the directions for using it as simple and clear as possible.* Avoid unnecessary complex language and format. Remember that you do not want these factors to prevent a person from making an appropriate response when he can otherwise do so.

2. *Increase the number of response options to a point where the chances of guessing the right answer are very small.* Guessing obviously introduces

chance errors into the record, since the particular credits earned on such items arise not from ability but from lucky guesses. By increasing the number of alternatives per question, we reduce the person's chances of guessing correctly. Theoretically, the chances of guessing right on a two-choice item are one out of two; on a three-choice item, one out of three; on a four-choice item, one out of four; and so on. Actually, the odds are generally somewhat better than chance since a person often has some knowledge of the point in question and can eliminate at least one incorrect alternative. Most published tests use five-choice questions, but the gain in reliability over a test with only four choices is probably small.

An excellent example of this principal is shown in the following item type used by Wesman and Seashore to measure verbal reasoning (3):

. . . is to diamond as circle is to . . .

| | | | |
|---|---|---|---|
| 1. square | 2. shape | 3. cube | 4. gold |
| A. triangle | B. oval | C. round | D. smooth [2] |

The task requires that the subject complete the analogy. To do so, he must find *two* terms, one for each relation. He records his choice on the answer sheet by marking the number and letter that include his two choices: 1A, 1B, 1C . . . or 4D. In effect, he records a *combination* of two answers. Here the chances are only one in sixteen that a person will guess any right answer. Hence, this item type is unusually reliable, and the authors do not find it necessary to correct for guessing. As the same authors point out, their item type achieves complexity and difficulty without introducing rare bits of knowledge or very unusual vocabulary terms as is often the case with the traditional analogy item. This ingenious item type thus improves the validity of the record in two ways: by minimizing chance errors due to lucky guesses; and by insuring that the subject's choices reflect real thinking rather than simple recall of information.

3. *Give the subject practice in doing the exercise and in recording his judgments.* This is especially desirable when the type of exercise and the manner of recording answers are rather unusual.

*Getting more information.* In the direct observation of behavior, the following practices seem desirable:

1. *Use several observers and collate the results.* Since a single observer is limited in what he can see, several observers are likely to give a more complete report.

2. *Use mechanical recording devices to replace the human observer*

[2] Reproduced by permission of the Psychological Corporation, New York.

*whenever practicable.* These devices can generally far surpass the human observer in what he can record.

On tests in which the subject must record his answers, and on self-report forms, we often can get more information through some simple changes in the original situation or in the manner of recording answers. Leading possibilities include those now to be listed.

1. *On fairly involved problems, attempt to get a record of the subject's decisions at several points in his solution.* These points would ordinarily be those subproblems leading up to the final solution. Such a record could permit one to reconstruct the subject's *sequence* of thinking, as well as to identify points at which his reasoning may have gone awry. It could also provide a basis for giving partial credit for correct judgments made along the way although an over-all satisfactory solution may not have been reached.

Two unusual attempts to devise such a record are those of Glaser and others (11) and Rimoldi (14), cited on page 105. Through the use of cards or tabs, these approaches permit the recording of choices at various points in a problem-solving procedure.

2. *Have the subject record the reasons for whatever choices he is called upon to make.* The choices by themselves represent only end results. A statement of reasons helps to give his rationale for the choices. In this connection, examine the simple illustration below (2, p. 86).

When a metal X is placed in a solution of hydrochloric acid, it goes into solution with the evolution of hydrogen. When metal Y combines with oxygen, considerably more heat per gram of oxygen is given off than when metal X combines with oxygen.

A reaction between metal Y and oxide of metal X:

———— will proceed with the evolution of heat.

———— will proceed with the absorption of heat.

———— will not proceed.

———— may or may not take place, depending upon the nature of the oxides.

The basis for the prediction is:

———— metal X is more active than metal Y.

———— metal X is above metal Y in the electromotive series.

———— more heat is given off in the formation of oxide of metal Y than is required to decompose the oxide of metal X.

———— less heat is given off in the formation of the oxide of metal Y than is required to decompose the oxide of metal X.

———— an equilibrium may shift to the right or to the left by the use of appropriate methods.

3. *List on the recording form the range of common answers likely to be given by the individuals for whom the instrument is intended.* Ideally, this would mean that each individual should be able to find after each question an answer similar to the kind he would make under free-response conditions. But, you may ask, how does this help us "get more information?" In this sense: that as many members of the group as possible will find response options that correspond closely to their real judgments.

In order to get such a range of functional response options, it is desirable to give the questions first in free-response form. Then one may choose the most common responses for listing on the recording form, wherever possible retaining the original phrasing used by the subjects. This procedure is desirable for getting incorrect answers for multiple-choice questions. It is further treated in Chapter 8.

4. *Consider having the subject mark the best and poorest alternatives, or rank the alternatives in order of merit or preference.* How each of these methods may improve the validity of test results was illustrated in Chapter 4, where we noted direct and indirect ways of appraising ability to plan experiments (pp. 102–3). In both illustrations, the students reacted to exactly the same items as those presented previously in best-answer form, except that they recorded the additional judgements asked for. As one might expect, each variation from the best-answer form did lead to more complicated scoring. It is well to recognize that this approach may be difficult to apply, and even when applicable requires great care in determining the item alternatives.

Another possibility is to have subjects mark the incorrect rather than the correct alternatives on multiple-choice tests. This contrasts with the custom of choosing the best or the correct answer. Coombs suggests that we might get more informaion by instructing people to cross out the wrong answers (6). According to this procedure, each individual would cross out as many of the wrong answers as he could recognize (or that he was willing to guess were wrong). On a four-alternative test item, a person could cross out one, two, or three alternatives. He would receive one point credit for each wrong alternative crossed out, but lose three points if he crossed out the correct alternative. Clearly, this procedure attempts to give credit for partial knowledge or understanding, and to provide some differentiation among those individuals who would ordinarily fail the item and be lumped together in one group. The research so far reported is not altogether conclusive (7) and we must wait for additional studies before recommending this procedure.

These illustrations do not exhaust all of the useful ways of enhancing the validity of a record. Indeed, further modifications are already appearing in the technical literature (9).

Through such refinements in procedure, we may get more information, but at the same time we may complicate the scoring. The issue then turns on whether the additional information is worth enough to offset the additional scoring; or, in short, whether the improved procedure is practicable.

11. In studying the functioning of small face-to-face groups, why is it desirable to have separate *process* and *content* recorders?
12. What educational arguments can be advanced for having the student record his reasons in addition to the conclusions he reaches?
13. Does the exercise on page 144 actually require the student to give his reasons? What technical question does this raise?
14. What possible range of scores would Coombs' cross-out system yield on a four-option test item?

## Practicability

### Meaning and implications

By practicability of a recording device or procedure we mean the ease with which it can be put into practice, apart from any considerations of validity. A particular type of record may allow us to get valid data, but it may not be practicable for everyday use.

To be practicable, a record should be relatively inexpensive to make. This means that it should keep cost in time, effort, and special facilities down to a minimum. But there is a further consideration that we must usually take into account, and that is the usability of the record once we have it. Does it lend itself readily to transcription? To scoring or summarization? To interpretation? These operations are no less important than the making of the record itself. This problem comes out forcefully in the case of sound recordings. We can get these with relative ease; in no time, we have reels of utterances from interviews, problem-solving sessions, or class discussion. But the cost of transcribing such records becomes formidable, since one hour of actual recording may take as much as seven to ten hours of transcribing (15, p. 81).

### Ways of enhancing practicability

In reviewing the main types of records, we touched upon the problem of enhancing practicability, sometimes in considerable detail. Rather than repeat much of this discussion here, we will concentrate on two important methods: simplifying records without sacrificing validity, and using special answer sheets.

*Try to simplify the record without sacrificing validity.* Check lists and other special recording forms for use in direct observation illustrate this approach. We noted earlier that such forms permit us to get down the essential facts with a minimum of writing.

Such devices have their counterparts in objective tests. One of the great advantages of objective tests is that they do reduce to a minimum the time needed to record answers, since usually all a person must do is to write down a letter or number corresponding to his choice or mark an answer sheet. This is an advantage only insofar as the test itself samples the appropriate behaviors. It is an advantage, in other words, only if the test does not distort the required tasks appreciably by casting them into multiple-choice or similar forms. We know that objective test items 'often do set up rather artificial situations, and that in such instances the efficiency of recording and scoring is illusory.

One of the frequent criticisms of objective test items is that they require the person only to *recognize* the correct response from among certain given alternatives, rather than to *produce* it without the aid of special cues. To overcome this limitation and yet retain the advantages of objective items, we must devise item types and records that do require the person to produce the correct response. While there are serious limitations on how far we can go in that direction, it is worth a try. Already we have come up with some noteworthy successes, two of which are shown below.

In the area of language, an important ability is that of recalling a word that fits a given definition or meaning. This would seem to be more important in writing than in reading, where the need seems to be the other way around—recalling the meaning of a given word. In any case, the direct way to test this ability is to present a series of definitions and have the subject write out the word that fits each one. This would amount to a completion-type exercise, and it would seem to be the only intrinsically valid way of testing this ability. Yet the item type used in the Cooperative English Test seems to set up a similar task, with the added advantage of a simpler and more easily scored record:

> 11. A flat, dull or commonplace statement (9)
>      1) O   2) P   3) R   4) S   5) T

The number in parentheses at the right tells the subject how many letters there are in the word, and he is to choose the letter that corresponds to the first letter of the exact word. This item type does present a few cues, of course, but it emphasizes active recall much more than the conventional vocabulary test item.

During the last war, the Army Air Forces developed an objective test of skill in reading numerical scales (16, p. 63). The test required the subject to read each scale example and record only the last digit of his answer. For this purpose, the AAF devised an answer sheet with spaces for ten different responses, the A position for any answer ending in o, the B position for any answer ending in 1, and so on. This recording procedure was satisfactory, since almost any error was sure to occur in the last digit. Thus, the procedure required the subject to produce the correct response, but it still retained the advantages of a simple, objective, and easily scorable record. In this regard, see Figure 3 on page 90.

*Consider the use of separate answer sheets.* Having the subject make the record is quite economical, and we can gain further advantages by using a separate answer sheet—when this is appropriate. Here we can either buy printed forms commercially available or devise our own. The major source of printed answer sheets is the International Business Machines Corporation, which prints a wide variety of them, all patented and suited for the IBM test-scoring machine. IBM answer sheets cost a few cents each and thus are more expensive than homemade mimeographed sheets. When hand scoring is to be done, the latter serve as well as the printed forms.

Separate answer sheets offer the following advantages. They permit us to use test booklets over again and, since the booklets generally cost much more than the answer sheets, to save a good sum of money. Furthermore, the compact arrangement of answers on a single sheet makes scoring so much easier, whether done by machine or by hand. This also facilitates statistical counts and analyses of the responses, such as are likely to be made if scoring machines are available.

Some patented answer sheets and pads offer a further advantage: as the subject records his choices, he automatically classifies them in terms of the scoring categories to be used. The Ohio State University Psychological Examination, which is a test of general intelligence, the Kuder Preference Record, which is an interest inventory, and other tests distributed by Science Research Associates, make use of a pin-prick technique. The Ohio State test uses an answer pad that contains three hidden scoring sheets which lie directly under the answer sheet itself. Each scoring sheet is spaced exactly like the answer sheet, except that after each question four of the five answer boxes are blacked out; these correspond to the incorrect alternatives. As the subject punches the pin through an answer space, he pricks all three scoring sheets in the same box. His score is simply the number of holes that appear in the white spaces. The pin-prick technique is even better suited to the Kuder Preference Record, since this instrument yields ten scores.

The SRA Self-Scorer makes use of a similar principle (17). This device consists of a folded answer sheet and a key inserted in a punchboard. The student punches holes in the answer sheet corresponding to his answers to the test questions. He is instructed to punch holes after each question until he sees red, or rather, until a red dot appears below the hole. The red dots correspond to correct answers and are distributed randomly on the opposite sheet, one red dot per question. The student's score is the sum of his punches (as in golf, a low score is better than a high score). There are several answer-sheet keys available from the publisher, and for each the instructor must see that the right answers on the test match the red dots on the key. This device has a further advantage: it gives the student *immediate* knowledge of his right and wrong answers.

On the whole, separate answer sheets constitute a very practical form of record. They will become more practical if economical scoring machines hit the market and become common in school systems. The cost of such forms may be a fraction of what it is today, and special paraphernalia such as electrographic pencils will probably be unnecessary. What we will then need is ingenuity in devising a variety of forms to fit many special testing needs.

## REFERENCES

1. Anderson, H. H., and Brewer, J. E. Studies of teachers' classroom personalities, II. *Appl psychol Monogr.*, 1946, No. 8.
2. Ashford T. A., and Shanner, W. M. Objective test items of the recognition type that test reasoning and minimize guessing. *J. chem. Educ.*, 1942, **19**, 86–90.
3. Bennett, G. K., and others. *Differential aptitude tests:* Verbal reasoning, form A. New York: Psych. Corp., 1947.
4. Bloom, B. S. Study of conscious thought processes by the method of stimulated recall. *Amer. Psychologist,* 1950, **5**, 342–343. (Abstract)
5. Bloom, B. S. Thought processes in lectures and discussions. *J. gen. Educ.,* 1953, **7**, 160–169.
6. Coombs, C. H. On the use of objective examinations. *Educ. psychol. Measmt,* 1953, **13**, 308–310.

7. Coombs, C. H., and Womer, F. B. The assessment of partial knowledge. *Educ. psychol. Measmt*, 1955, **16**, 13–37.

8. Cronbach L. J. *Essentials of psychological testing.* New York: Harper, 1949.

9. Dressel, P. L., and Schmid, J. Some modifications of the multiple-choice item. *Educ. psychol. Measmt*, 1953, **13**, 574–595.

10. Gaier E. L., Selected personality variables and the learning process. *Psychol. Monogr.*, 1952, **66**, No. 17 (Whole No. 349).

11. Glaser, R., and others. The tab item: a technique for the measurement of proficiency in diagnostic problem solving tasks. *Educ. psychol. Measmt*, 1954, **14**, 283–293.

12. Hobbs, N. (Ed.) *Psychological research on flexible gunnery training;* AAF Aviation Psychol. Prog. Res. Rep. No. 11. Washington: U. S. Govt. Print Ofc., 1947.

13. Lindahl, L. G., Movement analysis as an industrial training method. *J. appl. Psychol.*, 1945, **29**, 420–436.

14. Rimoldi, H. J. A. A technique for the study of problem solving. *Educ. psychol. Measmt*, 1955, **15**, 450–461.

15. Thelen, H. A., Educational dynamics: theory and research. *J. soc. Issues*, 1950, **6**, 2–95.

16. Thorndike, R. L. *Personnel selection:* test and measurement techniques. New York: John Wiley, 1949.

17. Troyer, M. E., and Angell, G. W. *SRA Self-Scorer.* Chicago: Science Research Associates, 1949.

18. Tyler, R. W. A test of skill in using a microscope. *Educ. Res. Bull.*, 1930, **9**, 493–496.

19. *A guide to the use of anecdotal records.* Prepared by Division of Tests and Measurements, Bd of Educ. of the City of New York, 1949.

20. *Teaching by discussion in the college program.* The College, University of Chicago, 1949. Copyright 1949 by The University of Chicago.

21. *The Wall Street Journal.* Chicago, June 13, 1956, Vol. 36, No. 169, p. 1.

# CHAPTER 6

# *Summarizing the Evidence*

**EVALUATION**

Illustrations
Judging essays. Evaluating responses to objective test items.
Special Problems in Evaluation
Determining the criteria for judgment. Applying the criteria
for judgment.

COUNTING OR "SCORING"

Varieties of Raw Scores
Special Problems in the Use of Raw Scores
Semantic difficulties. Further limitations of the scale. Absolute
vs. relative standards. Choosing appropriate units.

DESCRIPTION

Illustrations
A problem-solving sketch. Translation of scores.
Special Problems in Description
Choosing appropriate terms. Description vs. interpretation.

QUALITIES TO BE SOUGHT IN THE SUMMARIZATION

Relevance
Objectivity
Practicability

We have seen that efforts to study behavior normally yield a
variety of records. Regardless of their form, however, these records all
have one feature in common—they are abstractions. No record can pass
for the real thing, the behavior itself. Each is an abstraction in the sense
that it has not captured all aspects of the behavior under observation.
This feature is particularly evident in paper-and-pencil records where the
person has marked his choices or where the observer has checked certain
items. Such records are extremes, of course, but even records, such as

motion pictures, are abstractions because they, too, do not include all of the significant reactions that take place. It should be clear that the nature of the record places definite restriction upon whatever further treatments we might want to make of the data.

The next step in the development of an evaluation instrument is to devise and carry out some method of summarizing the evidence which has been recorded. Many readers will think of this step as the scoring problem, which of course it is in many cases. However, summarization does not always lead to numerical scores, and so it seems preferable to use the broader concept—summarizing the evidence.

The process of abstraction, which was begun in making a record of behavior, is now carried further. In this chapter, we will consider three important methods of summarizing such evidence: evaluation, counting or scoring, and description. For each method, we will present some concrete illustrations and then discuss special problems that arise in its use. Finally, toward the end of the chapter, we will highlight the three important qualities to be sought.

## EVALUATION

By far the most common way of treating a record of behavior, or a product of that behavior, is to evaluate it. To evaluate anything is to judge its value. And to judge the value of anything, one must have some standard or criterion against which the thing may be judged.

In order to understand this process better, let us first review some common illustrations.

### Illustrations

#### Judging essays

Suppose we have a set of English compositions written by a group of students and we want to appraise these papers. Being sophisticated in the ways of evaluation, we know that we must judge the papers in accordance with criteria and that these criteria should correspond to our educational objectives.

Suppose, further, that our educational objective in this area amounts to this: improved skill in writing compositions that give evidence of coherent organization, apt style, logical reasoning, and good content. These four qualities are what we mean by criteria; they are the things we would look for in the essays. As they stand, they are undefined and would not be helpful as a guide in appraising the essays. It is necessary to define them, not only in terms of the highest level of attainment that we might expect or hope for in the group, but also in terms of lesser degrees of attainment. This has been done for organization, in which we distinguish five levels of attainment (after Diederich, **3**, p. 588):

4—The paper has a discernible plan; a central idea or theme; a clearly marked beginning and ending; distinct and unified paragraphs; smooth transitions; and an order of development that fits the purpose, the logic of the subject matter, and the requirements of the audience.
3—Intermediate between 4 and 2.
2—The paper has a discernible plan but it presents some weaknesses in organization, such as a poor beginning and ending; overlapping and rather poorly organized paragraphs; awkward transitions; and/or an order of development that falls short of the requirements of the task.
1—Intermediate between 2 and 0.
0—The paper has no discernible plan; no central idea; no clearly marked beginning and ending; overlapping and poorly organized paragraphs; abrupt transitions; and an illogical sequence of ideas.

Essentially the same sort of definition would be done for the other three qualities.

Precisely what does this kind of analysis represent? More than anything else, it represents a *translation* of one aspect of an educational objective into various possible levels of attainment. But it also represents a *scale,* for we have assigned numerical values to each of these levels. In a very real sense, the quality represents a *dimension* along which different essays can vary.

It would be possible to extend this definition by giving concrete examples of each of the elements listed above, e.g., a paper that has a poor beginning and ending. This would represent another level of translation, and a desirable one for acquainting readers with the meaning of various statements on the scale.

Once we have translated the qualities into levels of attainment, we are in a favorable position to evaluate the essays. The process of evaluation consists of judging each essay in the light of the four qualities, or criteria. The elements in any process of evaluation are the following:

1. A product or specimen of behavior to be evaluated.
2. A criterion, or set of criteria, if more than one quality is to be considered, against which the specimen is to be evaluated.

3. An act of judgment relating the specimen to the criterion. This is a kind of matching operation in which the specimen is put in what seems to be its proper place on each criterion dimension.
4. A report of the judgment, usually expressed as a numerical score but sometimes as an adjective or descriptive statement.

Our own judgments of an essay might lead to the following ratings: organization—4; style—3; logical reasoning—3; content—3. These could just as well have been expressed as letter grades—A,B,B,B—except that the latter do not lend themselevs readily to quantitative treatment. Letter grades, however, are implicitly quantitative in that they reflect differences in degree. We might also have used adjectives, such as Excellent, Good, Fair, Poor, and Unsatisfactory. These would convey substantially the same information but they would be more cumbersome to work with. Should we so desire, there would be nothing to stop us from making an over-all judgment of the merit of the essay, and this too could be recorded in any one of the above ways. For such a purpose, it would be most desirable to retain the separate quality scores as a basis for ironing out disagreements between judges. Thus, if two judges disagree in their general impression of an essay, it is helpful to be able to localize rather quickly the sources of their disagreement.

The fact that we use numerical scores to record our judgments raises some interesting questions. Does the evaluation represent an act of measurement? Can we really "measure" such qualities? Isn't this, after all, a very subjective process?

To answer the first two questions, which ask essentially the same thing, let us recount briefly what we have done. We have taken a given quality and defined five levels of attainment. We have done this on the assumption that competent judges can take each essay and match it with the appropriate level—an assumption that can be reasonably well fulfilled. In other words, we have assumed that competent judges can distinguish between the relative quality of a set of essays and can sort them out accurately into five categories. The series of numerals that we use serves as a way of ordering, or indexing, the successive quality levels. It does not qualify as a measuring scale in the sense that we think of a ruler for measuring length. A ruler represents a physical scale containing equal units and an absolute zero (just not any length at all). If we accept this kind of physical scale as our model of measurement, then it should be clear that our evaluations of essays do not correspond to it. We cannot say, for instance, that John's essay, given a score of 4, is twice as good as Bill's, given a score of 2. This kind of statement assumes an absolute zero and a scale of equal units. However, if we accept a less rigorous definition of measurement, we can consider our numerical evaluations of the essays as acts of measurement. According to this view, measurement consists basically of "the assignment of a class of numerals to a class of objects" (8, p. 535). In our use, the series of numerals serves to index numerically the differentiations in quality that we are able to make. Fundamentally, this is an act of measurement.

To answer the third question, we need only remind ourselves that *somebody* has to make the evaluations. They are not made for us by a machine. This being the case, the answer should be clear: Yes, of course, the making of evaluations is a subjective process; it will always be that way. But because a process is subjective in the sense of being personal does not mean that it is necessarily whimsical or biased, as the question usually implies. Any one judge's evaluation *may* be whimsical or biased, but we can check that by comparing it with the evaluations of competent judges who are guided by an agreed-upon set of criteria.

### Evaluating responses to objective test items

Perhaps the first association that comes to mind, when we speak of "evaluating responses to objective test items," is that of counting up the correct answers. That is to say, we may think of this as simply the application of a scoring key and the counting of responses that agree with the key.

This view of evaluation is inadequate, for there is more to evaluation than applying a scoring key and totaling the correct answers. The scoring operation can be so thoroughly routine that an untrained clerk can do it. Does this mean that the scores do not reflect any evaluation whatsoever? No, for the *key itself* reflects the personal judgment of those who made it. In what ways does the key reflect personal judgment? In these:

1. The choice of the correct or best answer. (This element of judgment all but vanishes on certain types of problems or questions, such as those in mathematics and science, where there is often only one logically possible answer.)
2. The amount of credit given for particular responses, including here the less acceptable answers as well as the best answer. (This judgment affects all kinds of objective test items, regardless of the subject matter field.)

Other personal judgments enter at the point of *writing* of objective test items, such as the choice of alternatives to be offered the student in each item. These judgments, together with those made in the evaluation of responses, show clearly that the so-called objective test item is not free of subjective judgments.

The usual method of scoring objective tests is so simple that no doubt it obscures the system of weighting upon which it is based. This weighting may take place on all three levels: the weighting of responses to the individual item or question, the weighting of items themselves, and the weighting of part scores. Our concern here is with the first level. At this level, the usual weighting is 1, 0; that is, one point credit for the right answer and no credit for any other answer. This system may look so obvious and natural to you that you may fail to realize its arbitrary nature. Why, for example, couldn't one give 2 points for the right answer and subtract 1 point for choosing an incorrect answer? This second system is no more arbitrary than the first.

What important implications lie back of the usual system of weighting responses to objective test items? It is, first of all, an all-or-none kind of evaluation: one either gets credit or he doesn't. Thus, if we view the individual item as a *test*—and we may legitimately do so—then this one-item test sorts students into two groups: those who pass and those who fail. This is very severe rating in contrast to a test made up of many items, which permits a *range* of scores and hence gives credit for many degrees of ability in the group. The all-or-none system of weighting choices thus gives no credit for partial understanding short of choosing the best answer. Without a doubt, one would find in any group a range of individual differences in the specific ability tapped by a test item, not just a simple presence or absence of the  ability in question. The all-or-none system of scoring not only does not differentiate among those who fail the item but it does not further differentiate among those who pass the item. It is undoubtedly true that there are individual differences in the specific ability tapped by an item even among those who choose the right answer.

If the all-or-none system of scoring objective test items is so severe, can we improve upon it? Would it be possible to assign a series of weights to the several alternatives in an item according to their relative merit? These questions have intrigued other people, and we have some answers to the questions. Tyler's study, cited in Chapter 4, is appropriate here (16). In this study he found that differential weighting did improve considerably the validity of an objective test of ability to draw reasonable generalizations from experimental data. Whereas an objective test requiring students to check the best of five suggested generalizations, and scored on the usual right or wrong basis, correlated quite low with the direct method, one making use of special credit values correlated very highly with the direct method. This improved version required students to check both the best and the poorest of the five generalizations listed after each set of data. This test was scored by giving the student a credit value for each alternative chosen as the best and subtracting the credit value for each alternative chosen as the poorest. The credit value for an alternative was the average rating, on a five-point scale, given that generalization by three instructors who had previously evaluated it. A student's response for each item thus was not scored as either 1 or 0, but might take any value from +4 to −4.

As convincing as Tyler's study is, it is perhaps the exception rather than the rule. Present practice overwhelmingly favors the all-or-none scoring of objective test items and the equal weighting of each item. The experimental evidence generally shows that special weighting systems, either of item alternatives or of items, do not appreciably affect the ranking of scores obtained with the simpler 1, 0 system of weighting (14). This being the case, there is little to be gained by going through the extra labor. To repeat, there are exceptions where special weighting systems do improve the validity of scores, but they are few and far between.

## Special problems in evaluation

### Determining the criteria for judgment

As we pointed out in Chapter 3, the definition of an objective in behavioral terms is helpful but it is not sufficient for evaluating that behavior. It is also necessary to specify certain criteria by which we can appraise that behavior. As we illustrated in both that chapter and this, these criteria are the characteristics which we feel are basic to the educational objective in question. To the degree that a student's behavior gives evidence of these characteristics we can say that he has attained the educational objective.

For many evaluations of human behavior, the practice is to specify only one characteristic or dimension. This is the case with the bulk of ability tests, whether in the area of achievement or aptitude. Performance is appraised in terms of its goodness, or the success with which a sample of tasks is accomplished. Really what one has is a succession of criteria, each specific to a test item or task, but all of which amount to "success in performing a task." For many purposes of appraisal, a single score summarizing general excellence or standing is all that is needed.

Other evaluations of human behavior may require several attributes or dimensions to encompass the full complexity of the objective. A single score can hardly do justice to outcomes as complex as appreciation of good literature, attitude toward current social issues, and effective thinking.

Whether we use one or several characteristics to summarize our evaluations of some behavior, it is necessary to define these characteristics so that judges know what these mean. This is generally necessary because we cannot assume that all judges read the same meanings into the terms used.

This process of definition may be carried out in advance of testing or evaluation, and quite often it may be postponed until after the products or records of behavior are collected. If the latter course is followed, it is common practice to draw off a sample of products and to go through these carefully. This gives some idea of the variation among the products with respect to the characteristics under study, and some concrete examples which show different degrees of the several characteristics. A group of judges who are about to evaluate a set of essays can operate in this way.

At some point, definition should lead to the assignment of scale values for each characteristic to represent different degrees of its presence. We have already illustrated this with respect to the quality of organization in essays. However, we did not see an illustration in which definition was carried to the level of sample responses. This is brought out clearly in the scoring guide for the following question taken from the Wechsler-Bellevue Intelligence Scale (17, p. 174): "What should you do if while sitting in the movies (theater) you were the first person to discover a fire (or see smoke and fire)?" The question is one of a series designed to test general comprehension. Credit is given a response according to the degree to which it gives evidence of generalization and quality. The exact credit is determined by matching a person's response against sample answers as shown below (17, p. 192):

THEATER. General: Notify responsible person (prevent panic). Samples of
  2 *credits*
    Keep quiet and notify the manager immediately.
    Tell the manager about it.
    Call it to the attention of one of the ushers.
    Tell orchestra to play—and notify manager.
    Quietly call the usher and have him give the general alarm.
    Tell the man who shows you to your seat.

*1 credit*
   Give alarm quietly.
   Ring the fire alarm.
   Call the fire engines, or firemen.
   Investigate if fire is real and, if so, notify usher.
*0 credit*
   Warn the other people.
   Scream there is a fire.
   Run out.
   Walk to nearest exit.
   Tell people there is a fire and to use the nearest exit.
   Go for water.
   Try to get friends out as quickly as possible.[1]

How many scale values should we assign for a given characteristic? This is a question that deserves close study, for the tendency is to assign either too many or too few. The answer is clear enough: as many scale values as there are distinguishable levels. In the study of human behavior, rarely will these be more than seven. The human observer, no matter how carefully trained, generally cannot distinguish more than that number of levels reliably. This has implications for grading such products as essay examination papers. How many points to allow for a given question? This should depend upon the number of distinguishable levels of answer to the question (13). Thus, if six quality levels can be distinguished, a maximum of five points may be allowed: 5 for the best or correct response, 4 for the next best, and so on down to 0 for the poorest. This system is more defensible than any of the special weighting systems that teachers often use (13, p. 490).

1. For each of the following statements of educational objectives, indicate what characteristics you believe should be used as a basis for appraising or summarizing the evidence.

   a) Development of ability to apply principles of psychiatric nursing to concrete situations—that is, to do the right thing in a situation and to justify it on the basis of accepted principles.
   b) The development of increasingly broad and mature reading interests (h.s. literature).
2. Study carefully the alternatives in the items on page 89. Try to decide what attitude or approach each alternative exemplifies.

[1] Reproduced by permission of The Williams and Wilkins Company, Baltimore.

a) For the exercise as a whole, what possible criteria might one use to judge any student's responses?

b) What would be undesirable about summarizing a student's choices as simply the number of right answers?

3. Below is a verbatim reproduction of an essay written by a 9th grade student as part of a civics examination. The assignment was as follows: "Pretend that you are talking to a visitor from Russia who wants to know what the Bill of Rights is all about. Tell him all you can about it, including where it may be found, what it contains, times when the rights may be limited or curtailed, and so forth."

---

"They decided to have the Bill of Rights as part of the constitution, so that the government could not get to much power and form a ditatership. The Bill of Rights can be found in the constitution as the first ten amendments. Some of the rights are limited during War time, such as the right to a speedy trial. In the first amendment there are five rights; these are, freedom of speech, freedom of press, freedom of religion, freedom of assembly in proper places. In the other nine amendments there are rights such as, nobody can search your house without a warant, you do not have to provide a solider with lodgeing unless you want to. You have the right to a speedy trial, right to a trial before an impartial jury, right to refuse to testify against yourself, right to have a lawyer, right to keep arms in your house, and many others. Now these rights can be limited during war time and if your in jail. But you have a great deal of rights and are quite free here as compared to most other countries."

a) If you were teaching civics at the 9th grade level, what criteria would you lay down for judging such essays? (Be specific. You may find it profitable to refer to a copy of the Bill of Rights.)

b) If you were a teacher of English, what additional characteristics would you want to evaluate?

### Applying the criteria for judgment

Well-defined criteria are necessary, but they do not in themselves guarantee sound evaluations. There are other factors that enter the picture, not the least of which is the skill of the judges. In the first place, it is necessary that judges thoroughly understand the criteria, accept them wholeheartedly, and apply them skillfully. We are likely to get a high degree of agreement among judges to the extent that these conditions are fulfilled. The only other main factors that might stand in the way of sound judgments are the possible complexity of the task and the operation of various subtle biases.

Admittedly, the task of evaluation varies greatly, depending on the complexity of the behavior or objects under study. The evaluation of arithmetic computations may reduce to a matter of noting right and wrong answers; the evaluation of a piece of artistic work may demand our very best efforts. The evaluation of any object with esthetic appeal is especially difficult, for judges tend to be influenced by their own personal standards of appreciation—which may be different from those agreed upon by a committee. This becomes even more difficult when the evaluation deals with performance as it takes place and judges react subtly to the personality of the performer. One experimenter, who studied the evaluation of ability to interpret literature orally, has this to say (10, p. 10):

. . . In practice, it would appear that a grade recorded by a teacher of oral interpretation is more than not a report of the teacher's standards of appreciation, both of the reader and the literature, and not a report of the quality of performance.

This same experimenter concluded that it would be desirable to use forty or more judges if one wanted to get reliable measures of that particular ability.

The foregoing illustration probably represents the extreme in complexity. But even complex behaviors and products lend themselves to objective evaluation if certain precautions are taken. One important precaution is that students perform essentially the same tasks. This tends to eliminate variation that arises from differences in the task. In other words, it makes the behavior or products comparable from one individual to another. The other precautions relate to the use of well-defined criteria for evaluation and to the training of judges. The Traxler-Anderson experiment (15) on grading English themes is pertinent here. These experimenters found that when students wrote themes on the same topic, and when carefully defined criteria for scoring were used, it was possible to get a high degree of agreement among different readers, much higher than usually obtained for English compositions.

Even when judges mean well, they may let certain biases get the better of them. Biases are especially prominent in borderline judgments, as the following verse satirizes:

> 'Twixt Right and Wrong the Difference is dim;
> 'Tis settled by the Moderator's Whim.
> Perchance the Delta on your Paper marked
> Means that his Lunch has disagreed with him (7).

(This gem comes to us from days of old, when methods of marking were quite subjective—at least through the eyes of students!)

There are several important types of bias and error that tend to creep into evaluations. The following have been ferreted out as a result of many research studies:

1. *Tendency to focus on factors that are irrelevant to the purposes of the appraisal.* Perhaps the most notorious example is the tendency for graders to be influenced by the quality of handwriting on essay papers. Thus, some readers will tend to rate higher those papers that are more legibly and attractively written than others of similar content. Other factors that are often irrelevant, but nonetheless influential, are neatness of work and impressions of personality.

2. *Tendency to let a general impression or evaluation color one's evaluation of specific qualities.* This is sometimes termed the "halo effect." Thus, a reader may be so impressed with the over-all merits of an essay that he may assign high grades to several specific qualities, such as organization, style, reasoning, and content, when in fact only one or two of these may deserve such a high rating. This tendency is even more pronounced in the area of character judgments, where raters may score a man high on many characteristics because he is an efficient or trustworthy person. The way to forestall this effect is to rate only one quality at a time; or in the case of an essay examination, to evaluate one question at a time for a series of papers.

3. *Tendency to rate too high or too low.* These are usually termed "errors of leniency or severity," respectively. Apparently, many judges do have a tendency to lean toward one or the other extreme. One way to control this is to suggest that judges strive for an approximate distribution of scores across the scale, rather than to concentrate them at one or the other end. This is reasonable when there is in fact a distribution of merit in the group that corresponds pretty much to the recommendation. Otherwise, it smacks too much of an arbitrary grading on a curve.

4. *Tendency to concentrate ratings in the center of the scale.* This is usually termed the "error of central tendency." Since the judge does not give many ratings at the extremes of the scale, he fails to discriminate among a large share of the specimens in the sample. He does violence to the data to the extent that there is a wide range of individual differences in the sample. As with the previous tendency, this too can be partially corrected by suggesting an approximate distribution of ratings.

5. There is still another tendency, one that is difficult to phrase in a few words. That is the tendency to evaluate a specimen against the one rated immediately beforehand, rather than against one's concept of the several scale positions. It has been found, for example, that the rating given a theme depends considerably on contrast with the paper read immediately before. "A C paper may be graded B if it is read after an illiterate theme, but if it follows an A paper . . . it seems to be of D calibre" (12, p. 41). One way to forestall this effect is to sort the papers into five or so piles according to general merit or whatever specific quality is under study, and then to re-examine those in each pile. The few that obviously do not belong in the given pile can be moved up or down, as the case may be.

Tendencies such as these emphasize the many subtleties that affect the process of evaluation. The making of sound judgments is truly an art. It requires some sophistication to become sensitive to such tendencies in oneself, to control them, and to make judgments that reflect the best of which one is capable. This can only come through much training and experience.

This brief survey of evaluation hardly does justice to the complexity of the process or to its many variations. But the reader should not be able to lay this book aside and say that we have slighted the part that human judgment plays in the process.

## COUNTING OR SCORING

Let us turn now to a basically simpler process than evaluation—that of counting. By this we mean nothing more than the summing of items to give a total score. For all practical purposes, many of the operations included under the term "scoring" boil down to this. True, there may be an elaborate statistical treatment that finally emerges; but at bottom a simple frequency count that gives the raw data. However, some people do use the term "scoring" to refer to rating—which is a form of evaluation—and so we cannot use it here without creating confusion.

Because counting is a simpler process than evaluation, it does not mean that it generally comes before the latter. It may or it may not. More often than not, counting comes after evaluations have been made. This is the case with most tests of ability, where the count is a summing of the credits earned. It is not the case, for instance, where the count represents the number of trials needed to accomplish some task; here, evaluation of the goodness of performance comes later, and then usually in relation to group norms.

The total score that we arrive at through counting, together with certain simple transformations of this, is commonly called a "raw score." There are all sorts of raw scores, depending upon the items that are being summed. Let us review first some common types of raw score and then the basic assumptions that lie back of this process.

We might group the many varieties of raw scores into the following types:

1. *Number of points credit*. What we really mean here is that the raw score amounts to a sum of earned credits or numerical evaluations. This type of raw score is common in evaluations of human abilities. On the usual objective-type test, the score is a sum of the weights 1 and 0—in effect, the sum of the right answers. On an essay examination, it may be a sum of weights except that here the weights usually vary from 0 to several points for each question or exercise. On any other instrument that includes a series of parts each of which receives a numerical rating, the raw score is also a sum of numerical evaluations.

2. *Simple frequency count*. This would involve a summing of all items or acts of a given kind, but without the implication of totaling credits as in (1) above. Examples: spelling errors in several samples of writing; number of interests checked in a given area; number of times one broad life goal is preferred over all others in such a list of twenty (score of 19 is thus maximum for any goal in this list); number of personal problems checked in an inventory of that kind.

3. *Number of trials needed to accomplish a task or series of tasks*. This is probably a rare kind of score except for recording progress in certain kinds of motor skills. The SRA Self-Scorer, described on page 149, yields a total score that really amounts to the number of attempts needed to get the right answers on a test.

4. *Time score*. Usually this is a count of the time needed to perform a given task or series of tasks. It is also appropriate for recording speed of reaction, as in the traditional reaction-time experiments conducted in the psychological laboratory. You may not think of this type of score as a count inasmuch as the watch doesn't count but only ticks! But it is, after all, a frequency count.

5. *Rate score*. With a time score, the amount of work is fixed; it is a

question of finding how long it takes a person to do that amount. With a rate score, it is a question of the amount performed in a given period of time. The most common examples are the rate scores for reading comprehension and typewriting, both of which are expressed in words per minute. This type of score, by the way, is one of the simple transformations about which we spoke earlier (p. 164). This is also the case with the remaining two types of scores.

6. *Per cent score.* As this term implies, a count of some sort is converted into a per cent, usually though not always of the maximum possible score. Examples: per cent right on an ability test; per cent of the times an individual chooses "Like" for a list of activities in a given interest area. A per cent score is particularly desirable when different individuals respond to different numbers of items and what we want is some indication of the *proportion* of times each responds in some defined way.

7. *Corrected score.* Of the three transformations, this one remains essentially a count. By a corrected score we mean a score corrected for guessing. The usual formula is $S = R - W/(n - 1)$, where $S$ is the corrected score, $R$ is the number right, and $n$ is the number of choices offered. For a true-false type of test, the formula reduces to $S = R - W$. This problem of correcting for guessing is discussed in Chapter 12.

No doubt there are other types of raw scores that could be added to this list. Possibly some specialists would not want to regard rate and per cent scores as raw scores on the grounds that they are something more than a crude count. Our argument is that they are simple transformations of crude counts and therefore retain the basic limitation of a raw score, namely, that it has no significance in itself. A raw score can take on significance only when compared to a standard of some sort, as we shall presently see.

As an operation, counting itself is so simple that we often overlook the assumptions made in carrying it out and treating the resulting raw scores. There are at least two basic assumptions that we make:

1. That all the items belong together, i.e., are enough alike so as to deserve being counted together and included under a common classification. This is the assumption of *item homogeneity*.

2. That one item is as good as another, i.e., each item has equal significance as an indicator of the characteristic under study. This is the assumption of *equal or unit weighting*.

These are big assumptions and they deserve close study. Let us turn to a consideration of these and to some other special problems.

Special problems in the use of raw scores

### Semantic difficulties

Any total score derived from an instrument is inevitably a composite. It is a sum of specifics which are in fact not identical but which we assume to be reasonably similar. We assume further that the differences we have ignored in lumping these items together will not make a difference in the ultimate use which we will make of the scores. How sound are these assumptions? This is the nub of the problem.

It seems helpful to look at this problem from two levels: that of the equivalence of items and that of the equivalence of scores. At the first level, we concern ourselves with similarities and differences from item to item in any individual's pattern of choices or answers. At that level, you will recall, we assign a given numerical value to those items answered in one way and another numerical value to those items answered in a second way. This introduces a problem of semantics: [2] To what extent does the identical symbol (say the usual $r$ for right answers) stand for the same thing in different items? It is as though the little symbol $r$ were to rise up in righteous indignation and challenge us: "What right have you to throw me around with such abandon? What right have you to use me to label so many *different* things?" At the second level, we concern ourselves with similarities and differences between two total scores of the same numerical value. Here the problem of semantics enters in this way: To what extent do two equal total scores stand for the same things in different persons? Obviously, this second level includes those variations that arise at the level of the individual item, in addition to variation in the *pattern* of responses over the same sample of items.

To come down to the first level again, let us consider two items on the same achievement test. These items will not be identical in their content, of course, but will pose different questions from the same area. Let us assume further that an individual student got them both right, i.e., he chose the answer keyed as correct and got $r$ point credit. For all practical purposes, then, the items are equivalent. But *are* they? Might not they (i.e., the individual's responses to them) really differ in many ways, of which the following seem especially important?

---

[2] The term "semantics" has a number of common meanings. Here, we define it as a branch of language study that deals with the relationships between the words or symbols people use and the life facts which they intend these words or symbols to represent.

1. In the *mental processes* followed by the individual in arriving at his final decision about the answer. This in itself could include a wide range of different processes—careful reasoning, pat association, blind guess, or any of the response sets previously discussed. In other words, on one item an individual may have arrived at his choice through careful reasoning, and on the other through memory of that particular problem. Yet the unit weights treat the items as though they called forth similar processes.

2. In the *certainty* of the individual's judgment. Thus, on the second item the student may have felt much more sure of his answer because he happened to have met that particular point in his readings and recalled it, whereas on the first item he may have been unsure of the soundness of his reasoning. On the whole, teachers probably do not concern themselves with assessing the student's certainty of his judgments. Thus, on examinations they rarely ask the student how sure he is of his judgments. Yet this is a factor that probably varies from item to item.

In addition to such differences, there are other important ways peculiar to certain types of instruments. Take those instruments on which the student expresses judgments of like-dislike, agree-disagree, and so on. On such instruments it should be possible to detect a variable that might be called intensity of feeling, but which is actually ignored in the response categories and hence in the scores as well. Thus, a student may say that he likes two successive activities on the form, but one he may like much more intensely than the other. Here also is a variable of some importance that may be ignored entirely in the summing of units to give a total score.

On psychological grounds, we expect such *intra*individual variations to occur from item to item, and most likely there are reported experiments that confirm this expectation. We also expect individuals to differ in such variables, and we have many reported experiments that establish the fact of *inter*individual differences therein. The many studies on response set, synthesized by Cronbach, confirm this expectation. More recently, two independent experiments have detected individual differences in the variable certainty of judgment (4, 6). This takes us to the second level, that of the equivalence of total scores.

At the second level, the lack of identity between equal scores shows up as well in the pattern of choices on an instrument. On an achievement test, for instance, two persons may earn the same scores but through different combinations of right answers. This is probably the rule rather than the exception on devices of that kind. Obviously, the lack of equivalence increases to the degree that the particular combinations represent different things.

To summarize up to this point: If we consider any individual's score on a test or inventory, we have good grounds to question the homogeneity of his responses from item to item. To a degree, his score is a sum of items that are only more or less similar. Moreover, if we consider the scores of any two individuals, we have reason to question the equivalence of their scores if they are equal or approximately so, on these main grounds: first, that to a greater or lesser degree these individuals are likely to respond differently to the same items; and second, that they are much more likely than not to earn their scores through different combinations of choices. The effect of all such variations is to make scores impure, so that it becomes difficult to know exactly what an individual's score means or to compare the scores of different people.

What can we do about this state of affairs? There are three important possibilities before us:

1. Do nothing; use the scores as they are and assume that they will be useful in that form. As passive as this approach sounds, it is actually what we do in most cases. And despite the imperfection of our units and scores, they do provide us with helpful information about the relative status of individuals in different characteristics.

2. Purify the score which a given instrument yields. The usual way is to make psychological and statistical studies of the items, and then to throw out those items that don't seem to fit with the rest. This approach is generally beyond the resources of classroom teachers and others who develop instruments for informal use. However, such persons can often improve their instruments by removing ambiguities in directions, by abandoning forms such as the true-false, which encourage response sets, and so on.

3. Break the score down into two or more components if this is at all possible. Statistical studies are helpful here, but again they are practicable only in the development of instruments intended for large-scale use. However, findings that grow out of such large-scale studies can often be applied directly by the classroom teacher. Thus, on certain achievement tests it may be possible to come out with two scores: one for ability to recall facts and principles; another for ability to apply these to new problem situations. This enhances the usefulness of the results over that of a single, composite score.

At a number of points in this chapter we have touched upon the second assumption listed on page 165, but there are a few things we should say about the matter of weighting items (as against the weighting of item alternatives, which was discussed in the section on "evaluation"). On logical grounds, a good case could be made for the differential weighting of items or questions within a test. Thus, we could argue that some questions are more important than others and should therefore receive more credit. It is not unusual to find teachers who do just this sort of thing in scoring an examination, perhaps giving 2 points credit for the more important items and 1 point for the others. It is also possible to show that some questions are more difficult than others, and that some show a higher correlation with an outside criterion, such as success in later course work. These considerations would seem to justify the use of differential weights. However, the bulk of experimental evidence does not. It has been shown repeatedly that correlations between weighted and unweighted scores on tests tend to be very high. With the exception of certain standardized interest inventories and personality questionnaires, almost all tests make use of unit weighting of items.

Does this evidence mean that the second assumption is generally fulfilled, and that one item is as good as another? Not necessarily. What generally happens is this: that while test items may differ in importance, difficulty, and predictive power, such differences are minimized because they tend not to affect the rank order of individuals on the test. The better students will tend to get more of the important, difficult, and predictive items right than will the poorer students, and hence all will maintain about the same relative rank order on the total score.

4. A social beliefs inventory contains statements, such as, "Complete freedom of speech should be given to all groups and all individuals regardless of how radical their political views are." Individuals are to mark each statement Agree, Disagree, or Uncertain. One of the scores yielded is an uncertainty score, the percentage of times the individual marks U.

   a) What possible meanings might a U response have on any item?
   b) How would this limit the usefulness of the uncertainty score?

### Further limitations of the scale

Among other things, we have argued that the units which make up a raw score are not really equal in any sense of the term. We have also argued that the scale they form may not be unidimensional—that is, measuring only one variable—although we have noted that this can often be corrected by refining the instrument or procedure. There remain some further limitations.

Differences between the raw scores of different individuals are not in any sense absolute distances. The differences can always be changed by adding or removing items that discriminate between the persons involved. To illustrate: Tom, Dick, and Harry earn scores of 30, 45, and 60, respectively, on a test. Apparently, Dick is as different from Tom as Harry is from Dick. But suppose we add to the test ten items, all of which Harry can pass, four of which Dick can pass, and none of which Tom can pass. This alters the scores as follows:

|                | Tom | Dick | Harry |
|----------------|-----|------|-------|
| Original score | 30  | 45   | 60    |
| Change         | 0   | 4    | 10    |
| Revised score  | 30  | 49   | 70    |

It should be clear that all three of the differences have been stretched. In other words, because our units have no constant meaning, we are not able to pin down the exact amount of the difference between any two of the scores. We do not have an additive scale like a yardstick against which we can place the scores of different people and tell exactly how far apart they are.

With psychological variables, raw scores do not represent distances from an absolute zero—some point at which there is "just not any of" the variable present. This means that it is really not possible to tell how much of a given characteristic a person has. We cannot say that Harry, with his score of 60, did twice as well as Tom, with his score of 30; or that he has twice as much ability as Tom. We can only say that Harry did better than Tom. About all we can ask of raw scores is that they rank people consistently on the underlying variable.

### Absolute versus relative standards

In the absence of a true zero, a raw score means very little by itself. Johnny likes twelve activities out of twenty that deal with mechanical things. Does this show high, moderate, or low interest in mechanical things? Does this mean that he likes such activities more than he does taking part in artistic activities? We cannot really say.

Even a per cent score, which may seem to convey a definite meaning, means very little by itself. We can say that Johnny likes 60 per cent of the activities that fall in the mechanical area. But this has no further significance, for we can alter this per cent very easily by adding more items to the inventory. This possibility is especially evident on ability tests, where we can alter per cent scores at will by adding either very easy or very difficult items. The effect of adding very easy items is to add a constant to everybody's score; hence, per cent scores will rise accordingly. The effect of adding very hard items is to add no further points to scores but to increase the maximum possible; hence, per cent scores will fall accordingly.

Only as we compare raw scores to some standard do they take on meaning. Standards may be of two sorts: absolute and relative. Absolute standards are those that exist independently of the performance of other persons. An absolute standard for a person's word knowledge is the unabridged edition of Webster's *Dictionary*. This contains practically all of the known words in the English language, and to measure a person's word knowledge it is only necessary to have him define a representative sample of words drawn from this dictionary. The per cent of words he correctly defines gives an absolute measure of his vocabulary. Such standards are rare in the study of human behavior. Most of the time we must resort to relative standards. Even in the case of vocabulary, questions would arise: "How does this person's vocabulary compare with others of his educational background? With the norms for his age? With that needed to do acceptable college work?" These are all questions of relative performance.

Most standards for the evaluation of human behavior go back to group norms of some kind, and for this we make extensive use of derived scores. The latter are relative scores that are derived from a distribution of raw scores. The two most common types of derived score are percentile ranks and standard scores. A percentile rank expresses a person's rank as a percentage of the group he surpasses in standing. Thus, a percentile rank of 67 indicates that he surpasses 67 per cent of the group upon which the percentiles are based. A standard score shows how far a person deviates from the average, either above or below, in units of standard deviations. Both of these types of derived scores are explained in elementary statistics books.

In spite of the wide use of derived scores, and the general practice of comparing an individual's score to some set of norms, there is a definite need for resorting to standards that are in a certain sense absolute. One such standard is that of the individual's earlier scores on the same variable. This permits us to determine growth or decline in the functions being measured—a much neglected procedure at all levels of education. Another such standard is the definition of minimum competence needed to pass a course, to qualify for advanced study, or to qualify for a position or professional license. In this connection, the College of the University of Chicago is currently experimenting with a technique for determining the minimum passing score on comprehensive examinations in various general education courses (9). This is in contrast to grading on a curve— assigning grades on some arbitrary percentage basis. The technique relies upon the judgment of instructors as to what constitutes adequate achievement on the part of a student. Instructors determine the minimum passing score by identifying those incorrect alternatives in objective-type test items that D students should be able to recognize. This provides a rather straightforward method of defining minimum competence in terms of specific knowledge and skills.

### Choosing appropriate units

Had we followed an approach parallel to that under evaluation, we would have taken this problem up first. However, it did seem convenient to follow through on the several logical problems involved in arriving at and using raw scores.

The expression, "choosing appropriate units," refers to the problem of choosing one or more dimensions for the purpose of measuring the characteristic(s) in question. Again the basic requirement is that of relevance. The particular unit chosen must be appropriate for the purposes of the measurement.

To many, this problem may seem so straightforward as not to call for discussion. Given the responses to an instrument such as a classroom test, the obvious procedure is to treat the individual item as the unit, to allow one point credit for each correct answer, and to sum the correct answers to get a score.

Yet there are situations in which this procedure is not necessarily the only or the best one to follow. As Ashford and Shanner (1) argue, it would be possible to score as a *combination* certain item pairs such as the one on page 144, rather than to treat them as two separate items. To earn a credit of 1, a student would need to get both the prediction and the reason correct. It is assumed that the prediction and the reason together test a *single* understanding, and that a student really does not have this understanding unless he answers *both* items correctly. The pair of items, in other words, may be regarded as the unit of measurement. This method of scoring may be extended to any pair of items that tests such an integrated response. Other possible pairs include "cause" and "effect"; a "theoretical statement" and its "experimental basis"; "knowledge of a phenomenon" and its "explanation in terms of principles, generalizations, or theories" (1, p. 88). Of course, this method of scoring is appropriate only if there are such logically related pairs of items, and enough of them in a test to justify a separate score.

To look at the problem again from a rather different perspective, let us consider a scoring system developed for an interpretation of data test (11, pp. 51–65). Suppose we have a test consisting of sets of data, such as graphs, tables, and so on, followed in each case by a series of statements purporting to be interpretations of the data. Let us further assume that on the total test, twenty statements have been classified as true, twenty as false, and twenty as based on data insufficient for one to judge truth or falsity. Given this key, it is then possible to classify any student's judgments on the basis of the chart below.

| Key ⟍ Student | True (20) | False (20) | Insufficient Data (20) |
|---|---|---|---|
| True | Accurate | Crude Error | Beyond Data |
| False | Crude Error | Accurate | Beyond Data |
| Insufficient Data | "Caution" | "Caution" | Accurate |

As indicated by the chart, a student's judgments can be categorized into *general accuracy, beyond data, caution,* and *crude errors.* General accuracy means the extent to which the student agrees with the key. This score is simply a count of the total number of statements falling in the diagonal cells. It may be converted into a per cent of maximum possible number of correct judgments (60). The beyond data score indicates the extent to which the student marks statements keyed insufficient data as either true or false. The caution score indicates the extent to which the student has marked true or false statements as insufficient data. The crude errors score indicates gross misinterpretations: true marked as false and false marked as true.

According to the conventional method of summarizing a student's judgments, only a total score would be obtained. While a total score is still the best single index, it obscures certain tendencies on the part of the less proficient students. Thus, if a student scores low in general accuracy, the total score alone will give no indication of whether this arises primarily from a tendency to go beyond the data, to be overly cautious, to make a large number of crude errors, or from some combination of these. The use of a pattern of scores, on the other hand, helps to show what the student did when he was not accurate. Hence, the pattern of scores has diagnostic value.

The two illustrations which have now been presented show quite unusual ways of summarizing a record. The striking thing about the first is the *unit* chosen—a combination of items rather than the single item. The striking features of the second are the use of a grid for classifying responses in relation to the key, and the derivation of a *pattern of scores* which have diagnostic value. Although equally striking illustrations could have been cited from other areas, it is hoped that these two will encourage you to take an occasional fresh slant toward this general problem.

5. In the chart on page 173, why has the term "caution" been put in quotation marks?
6. For the given example, use the chart to determine the number of *opportunities* for a student to:
   a) go beyond the data.
   b) show "caution."
   c) make crude errors.
7. How would the *general accuracy* score differ from the three above?
8. What sort of correlation would you expect between *beyond data* and *"caution"* scores?
9. In prediction-reason pairs, such as on page 144, there are two types of response which are especially significant for diagnostic purposes:
   I. Prediction right—reason wrong
   II. Prediction wrong—reason right
   What deficiencies might account for each of these types of response?
10. For the pair on page 144, what is the probability of getting both prediction and reason correct through chance guessing? Would this system of scoring combinations tend to reduce the effects of guessing?

## DESCRIPTION

Perhaps the simplest way to summarize a record of behavior is to describe that behavior: to tell what a person did and how he did it. This contrasts with evaluation, at the other extreme, which necessarily involves interpretive judgments. Description requires very little interpretation in the sense that evaluation does. The emphasis in description is on *how*, rather than upon *how much* or *how well*.

It is possible to be very specific in describing performance by giving an item by item or part by part account: "On item 3 James K. correctly recognized the danger of generalizing from a single case . . ."; "In the first paragraph of her theme, Nancy Y. used 'infers' where she should have used 'implies'"; and so on. Perhaps there are times when such detail is necessary, but this approach seems hardly different from simply recording the responses as they take place or restating them in essentially the same form. There is usually little to be gained from such detail—at least in a final summary. If the purpose of the study warrants it, such detail might well be of preliminary value. The purpose of description, as a method of summarization, is rather to transcend the specifics and to generalize from them: to dig out the salient characteristics or to build a coherent sketch of a person's manner of functioning.

Although description is a rather time-consuming and cumbersome procedure, it does have a place. It offers advantages that other procedures lack. To see its usefulness, let us turn to some important illustrations.

### Illustrations

#### A problem-solving sketch

As mentioned in Chapter 2, a fruitful approach in studying problem-solving or reasoning is to present a student with a series of problems, have him verbalize his thoughts as he tries to solve them, and record his utterances by means of sound recorder. This method yields rather rich data which must then be summarized in some meaningful fashion. The usual procedure is to transcribe the utterances, search for characteristic tendencies, and then prepare a summary sketch. Such a sketch appears below. This sketch is taken from the author's own files; it is based on two one-hour sessions in which the student tried to work out loud some twenty problems drawn from achievement test exercises.

Problem-solving Report of R. G.

1. *Understanding of the nature of the problem.* Although this student reads the directions to a problem with great care, he does not probe deeply enough to grasp the problem in its full import. Moreover, he pays too little attention to the details of the directions, often forgetting these as he tries to arrive at a solution.

2. *Understanding of the ideas contained in the problem.* Here R. G. does pick out key words in the problem and the alternatives. However, he tends to avoid those he does not understand: and often he either works with a vague definition of key words or he makes dubious assumptions about their meaning. He makes little attempt to translate these terms into more familiar terms or into concrete examples.

3. *General approach to the solution of problems.* R. G. seems to do little independent thinking in arriving at a solution, preferring again and again to recall the solution from previous schooling. He finds many side issues that he cannot resolve and consequently does not attempt a solution of the main problem. His superficial approach shows up in several ways: once having made a choice, he tends to gloss over the other alternatives; he may ignore the problem entirely and search through the alternatives for some incidental clue; and frequently he selects an answer on the basis of feel—"it seems right."

4. *Attitude toward the solution of problems.* R. G. shows very little confidence in his own thinking; uncertainty characterizes most of his choices. He prefers to rely upon knowledge of a topic rather than to use reasoning to solve the problem. His personal biases frequently interfere with his thinking.

The outstanding advantage of such a sketch is that it focuses on processes rather than upon products of thinking. Had we merely counted the number of problems correctly solved, we would have summarized the record in terms of products—in this case, correct answers—and missed a wealth of data that throw light on this student's characteristic habits of problem-solving. A single score is useful for indicating the general level of a student's ability to think but it leaves out all the idiosyncrasies that brought the score about. We now know that two individuals may attain the same scores, yet through rather different processes. Only if there is a one-to-one correspondence between particular thought processes and particular solutions can we rely upon a single score to stand for similar processes. This seems unlikely.

Because it does focus on processes, such a descriptive sketch tends to be analytic and hence is helpful for diagnostic purposes. The sketch gives some indication of what processes and attitudes aid the student's reasoning, and what hinder it. Furthermore, when such sketches are obtained at widely spaced intervals of several months or a year, they permit us to note changes in the level or manner of performance—qualitative changes, as they are sometimes called. A change in score cannot adequately portray such specific qualitative changes.

11. To what extent does the problem-solving sketch contain quantitative statements? Identify any expressions that you think are essentially quantitative in nature.

### Translation of scores

Description may also start from a different base. Instead of working directly from a record of behavior or some other primary evidence, we sometimes begin with the scores on an instrument and *translate* these into descriptions of behavior. This is a necessary step in the interpretation of instruments that yield several scores.

For an excellent example of this, let us consider the *General Goals of Life Inventory*. This instrument yields no fewer than twenty scores. It consists of 190 pairs of statements, each statement expressing an important goal of life. The student's task is to encircle that goal in each pair which more adequately reflects his main life goal. The maximum raw score for any of the twenty goals is 19 points; this would result if that goal were preferred over every other goal. Anne, a college student, came out with these scores (5, p. 28):

| *Score* | *Goal* |
|---|---|
| 19 | Serving God, doing God's will. |
| 18 | Self-sacrifice for the sake of a better world. |
| 17 | Promoting the most deep and lasting pleasures for the greatest number of people. |
| 15 | Serving the community of which I am a part. |
| 13 | Handling the specific problems of life as they arise. |
| 12 | Self-development—becoming a real, genuine person. |
| 12 | Finding my place in life and accepting it. |
| 11 | Peace of mind, contentment, stillness of spirit. |
| 11 | Realizing that I cannot change the bad features of the world, and doing the best I can for myself and those dear to me. |
| 11 | Overcoming my irrational emotions and sensuous desires. |
| 9 | Doing my duty. |
| 9 | Fine relations with other persons. |
| 8 | Getting as many deep and lasting pleasures out of life as I can. |
| 8 | Being able to "take it"; brave and uncomplaining acceptance of what circumstances bring. |
| 6 | Achieving personal immortality in heaven. |
| 3 | Making a place for myself in the world; getting ahead. |

3   Survival, continued existence.
3   Security—protecting my way of life against adverse changes.
1   Living for the pleasure of the moment.
0   Power; control over people and things.[3]

The scores are of some value in this form, since they indicate the order in which the student ranked the goals. However, they take on more meaning when they are compared and translated into the following sketch (5, p. 29):

> Looking at this pattern, we can make certain comments about it as a whole. First, Anne has given a fairly definite response to the inventory. Had she been confused or careless, her scores would have clustered about the middle of the scale (between 8 and 11). As it is, they cover the entire possible range from 0 to 19. She has been willing to accept some goals quite readily and much less willing to accept certain others. Her ties, except for the 3's, fall toward the middle of her list, the place in the ranking where these goals usually appear about which the student is confused or indifferent.
>
> Anne's pattern is also coherent. Considering the goals which she ranked high, we see that they are generally religious and altruistic. The goal which she ranked first, choosing it each time it appeared, is "Serving God, doing God's will." Apparently this service of God consists, at least in part, of service to her fellow-men also, for immediately after the service of God she ranked: self-sacrifice, the promotion of the pleasures of others, and service to the community. The goals she ranked low are also consistent with this pattern. They have to do primarily with her own personal interest—her power, momentary pleasure, personal security, survival, and advancement. . . . In short, if we consider Anne's pattern by itself, we see a coherent and consistent emphasis on service to God and man and a lack of interest in the goals (or even a renunciation of them) which have to do with her personal advantage.[4]

To arrive at such a sketch, a person must know something of the make-up of the instrument, particularly the philosophical significance of the different statements; he must also look for patterns of relationships, contrasts, and possible inconsistencies between different scores. In short, he must relate the different scores one to another to give them meaning.

12. In using the above inventory, it is not necessary to refer to group norms to give meaning to a person's pattern of scores.

   a) How do you account for this happy state of affairs?
   b) How could norms based on other college girls' scores help one interpret Anne's scores?

[3] Reproduced by permission of the American Council on Education, Washington.
[4] Reproduced by permission of the American Council on Education, Washington.

**13.** One of the major needs in comprehensive achievement testing is to be able to translate scores at several points along a score continuum into descriptions of what individuals can do at each of those levels. This is a highly technical problem but some readers may want to refer to one of the pioneer efforts (see **18**).

### Special problems in description

#### Choosing appropriate terms

The major problem in developing a description is to choose categories and terms that will best serve one's purposes. This is again a problem of relevance and means that the description should be couched in such terms as will throw light on the significant aspects of behavior.

The translation of scores into a description of behavior would seem to be inherently easier than working directly from unclassified data. In translation, the scores often provide a satisfactory set of categories, and so this problem is more or less solved in advance.

On the other hand, when one works directly from unclassified data, such as problem-solving protocols, the problem of choosing appropriate categories becomes formidable. Thus, there may be several different ways of organizing the descriptive sketches, and at the outset the superiority of any one of these may not be evident. Bloom and Broder report making several attempts to classify and organize their descriptive sketches of problem-solving before deciding upon the system outlined in Chapter 2. They rejected ready-made classifications, such as John Dewey's well-known steps of reflective thinking, in favor of one that seemed to do justice to the ways in which students *actually* go about reasoning.

There are a few other considerations that enter here, in addition to the relevance of the categories. These have come up before in our discussion of the formulation of educational objectives. The categories should be reasonably independent rather than overlapping: this is a plea for parsimony of description. Finally, the body of the description should be at the right level of generality: not so general as to be vague or to leave out much that is important, yet not so specific as to clutter up the sketch with unnecessary detail.

#### Description versus interpretation

Some writers make a distinction between description and measurement, and interpretation. This distinction seems fundamental, and it may be helpful to explore it briefly.

As noted, description deals with the *how*—that is, how the individual responded, how he typically behaves in some defined class of situations, what features characterize his work, and so on. Correspondingly, many forms of measurement simply answer the question, How much of this characteristic is present? or, To what degree does the individual show this behavior?

Other forms of measurement, however, go beyond simple quantification; they carry with them an implied evaluation. This is certainly true of most numerical ratings, which really amount to acts of judgment or interpretation.

Many descriptions and measurements are more or less devoid of interpretation. They provide the raw data from which interpretations can be made. One form of interpretation we have already discussed—the evaluation of behavior. Another important form of interpretation deals with the explanation of behavior as described or measured: How can we account for its occurrence or relative strength? Still another form of interpretation aims at prediction on the basis of the behavior as described or measured: How is the individual likely to perform in such and such situations?

It is important to recognize that our survey of basic problems, as taken up in Chapters 2–6, does not carry us very far into the problem of interpretation. For the purposes of this book, it does not seem necessary to go into this further problem.

## QUALITIES TO BE SOUGHT IN THE SUMMARIZATION

### Relevance

The method adopted for summarizing the evidence should be appropriate to one's purposes. It should yield scores or summaries that throw light on the characteristics which are the objects of one's study. It should, in brief, treat the data in such a way as to do least violence to them, and yet permit the kinds of interpretations that we want to make.

Summarization is a crucial step. Even a carefully devised test or procedure may fail at this point. It may call forth the relevant responses from students but still yield invalid results because the system of scoring or summarization is wholly inappropriate. Consider the following examples, which are by no means farfetched:

| *Purpose of the observation or evaluation* | *Inappropriate method of summarizing the evidence* |
|---|---|
| To evaluate the student's skill in writing English compositions; to provide him with diagnostic data on his strengths and weaknesses in writing. | Count the number of errors in grammar, punctuation, etc. Provide a separate count for each of these categories. Convert the total number of errors into a letter grade. |
| To describe an individual's characteristic methods of problem-solving. | Rate his performance on the basis of the number of problems correctly solved. |

In the first example, the method of summarization focuses almost entirely on the mechanics of writing. It fails to take into account more critical features of the composition, such as its organization, the soundness of the reasoning, and the degree to which the writer has achieved his aim. By classifying the errors, the method does provide some limited diagnostic data. The summing of these errors and their conversion into a letter grade gives a single index of dubious value because again it reflects a narrow range of characteristics.

In the second example, the method results in a summary index which is far too abstract to convey any useful information about individual habits of problem-solving. The method suggests an overemphasis upon answers per se, as against the processes followed in arriving at the answers or solutions.

Appropriateness works in another way too: the method of summarization should be appropriate to the data. That is, it should be in keeping with what the data will permit. There is little point in trying to derive a pattern of part scores from an instrument, when in fact these scores are much too short to give stable results, or when they are so highly intercorrelated that they are measures of pretty much the same thing.

This completes our discussion of relevance. It does not seem necessary to carry this discussion any further, since, under each of the three main methods of summarization, we have already devoted considerable space to this requirement. We have not, however, devoted much space to objectivity, the second important requirement of a satisfactory summary or evaluation. Hence, this requirement will come in for a somewhat longer treatment in this final section.

The system of scoring, or whatever method of summarization is adopted, should be relevant to one's purposes; but it should also be skillfully applied—and that's where objectivity comes in. Taken together, these two qualities of relevance and objectivity determine whether summarization *as a process* yields valid results.

## Objectivity

At some point in the development of an evaluation instrument it is necessary to see how far the method of scoring or summarization is objective, that is, to determine the degree to which different persons, presumed to be competent judges, would be able to reach similar scores or summaries after they had a chance to score or summarize the same records of behavior. Objectivity is associated with repeatability and freedom from bias.

The basic procedure for determining objectivity is quite straightforward: have several competent judges independently evaluate or summarize the recorded behavior, then compare their results. There are a few basic ways of comparing the results, depending somewhat upon the form in which the latter happen to be.

If the results are in the form of numerical ratings, one good way is to tally them in a scatter diagram. This has been done in the hypothetical example below, where it is assumed that two readers have graded the same essay question of fifty students on a 5-point scale.

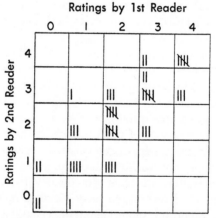

Fig. 6. Plot showing grades assigned by two readers

The agreement, though not perfect, is quite high. The obtained coefficient of correlation between the two sets of scores is .81. Had the tallies all fallen in the diagonal cells, the correlation would have been perfect. As it is, the readers differ by two points on only one case, by one point on twenty-one cases, and on twenty-eight cases they agree. The respective percentages are 2, 42, and 56. This suggests a second way of comparing the extent of agreement.

Let us assume that we have also the ratings of a third reader, and that these are correlated with those of the first reader to give the scatter diagram below.

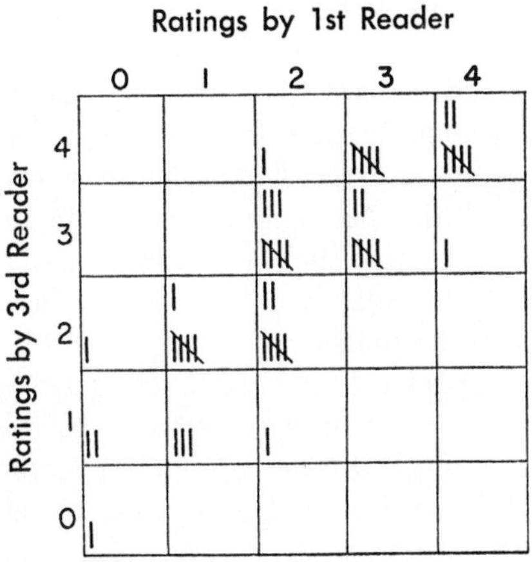

Fig. 7. Plot showing grades assigned by two readers

If we calculate either a coefficient of correlation or percentages as above, the agreement turns out to be similar to that between the first and second readers. Yet there is a systematic difference between the first and third readers. A closer inspection of the scatter diagram shows that the third reader tends to assign higher ratings on the average than does the first. The coefficient of correlation does not reveal this kind of discrepancy, for it is basically an index of relative ranking of the cases.

Now let us assume that Figure 6 represents the numerical ratings assigned by the first reader to the same set of papers, but on two separate occasions—a week apart and without knowing the identity of the papers on either occasion. The correlation between his two sets of ratings would represent an index of his reliability of rating. This correlation can be high, yet not tell anything about the objectivity of the evaluations. All it would tell is that on these two occasions the first reader agreed very closely with himself. To get evidence of objectivity, it is necessary to compare the evaluations of at least two competent judges; theoretically, of an indefinitely large number. The notion of objectivity includes that of rater reliability, for it is not possible for a judge to agree consistently with others unless he can first agree consistently with himself.

In the case of descriptions, the procedure for determining objectivity is more cumbersome. The question then becomes: To what extent will two or more competent observers arrive at similar descriptive sketches based upon the same records of behavior? This check requires a careful reading and comparison by another person to note points of agreement and disagreement between sketches. It may also lead to some form of numerical rating purporting to show the extent of agreement, but it need not.

Objectivity becomes critical whenever personal judgment plays a large part in the process of summarization. In that case, there is more room for personal biases to operate and the summaries may vary markedly from person to person. The solution here is to get judges to agree on the criteria which they will use, and to give them training in applying these. But, of course, even here limits to objectivity are set by the complexity of the behavior or specimens to be judged.

It is important to recognize that objectivity is not a sufficient condition for a valid appraisal or summary. Objectivity by itself is not enough; the scores or summaries must also be appropriate to the purpose. This is particularly important because it is often so easy to get high objectivity, but at the expense of relevance. Thus, it is no trick to get high agreement among scorers who tabulate the number of different kinds of errors made in English compositions. But as noted previously, these may not be the most important qualities to look for. In the history of educational measurement and evaluation there has been too great a concern over objectivity of scoring, with correspondingly too little concern over the appropriateness of what is being evaluated. This has also been true of many studies in other areas of human endeavor, so much so that one writer has been moved to call this pitfall the "fallacy of irrelevant objectivity" (2, p. 153).

### Practicability

The third and final quality to seek in the method of summarization is practicability. This condition is largely a function of the effort and skill needed to arrive at the summarization. The more time-consuming the method, the less practicable it becomes. While some published instruments suffer from a too complicated system of scoring, it is unlikely that this is a very serious problem with the general run of informal devices in use. If anything, instructors err in using too simple a method of summarization.

### REFERENCES

1. Ashford, T. A., and Shanner, W. M. Objective test items of the recognition type that test reasoning and minimize guessing. *J. chem. Educ.*, 1942, **19**, 86–90.

2. Bross, I. D. J., *Design for decision*. New York: Macmillan, 1953.

3. Diederich, P. B., Measurement of skill in writing. *Sch. Rev.*, 1946, **54**, 584–592.

4. Dressel, P. L., and Schmid, J. Some modifications of the multiple-choice item. *Educ. psychol. Measmt*, 1953, **13**, 574–595.

5. Dunkel, H. B. *General education in the humanities*. Washington: Amer. Coun. on Educ., 1947.

6. Gaier, E. L., Lee, Marilyn C., and McQuitty, L. L. Response patterns in a test of logical inference. *Educ. psychol. Measmt*, 1953, **13**, 550–567.

7. Kandel, I. L. Society—the chief examiner. *Coll. Bd Rev.*, 1953, **21**, 375–381.

8. Lorge, I. The fundamental nature of measurement. In E. F. Lindquist (Ed.), *Educational measurement*. Washington: Amer. Coun. on Educ., 1951. Pp. 533–559.

9. Nedelsky, L. Absolute grading standards for objective tests. *Educ. psychol. Measmt*, 1954, **14**, 3–19.

10. Seedorf, Evelyn H. An experimental study in the amount of agreement among judges in evaluating oral interpretations. *J. educ. Res.*, 1949, **43**, 10–21.

11. Smith, E. R., Tyler, R. W., and others. *Appraising and recording student progress*. New York: McGraw-Hill, 1942.

12. Stalnaker, J. M. The problem of the English examination. *Educ. Rec. Suppl.*, 1936, **17**, 35–48.

13. Stalnaker, J. M. Weighting questions in the essay type examination. *J. educ. Psychol.*, 1938, **29**, 481–490.

14. Traxler, A. E. Administering and scoring the objective test. In E. F. Lindquist (Ed.), *Educational measurement*. Washington: Amer. Coun. on Educ., 1951. Pp. 329–416.

15. Traxler, A. E., and Anderson, H. A. The reliability of an essay test in English. *Sch. Rev.*, 1935, **43**, 534–539.

16. Tyler, R. W. Ability to use scientific method. *Educ. Res. Bull.*, 1932, **11**, 1–9.

17. Wechsler, D. *The measurement of adult intelligence*. (3rd Ed.), Baltimore: Williams and Wilkins, 1944.

18. *Construction of comprehensive achievement examinations for Navy officer candidate programs*. Pittsburgh: Amer. Inst. for Res., 1953.

## FURTHER READINGS

Lorge, I. The fundamental nature of measurement. In E. F. Lindquist (Ed.), *Educational measurement*. Washington: Amer. Coun. on Educ., 1951. Pp. 533–559.

Remmers. H. H., and Gage, N. L. Product and procedure evaluation. *Educational measurement and evaluation*. (Rev. Ed.) New York: Harper, 1955. Pp. 150–175.

Smith, E. R., Tyler, R. W., and others. Selected chapters. *Appraising and recording student progress*. New York: McGraw-Hill, 1942.

# Summary of Part 1

We began with the assumption that we could abstract, out of the great variety of techniques for evaluating human behavior, certain basic problems common to all of them; and further, with the belief that there was considerable educational value to be gained from such an approach. In following this approach, we were able to isolate each problem and subject it to rather intensive study. We were also able to see variations that each problem might take, and alternative ways of meeting it.

In the second chapter, we introduced this thought: that every effort to evaluate human behavior must begin with a concept, however vague or clear, of *what* to evaluate. Ultimately, the concept must refer to some characteristic of behavior. The problem of forming such a concept is a problem in definition, but it is also much more than that. It is basically a problem of establishing the significance of the characteristics one proposes to evaluate for a given purpose. There are so many possible characteristics that we might study that we must *determine* those which are especially critical. We then reviewed some general, empirical procedures for helping us isolate the critical aspects of behavior. Following this, we reviewed a rationale for selecting educational objectives—for determining those aspects of behavior which we regard as important in our teaching, or in the development of children and youth generally. This brought us to the point of stating the characteristics in outline form.

Chapter 2 began the larger problem of developing specifications; Chapter 3 carried this to its conclusion. Here we recognized that abstract statements of attributes are not clear enough to guide us in test development or in making observations. It is necessary to define the characteristics in terms of student or worker behavior so that we may know what to look for. We also recognized that behavior does not take place in a vacuum nor is it always highly consistent from one type of situation to another. This led us to consider a variety of limiting conditions that must also be specified. Toward the end of the chapter, we carried the discussion well beyond the definition of behavior to other sorts of specifications that should be laid down.

The importance of clear specifications was made evident in the next three chapters, which dealt respectively with the following technical problems: selecting appropriate situations, getting a record of behavior or of its products, and summarizing the evidence so recorded. In each of these chapters, we first went through some concrete illustrations of the general problem and then we used this background as a basis for elaborating the requirements which a satisfactory solution should meet. The following outline summarizes these requirements and also gives a bird's-eye view of Part I.

|  | Basic Problem | General Requirements |
|---|---|---|
| Specifications | Determining what to evaluate | Validation of the characteristics of behavior one proposes to evaluate. They must be established as being highly relevant to one's purposes. |
| Specifications | Defining the behavior | The characteristics should be clearly defined in behavioral terms, neither too general nor too specific. It is also necessary to specify the limiting conditions under which the behavior is to take place. |
| Technique | Selecting appropriate situations | The situations should meet the specifications—i.e., be relevant to the purposes. The sample should be sufficiently large and representative so as to yield reliable results. Practicability. |
| Technique | Getting a record | The record should indicate accurately the reactions which are relevant (to the purposes of the study). Practicability. |
| Technique | Summarizing the evidence | The method of summarization should be relevant to the purposes. Competent judges should be able to apply the method with a high degree of objectivity. Practicability. |

In summary fashion the outline indicates the requirements that must be met at each stage of work. It should be clear that the validity of the results we come out with at the point of summarization depends as much upon the soundness of the ideas with which we began as upon the success with which the technical problems have been solved.

This last point warrants further scrutiny. It implies that one cannot look at the technique merely *as technique* in judging its validity. One must first examine the relevance of what is being evaluated, and consider the technique in relation to this. According to this view, a test might be measuring something quite accurately but not be a valid test because that "something" is not relevant to the given purpose. Thus, an achievement test cannot be considered a good test if it does not measure something that is highly significant for educational purposes.

According to our view, then, everything goes back to purpose. This shows up in each chapter. It shows up in the outline which has just been presented. Indeed, when reading the outline you may have gotten the feeling that you were going through a revolving door, seeing the same thing over and over again: ". . . should be relevant to . . . purposes." If there is any concept that runs through all of Part I, it is the notion of relevance. Relevance to purpose is the single most important requirement at each stage in the development of an evaluation instrument or procedure.

Another key concept that runs through Part I is the notion of abstracting. We abstract when, in the beginning, we isolate out of the total complex of human behavior those few aspects that concern our immediate purposes; when, at the point of collecting evidence, we draw a sample of situations from the indefinitely large universe of such situations; when, at the point of getting a record, we record only certain of the reactions taking place and ignore all others (of necessity); and when, at the point of summarizing the recorded evidence, we focus on certain characteristics and reduce our judgments to a single score or a short description. We cannot get away from abstracting, but we can try our best to keep the inevitable distortions down to a minimum.

One final point needs mentioning, and that is the order in which the basic problems appear. Although Chapters 2–6 do take up the basic problems in logical order, that is, in the order in which they would ordinarily be met, there is a slight irregularity. That occurs in Chapter 4, in which we discuss reliability as one quality to seek in a sample of evaluation situations. Actually, reliability cannot be estimated until *after* we have presented or observed a sample of situations, obtained a record, and summarized the evidence. In other words, the notion of reliability takes on meaning only in reference to obtained results. The logical point to determine reliability is after the evidence has been summarized and objectivity determined.

# PART II

# Constructing Achievement Tests

# Planning the Test

To insure the best possible test, one must plan for it. A good test does not just happen; it results from careful planning. Above all, planning helps to insure that a test has balance and comprehensiveness.

Planning takes in virtually all phases of test development, administration, and use. Its scope is broad. Moreover, it may continue right along with test development rather than be terminated abruptly during the initial stages of work.

This chapter will concern itself with the central tasks of planning, which are as follows:

1. To clarify the purposes which the test is to serve.
2. To outline the general features of the technique which will help to accomplish these purposes.

Subsequent chapters will go into detail on other aspects of test development and use.

## CLARIFYING THE PURPOSES

### Formulating a general statement of purposes

Ask an instructor for what purpose he is developing a test and he is likely to answer: "To measure achievement in the course." Such a statement has a familiar ring. Usually it implies testing for the sake of grading.

This may be a legitimate purpose, but is the statement satisfactory as a *general* statement of purpose? One who has thought through the implications would feel compelled to say no. Achievement can mean final level of accomplishment, but it can also mean a degree of progress from one level of accomplishment to another. Our instructor may readily concede that he means only to measure achievement in the sense of final status. To him, this is sufficient, for what he wants to do is to be able to assign grades fairly. This being the case, he could have said this at the outset.

Even with such a restatement of purpose, important questions of a general nature remain. Is the student's score on the test to indicate only his relative, over-all standing? Or is it to mean something more tangible in the way of *what he can do*—his level of functioning with the subject matter? Is the test to cover minimum essentials or is it to sample a wide range of achievement? Moreover, what are the general objectives and the areas of subject matter to which the objectives are to be related in the test?

The point to be made here is that the statement, "To measure achievement in the course," is too vague to indicate even in a general way what purpose the test is to serve. One may conceive of several possible general statements, as follows:

1. To measure the over-all level of achievement in the subject matter of the course for the purpose of assigning accurate grades.

2. To determine the level of functioning of students at several possible quality levels—that is, to be able to translate the student's pattern of successes and failures on parts of the test into a description of what he can do.

3. To determine the degree to which individual students and the group as a whole have mastered the minimum essentials of the course.

4. To develop a test parallel to the pretest for the purpose of measuring student progress in the course—that is, gains beyond the level of accomplishment indicated by the pretest.

While these purposes are somewhat incompatible when taken as a group, a few can be served simultaneously by the same test.

The above list represents some of the more common purposes for which tests may be developed, but of course there are other, and often broader, purposes. Chapter 1 should have made these other possibilities clear.

Regardless of the purpose, however, the general statement should include at least a tentative answer to the following two questions:

1. *What decisions do you want the test results to help you make?*

2. *What data do you need in order to make these decisions?*

When these two questions have been satisfactorily answered, the general features of the technique should become readily apparent.

To be sure, one can build a test without having made explicit the decisions to be reached—except for the usual purpose of deciding what grade to give a student. But this is, after all, a limited use of test results. Even a grade may fail to satisfy the student who says, "Yes, but where did I fall down on the examination?" or the one who asks, "What were my special strengths and weaknesses? I'd like to know where to improve myself in this area."

An illustration comes from the writer's experience as a consultant to the psychiatric nursing staff of a school of nursing. The staff of three instructors was preparing to revise a course examination and had called for some technical assistance. (There was a felt need for improving evaluation practices.) A discussion of the purposes of the course and a review of the previous course examination led to the formulation of these objectives for the introductory course in psychiatric nursing:

1. The acquisition of a fund of basic information.
2. The development of ability to apply principles to problem situations.
    2.1 To choose the best course of action.
    2.2 To justify these choices on the basis of supporting principles.

Such a statement of objectives is an important part of the specifications for a test, but it does not make clear the decisions which the staff hoped to make on the basis of the test results. After an extended discussion, members of the staff concluded that the decisions below were of most concern to them. (Opposite each decision is a brief comment on the data needed for that purpose.)

This list of decisions did not exhaust all the important possibilities. There were others on which this staff was not yet ready to seek help. But it did go considerably beyond a concern for grading only—a concern with which the staff had heretofore preoccupied itself.

Nor was the proposed test the only technique these instructors planned to rely upon. Other valuable information was to come from observation of students in clinical settings and in class discussions of ways of meeting problem situations. The availability of such additional data does raise questions as to the *optimum* contribution and make-up of the test. Such questions of how the test results can best be teamed with other data should also be considered during the planning of a test.

| *Decision* | *Data Needed* |
|---|---|
| 1. We want to determine a fair grade for each student based on over-all performance. | A total score based on a representative sampling of the course. |
| 2. We want to be able to tell a student her pattern of strengths and weaknesses:<br><br>a) the degree to which she has acquired the basic information<br>b) the degree to which she can choose the right course of action<br>c) the degree to which she can support her choices by citing the appropriate principles | Part scores for each type of outcome. Each part score must show relative level of accomplishment so that part scores may be compared. |
| 3. We want to be able to identify students who have acquired a good fund of information but have not developed much facility in applying it. | Similar to those immediately above. A scatter plot relating scores on 2 (a) with scores on a composite of (b) and (c) would be helpful for spotting such cases graphically. |
| 4. We want to be able to identify students who are good at choosing the right course of action but are unable to *rationalize* their choices. | Part scores corresponding to (b) and (c) under 2 above. |
| 5. We want to be able to determine whether there is a high correlation between scores on information and scores on application. | Similar to the data needed for 3. A coefficient of correlation would give a summary index of the degree of relationship. |
| 6. We want to be able to decide where our instruction has been effective and where it needs improvement. We hope to get some leads from the test results for the group as a whole. | All of the above data would be helpful. In addition, it would be most desirable to get item analysis data showing the proportion of students who have been successful on the various items in the test. |

In summary, a general statement of the purposes of a test should clearly indicate the nature of the decisions to be made, the nature of the data needed, and the nature of the individuals and groups about whom the decisions are to be made. A careful analysis here will go a long way in the direction of working out specifications. The details of these are numerous, and we have not in this section touched upon all phases of planning. Chapter 3, which covers the development of specifications, should be reviewed at this point for further details. Our immediate concern will be with the preparation of a table of specifications.

1. Why is it important to define carefully the nature of the individuals or groups for whom a test is intended? List as many reasons as you can.

2. How might the purposes best served by a final examination differ from those of tests covering shorter units of instruction?

3. In planning an achievement test, why is it desirable to take into consideration what data are already available on student progress?

### Preparing a table of specifications

Some thirty years ago it was the accepted practice in planning an achievement test to outline the content of a course or subject, and then to write questions that sampled specific elements of this content. It was not thought necessary to draw distinctions among the different ways in which a student might use these elements of content in his thinking. This meant that, although a test might sample different areas of content in a systematic fashion, it most likely did not sample different types of ability in any systematic fashion.

Today, this practice may be still in vogue with teachers. With many professional examiners, however, this is probably not the case; the cultural lag is much less here. The specialists now believe it desirable to supplement an outline of content to be covered with an outline of instructional objectives. The outline of objectives defines the major ways in which students are expected to deal with the particular content.

In addition to these two specific outlines, many examiners prepare a two-way chart or table of specifications. One such chart is reproduced in Figure 8. This was prepared by a college instructor who had responsibility for writing a year-end comprehensive examination in a physical sciences introductory course. Across the top of the chart we have listed the various content areas of the course; down the left side, a breakdown of the major types of objectives. Under each area we have an indication of the amount of time devoted to it in class—this gives some notion of the relative emphasis given the area.

How does an examiner fill in such a grid? He first enters the total number of items allotted for the examination in the lower right-hand corner of the table. He then subdivides this total in two ways: down the right-hand column, showing how the total number of items should be apportioned by type of objective; across the bottom row, showing how the total number of items should be apportioned by content area. These figures are tentative estimates, reflecting the instructor's judgment as to the relative emphasis to be given these various aspects of the course. Next, he works across each row in turn, apportioning items for each objective among the content areas in proportion to the weighting already given to each

| OBJECTIVES \ CONTENT | The Universe and Solar System, Scientific Method | Origin and Composition of Earth, Rocks-Minerals | Atmospheric Movements, Clouds, Weather | Atomic and Kinetic Theory, Gas Laws, Heat | Mathematics, Variation, Functions, Right Triangles | Weathering, Erosional Agents, Deposition of Sediments, Field Trip | Mechanical Energy, Gravitation, Forces and Motion | Electrical Energy, Statics, Magnetism, Electrical Effects | Chemical Energy and Changes, Acids-Bases | Earth Movements, Diastrophism, Vulcanism, Isostasy | Wave Motion, Light, Sound, Electro-magnetic Radiation | Metals, Non-Metals, Fuels, Carbon Compounds, Periodic Chart | *Total Number of Items |
|---|---|---|---|---|---|---|---|---|---|---|---|---|---|
| * Number of Lectures | 4 | 5 | 3 | 6 | 5 | 3 | 3 | 6 | 5 | 3 | 5 | 5 | … |
| ** Number of Laboratory periods | 1 | 4 | 1 | 3 | 4 | 1 | 3 | 2 | 5 | 0 | 5 | 1 | … |
| * Total time in each area | 5 | 9 | 4 | 9 | 9 | 4 | 6 | 8 | 10 | 3 | 10 | 6 | |
| **I. KNOWLEDGE AND UNDERSTANDING OF** | | | | | | | | | | | | | |
| A. Scientific facts and terminology | 5 | 12 | 3 | 4 | 2 | 6 | 3 | 6 | 8 | 2 | 8 | 4 | 63 |
| B. Principles, laws, and theories | 2 | 3 | 2 | 4 | 2 | 4 | 3 | 3 | 4 | 2 | 4 | 3 | 36 |
| C. The mathematical treatment of physical concepts | 1 | | 1 | 2 | | | 2 | 2 | 2 | | 2 | 2 | 14 |
| D. Theoretical assumptions and valid experimentation | 1 | 1 | | 4 | | 2 | 2 | 2 | 3 | | 3 | 2 | 18 |
| E. Definitions and generalizations | 2 | 4 | 2 | 2 | 2 | | 2 | 2 | 3 | 2 | 3 | 2 | 28 |
| | | | | | | | | | | | | | 159 |
| **II. SKILLS AND ABILITIES IN** | | | | | | | | | | | | | |
| A. The solution of mathematical problems | 1 | | | 4 | 6 | | 3 | 4 | 4 | | 4 | | 26 |
| B. The application of principles to familiar problem situations | 2 | 4 | 1 | 3 | 2 | 2 | 3 | 2 | 2 | 2 | 4 | 3 | 30 |
| C. The application of principles to new problem situations | 1 | 2 | 1 | 4 | 2 | 2 | 2 | 2 | 4 | 1 | 2 | 1 | 24 |
| D. Laboratory procedures and techniques | | 2 | | 1 | | | 1 | 2 | 3 | | 1 | 1 | 11 |
| E. The formulation of generalizations from specific facts | 2 | 2 | 1 | 2 | | 2 | 2 | 1 | 2 | | 3 | | 17 |
| F. The interpretation and use of data, tables and pictorial material | 1 | 3 | 3 | 3 | 4 | 2 | 2 | 2 | 3 | 2 | 4 | 4 | 33 |
| **Total** | 18 | 33 | 14 | 33 | 20 | 20 | 25 | 28 | 38 | 11 | 38 | 22 | 300 Total |

Fig. 8. Chart for a physical science examination. (From Comprehensive Examinations in a Program of General Education [1]. Reproduced by permission of the Michigan State University Press, East Lansing.)

area. This gives the figures in the individual cells, or the body of the table. The numbers in Figure 8, by the way, are the final distribution of items for the completed examination. They probably were not the exact distribution initially allotted by this examiner, for in the course of writing items he doubtless made minor changes here and there.

With such a chart or blueprint before him, an instructor or examiner can sample the outcomes of instruction in a balanced fashion, giving adequate emphasis to types of objectives as well as to content areas. Normally, he would use the chart as a flexible guide in writing items to fit objectives.

The chart in Figure 8 represents the extreme in detail and comprehensiveness. Other charts prepared for less comprehensive purposes need not be so detailed. A simpler chart, suitable for a course such as the one discussed in the previous section, appears in Figure 9 in a rather generalized form.

| Objectives of Instruction | Subject-Matter Areas | | | | |
|---|---|---|---|---|---|
| | AREA I | AREA II | AREA III | AREA IV | ETC. |
| 1. Knowledge of basic information .............. | | | | | |
| 1.1 Facts ................ | | | | | |
| 1.2 Terms and concepts ..... | | | | | |
| 1.3 Principles ............ | | | | | |
| 2. Application of principles to problem situations ........ | | | | | |

Fig. 9. Two-way chart relating objectives of instruction to subject-matter areas. (Relative weighting of objectives and areas not shown.)

4. Prepare a table of specifications for an achievement test, based on a statement of objectives and an outline of content to cover a course or unit of instruction.

5. Identify any objectives in 4 above which your test could not adequately appraise. Suggest other, more suitable techniques for these.

6. What factors should be taken into account in determining the length of a test?

## DECIDING MATTERS OF TECHNIQUE

### An overview of decisions to be made

After outlining purposes and specifications, one must make some preliminary technical decisions. The following list covers the usual run of such decisions.

1. Form of test—types of questions or problems; item types.
2. Reference materials needed or permitted.
3. Length of test—total number of questions.
4. Level and range of difficulty of questions.
5. Level and range of discriminating power desired in individual questions.
6. Arrangement of questions within the booklet. Basis of grouping: by subject matter, by objective, etc.
7. Manner of recording answers. Format of special answer sheet, if there is to be one.
8. Time limits, if any. Relative emphasis upon speed, accuracy, and power (ability at its maximum).
9. Directions relative to guessing.
10. Physical make-up of test—type of paper, format, kind of printing.
11. Scoring system.
12. Manner of reporting results to those concerned.

A number of these problems have already been considered in detail in Part I, and for that reason will not be reviewed here. A few will be considered in the following sections; others will be discussed in subsequent chapters.

### Form of test

#### Types of questions or problems

Questions and problems suitable for paper-and-pencil tests take a variety of forms. Yet essentially they group themselves into two broad types:

1. SUPPLY OR FREE-RESPONSE TYPE—*those in which the person must supply the answer to a question or the solution to a problem.*
2. CHOICE TYPE—*those in which the person must record a choice from among given alternatives.*

In the supply type, the person may write out his answer, however brief; work out on paper his solution to a problem; or otherwise produce the responses directly. In the choice type, two or more alternatives are given for each item and the person is merely required to make a choice from among them.

These two types may be further subdivided:

1. SUPPLY OR FREE-RESPONSE TYPE

   a) Extended answer
   b) Short answer

2. CHOICE TYPE

   a) Multiple-choice
   b) Classification

This breakdown differs from others in vogue. First, it is simpler. Thus, it does not overemphasize minor differences in form among essentially similar item types. Second, it departs somewhat from the conventional distinction between essay and objective types. This it does by classifying short-answer questions with supply-type questions rather than with choice items. (Hence, the definition of short-answer adopted here is more restrictive than that often found elsewhere.)

Illustrations of extended-answer, short-answer, and multiple-choice questions have already appeared in this book. No doubt most readers were familiar with these types to begin with, and with true-false—which is a special variety of classification exercise. Illustrations of classification exercises may be found on pages 262–65.

### Comparative advantages

No one form of question or problem is best for all purposes. Each has its special advantages and limitations. At this point let us consider the comparative advantages and limitations of the two broad categories, leaving discussion of specific types to subsequent chapters. Our interest here will be upon technical advantages. Other considerations, such as the educational value of a particular form of examination, we will omit. Educational values are certainly appropriate to the choice of question form; this we recognized in Chapter 4.

The technical advantages of supply-type questions or problems are these:

1. *They represent the most direct way of testing many outcomes, especially cognitive ones.* Table 2 in Chapter 4 amply illustrated this point. What we mean to say here is that the tasks set by many supply-type exercises are no different from, or so much like, their counterparts in everyday life that we can accept them as the same thing. Or, in more ele-

gant terms, the tasks define the behavior and they themselves constitute the criterion. This is not true of many test situations because they depart too much from the real thing.

Two very important types of ability for which it is necessary to elicit free responses are creativity and the ability to organize ideas. At the present time we have no really good evidence that creativity can be assessed through indirect approaches. Nor do we have any good evidence that there is a near-perfect substitute for an essay to test the ability to organize ideas. These outcomes are apparently beyond the scope of choice-type situations.

2. *They tend to give a better estimate of level of competency.* This point is a corollary of the preceding. What we mean here is that it is generally harder to *produce* the right response than to recognize it in a choice item. Stalnaker and Kurath demonstrated this in their study of vocabulary, cited in Chapter 4, and noted that other studies of learning had done likewise. Thus, two parallel forms of a test may rank students in about the same order, but students will tend to score lower on the free-response form. The high correlation which may result obscures the systematic difference in the average scores.

This notion of level of competency needs clarification. Suppose an instructor has as an objective, "the ability to complete chemical equations, given only one side of the equation," as in this example:

$$NaNH_2 + H_2O \rightarrow$$

The most direct approach is to have students complete each equation as it stands. While results on a choice test of the same material may correlate highly with results on the supply-type test, not all students who are able to *recognize* the correct completion in a choice item may be able to supply it. To the extent that this happens, inferences about level of competency will be misleading. The instructor cannot properly conclude that instruction or learning has been effective, if his standard is "the ability to complete chemical equations. . . ." For some purposes of evaluation, then, it is important to distinguish between level of competency and relative competency, or rank in some defined group.

3. *They minimize the possibility of getting the right answer through guessing.* Since the examinee must produce the right answer, he operates without the aid of special cues as appear in choice items. He can, of course, still guess, but his chances of guessing correctly are much less favorable here.

4. *They are relatively easy to prepare.* This is not to say that good free-response questions can be dashed off in a hurry, as they no doubt frequently are. They require as careful preparation as choice items. The difference in labor lies in the preparation of suggested answers for choice items. It is this additional time-consuming task which one can dispense with when he prepares free-response questions.

5. *They are much more likely to reveal individuality.* While a choice item restricts the response to a few suggested answers, a free-response question usually invites some individuality of expression. Thus, in any group, a free-response question tends to evoke a variety of responses reflecting individual differences in meanings, in attitudes, in manner of expression, and in methods of problem-solving. Such idiosyncrasies often provide rich data useful for understanding individual learning and development.

The technical advantages of choice-type questions or problems are these:

1. *They set up a forced-choice situation* which requires that the individual demonstrate the specific ability called for by each item. Because they are highly structured, choice items sharply channel or focus the individual's thinking. By contrast, a free-response question may give the individual the *opportunity* to demonstrate certain competencies, but there is no guarantee that it will evoke these. He may deliberately avoid coming to grips with the question, preferring to conceal his ignorance or lack of ability; or he may unwittingly respond in ways other than the examiner intended.

2. *They do not depend upon skill in expression and handwriting.* Neither facility in written expression nor speed of handwriting can affect how well a person does.

3. *They permit a wide sampling in a relatively short period of time.* This advantage follows from the fact that each item is brief and that the respondent does not have to take the time to write out an answer.

4. *They permit highly objective scoring.* Once a key has been worked out in advance—and this is usually not a difficult problem—scoring becomes a routine matter. Even clerks unfamiliar with the subject matter can score the test uniformly.

5. *They permit rapid and easy scoring.* This advantage follows again from the simple manner in which responses have been recorded and from the fact that a predetermined key can be routinely applied.

6. *They lend themselves more readily to statistical analysis.* This ad-

vantage especially holds when the choices have been recorded on an IBM answer sheet. It is then possible to obtain a count of the number of times each item alternative has been chosen by the total group or by subgroups, such as the upper and lower quarters on the total score. Such data then make possible the derivation of statistical indexes helpful in assessing the effectiveness of the individual items and the test as a whole. While these procedures are possible with supply-type examinations, they are quite cumbersome. Chapter 13 goes into these procedures in detail.

It should be noted, in passing, that the first four of the preceding advantages are also possessed by short-answer questions to a considerable degree.

7. Can you think of any outcomes or characteristics for which a choice-type test would constitute a more direct approach than a free-response test?
8. Some instructors prefer to use several different types of items or questions on the grounds that this produces a more interesting and flexible examination. How do you evaluate these arguments?
9. The joint use of supply and choice types may often be advantageous. Illustrate some important uses in which, for example, essay questions may be combined with multiple-choice items.

### REFERENCE

1. *Comprehensive examinations in a program of general education.* East Lansing: Mich. State Univer. 1949.

# Constructing Items to Fit Specifications

The title of this chapter suggests a focus similar to that of Chapter 4. This is true except for scope. Chapter 4 dealt with principles basic to the development of any kind of evaluation technique. Thus, the principles set forth there apply here, as do many of the illustrations, but here the scope is more restricted, since it deals largely with situations of the paper-and-pencil variety. Moreover, this chapter does not repeat many of the points discussed at length in 4. A review of that chapter would thus be highly desirable at this point.

Our purpose now is to expand on certain of the principles introduced earlier, showing how they may be applied to paper-and-pencil tests in particular. Please be clear on this point, however: Chapter 8 *is* intended to be general. It is intended to emphasize certain principles and practices applicable to *both* supply and choice types of test situations. It continues the theme set forth in Part I that the purpose of appraisal should primarily determine matters of technique.

## WORKING FROM SPECIFICATIONS

### General considerations

If you intend to build a test and you have worked out an adequate set of specifications, you have a flying start. A substantial part of the job of building the test lies behind you. The next part of the job is to devise situations to fit these specifications; in narrower perspective, to construct items.

How to proceed? You may follow the chart of specifications in either direction: by objective or by content area. You may, if you choose, concentrate on one type of objective at a time, composing items for that objective as you go through the various content areas; or you may choose to concentrate on one area of content at a time, composing items testing for different objectives. Which procedure is generally more economical and productive is hard to say; we lack evidence on this point. From the standpoint of convenience, the second approach would seem to have some advantages. By concentrating on a single area, you are at least able to keep the material fresh in mind as you work through it and you may then be in a better position to see ways in which the particular content relates to different objectives.

But this is a general question of procedure, and most of your concern will be with a further question: What is the best way to test for this specific objective with this particular content? Clearly, this is the sort of question that comes up continually in constructing items, and one for which there is no simple answer. Yet we can offer general suggestions for getting ideas and general principles for selecting situations, as was done in Chapter 4. In addition, we can illustrate in this and other chapters types of situations suitable for testing common educational goals; and we can refer you to general references, such as the *Taxonomy* (1), which illustrate ways of testing for important kinds of objectives. Through such illustrations, you should be able to develop your know-how considerably.

1. As a warm-up to the task of constructing test situations, take a single concept or principle from your field and compose questions which will

test this concept at several levels of understanding. Then try to decide for what particular instructional aim and group each question would be most suitable. This exercise should help to sensitize you to the range of possible objectives with which an element of content such as a concept or principle may deal, and with the importance of having clear specifications from which to work.

### Illustrations

To see how test items or situations may be developed to fit specifications, let us turn to a few pertinent illustrations. The first of these comes from a report on the development of tests for evaluating the research proficiency of physical scientists (17). This project is the same one which utilized the critical incident technique described in Chapters 2 and 3. Figure 10 contains the specifications—what Flanagan has called the "item rationale"—consisting of a detailed definition and description of the critical behavior, a breakdown of the behavior into its component parts, and specifications for an item to sample that behavior. Figure 11 shows an item written to fit these specifications.

This first illustration represents an extremely careful and elaborate approach to item writing. Such a formal approach is desirable, if not essential, in the development of tests for large-scale use. Perhaps this should represent a good model for less formal and more restricted test development projects. Our purposes in including this illustration here are to follow through on the earlier discussion of the critical incident technique and to present an example of an unusually rational approach to item writing.

Our second illustration ties in with one of the objectives of the nursing course mentioned in the previous chapter.

*Statement of objective:* 2. The development of ability to apply principles to problem situations.

2.1 To choose the best course of action.
2.2 To justify these choices on the basis of supporting principles.

*A situation designed to evaluate the attainment of this objective:*
Jerry, a twelve-year-old boy on the children's unit, has been described as a very friendly, ingratiating child who has difficulty relating to the staff. Today he approached the attendant and asked to be let out of the ward to go to the party for hospital children, but was refused as he did not have privileges. Later Jerry offered to take a smaller boy to the library when the nurse was unable to do so because of her work load.

*Behavior to be Sampled*

AREA VIII. Accepting Personal Responsibility

Subarea D. Being Fair and Ethical

Behavior 2. GAVE CREDIT FOR IDEAS OR WORK TO THOSE RESPONSIBLE.

*Description of Behavior*

Effective performance of this behavior involves giving appropriate acknowledgment to persons responsible for work which is reported publicly, or merely discussed informally. It involves judgments concerning scientific ethics and conventions which permit some variation in practice, yet follow certain general princples.

Ineffective performance would be shown by a failure to give credit to individuals participating in work, or failure to make acknowledgment appropriately.

*Identification of Behavioral Components*

(General)* 1. Recognizing the specific contributions made by various individuals in the conception and conduct of an investigation

(General)  2. Giving appropriate credit for ideas or work

*Item Specifications*

1. Objective, five-choice item

2. This item should be suitable for examinees in both physics and chemistry, as well as other fields.

3. *Description of Proposed Item*

Describe a situation where an individual takes over an investigation after preliminary planning or work has been done by another person. Include enough details to make the contributions of the latter clear. Ask the examinee to select the best way of referring to this individual's work in a report of the completed project. The correct choice should specify that all of his specific contributions be mentioned. Wrong choices might include brief mention that he participated, mention of only part of his contribution, or rationalizations for failure to give appropriate credit.

This is intended to sample components (1) and (2).

* Each behavioral component was labeled "specific" or "general" depending on whether it would require specific technical knowledge or a general scientific background common to most research scientists.

Fig. 10. Example of an item rationale.

*NONTECHNICAL ITEM (VIII-D-2)*

Carson, a research associate in an industrial laboratory, had been working on the design of a new device for measuring the thickness of plastic sheets. In the course of his work he thought of a way to improve an automatic counter and use it with the measuring device so that the measuring and counting processes could be done in a single operation. When Carson was just beginning the planning stages of the automatic counter, he was asked to come to Washington to work on an urgent government project. The laboratory granted him a leave of absence and appointed Hardy to continue the work of Carson's project.

Hardy finished the development of both the measuring device and the counter, making a number of basic improvements on the original idea of the counter, and was ready to write the report which would accompany the completed design. Because he had not assumed responsibility for the project in the beginning Hardy was wondering how to refer to Carson's work in the report.

Of the following the best thing for him to do would be to

A. mention that Carson worked on the project, but he need not give any details.

B. make no mention of Carson's work since the final responsibility of the design and the report are his.

C. mention Carson's work on the measuring device, but not on the automatic counter since Carson did very little work on that.

D. make no mention of Carson's work since at present he is not directly associated with the company.

E. mention everything that Carson did on the project, even though his preliminary plans of the counter were changed considerably.

Intended Answer: E

Fig. 11. Test item written to fit specifications in Fig. 10. (Reproduced by permission of the American Institute for Research.)

What is the best thing for the nurse to do in this situation?

a) Accept Jerry's offer because he needs to assume responsibility on the ward.
b) Refuse his offer, reminding him again that he does not have privileges and cannot therefore leave the ward unsupervised.
c) Accept Jerry's offer because he could then get some books for himself and thus keep busy.
d) Refuse Jerry's offer but encourage him to associate with the older children.
e) Refuse Jerry's offer because one child cannot assume responsibility for another child, but express appreciation to Jerry for offering his services.

Indicate below the psychiatric nursing principles upon which you based your choice: (The key is given here.)

1. (Do not allow child to manipulate the situation.)
2. (Set limits in a consistent way.)
3. (Avoid praise as this encourages his ingratiation.)

When we compare this exercise with the statement of the objective, we can conclude that the situation does afford an opportunity for the student to demonstrate her ability to apply principles. Although we do not have in the specifications any indication of the range of problem situations to be encountered, the situation described does appear to be both realistic and important. This exercise, it should be noted, illustrates well the joint use of multiple-choice and free-response questions.

   2. Assume that the two items below had been written in order to test "ability to recognize the meanings of words in context." To what extent do you think they fit this specification? If they had been written to test knowledge of vocabulary as such, to what extent do you think the additional content (i.e., context) is desirable?

   Those HALCYON days. 1-holy 2-robust 3-busy 4-peaceful 5-childhood
   A lamentable HIATUS. 1-accident 2-death 3-flight 4-reaction 5-break

### Special problems

#### Testing for understanding

There are many special problems that one faces in writing items to fit specifications. One of the most important of these by far is the problem of testing for understanding. We have dealt with this problem before but it deserves repeated emphasis.

For an exceptionally lucid statement on the problem of testing for understanding, we shall quote Professor Walker H. Hill, of Michigan State University, an expert examiner who has faced this problem many times. In the quotation below, he explains the kind of distinction he made between knowledge and understanding, and how he carried this out in writing items for comprehensive examinations (after 15, pp. 29–30).

. . . The examiner's distinction between knowledge and understanding is relatively easy to apply, and to explain. An item is considered to be a test of *knowledge* when it can be answered on the basis of rote learning, when all that is required is recall of something the student has read or heard in the course. In this sense many students will have considerable knowledge of the facts, principles, concepts, etc., which have been taught in the course, and one thing we wish to test is the extent of their knowledge. A student not only knows facts but *understands* them when he can see their relation to one another—see it in a way not specifically taught in the course. He not only knows a principle but understands it when he can recognize it in a new context or when it is stated in different words; when he can distinguish it from some other principle that is similar to it (e.g., one that uses some of the same words); when he can recognize it in, or apply it to, a new situation or problem; when he can recognize what facts are pertinent to it (or distinguish facts which support it from those which do not). This is not an exhaustive list of criteria, but it illustrates what the examiner has in mind when he speaks of understanding.

The distinction may be illustrated by two examples:

"The mores determine to considerable degree our attitudes toward morals, monogamy, courtship, etc."

By *mores* is meant
1. legal regulations.
2. the folkways of a society.
3. customs considered essential to social welfare.
4. patterns of behavior common to all cultures.
5. ideals which are everlasting.

In a comparison of happily married men with unhappily married men, which of the following traits has been found to be more characteristic of the former?
1. Liking for power.
2. Sensitivity to social opinion.
3. Liking for bureaucratic procedures.
4. Autocratic attitudes.
5. Feelings of inferiority.

Both of these items deal with concepts. The first is designed to test whether the student *knows* what is meant by *mores*. The correct answer is very much like a definition given in his textbook. He need only remember that definition to answer the item correctly. We do not know whether he could give or recognize an example, or whether he could by example distinguish between mores and folkways (which distinction is a key to the concept).

The second item requires more of the student. He has not been told that a liking for bureaucratic procedures is characteristic of happily married men. But he has read that, more often than is true of unhappily married men, they work well with business superiors, are willing to give close attention to detail in their daily work, like methodical procedures and methodical people, and are cautious and conservative. In another part of the course, quite outside the context of marriage, the student has learned that such traits are characteristic of bureaucracy. The item is designed to require him to combine specific facts he has learned in one connection and to see their relation to a concept learned in another connection—to *understand* both the meaning of the facts and the meaning of the concept.

While we are discussing this particular item, it may be instructive to digress long enough to point out that it exemplifies a possible weakness. It is possible that a student could remember that all the other traits mentioned are *not* characteristic of happily married men and therefore No. 3 must be the correct answer. In that case he would arrive at the correct answer by elimination, and the item would test his knowledge rather than his understanding. This would require a detailed recollection of facts which the examiner considered extremely unlikely. But, insofar as it is possible, it is a real weakness of the item, a kind of weakness which the examiner tries to avoid. The item might still be a good test of something, but not of what it was intended to test.[1]

### The role of memory

To test for understanding, you must use situations that contain an element of novelty—you must, in other words, play down the role of memory. Does this mean that memory is unimportant in situations that call for a display of thinking? Just what is the proper role of memory in examinations?

If the intended purpose is to test for knowledge, then the role of memory should be clear enough. The test situations must call for a demonstration of specific information. On the other hand, where the purpose is to appraise thinking, there is a real possibility that the role of memory will be misunderstood.

For a pointed discussion of the role of memory on examinations, we shall reproduce portions of a statement prepared by a college humanities staff (16). The original purpose of the statement was to acquaint students with the purpose and nature of the examinations in a general humanities course. This particular course emphasized the arts by which one analyzes works in history, rhetoric, drama, fiction, and philosophy. Classroom discussion was devoted to an analysis of appropriate texts (original works), but students were also expected to study assigned supplementary works

[1] Reproduced by permission of the author and the Michigan State University Press.

outside of class. Examinations dealt with both the works studied in class and those studied outside.

One part of the statement below consists of a sample of questions for the major types of objectives. This part illustrates again how items are written to fit specifications. The remaining part consists of discussion. In this excerpt, the references pertain to Gibbon, *The History of the Decline and Fall of the Roman Empire*; to Herodotus, *The Persian Wars*; and to Thucydides, *The Peloponnesian War*. Milton's *Areopagitica* is his speech for the liberty of unlicensed printing, addressed in 1644 to Parliament, which had just restricted the freedom of the press.

I. *Knowledge of the significant facts in assigned readings.*

Item 1. According to Gibbon, the religious policy of the Emperors from Augustus through the Antonines was, in general—
A. to consider all religions as equally true.
B. to consider all religions as equally useful.
C. to assimilate all religions to the Roman pattern.
D. to encourage the old Roman religion and discourage others.

II. *Ability to draw correct inferences from recalled or given texts.*

Item 2. It may be assumed from Milton's *Areopagitica* that his audience at the beginning of the work was favorably disposed toward—
A. both booksellers and bishops.
B. both learning and licensing.
C. both monks and Moses.
D. both Italy and Spain.
E. none of the foregoings pairs.

III. *Ability to make correct interpretations of texts in terms of principles, processes of reasoning, and other factors appropriate to the form of writing involved.*

Item 3. Engels in his *Germany: Revolution and Counter-Revolution* (A—includes B—does not include) an account of the relationship between German philosophy and the political enlightenment of Germany

Item 4. because he believes that the philosophers—
A. exemplify, in their theories, a shift in the political thought of the middle class.
B. first reached and stirred the slumbering masses of the proletariat, the class which took the initiative in 1848.
C. by means of their clear and simple exposition of the situation, were the first to reach and unite all the classes of Germany.
D. played no part in informing any class of the German people.
E. had no understanding of the revolutionary movement, either inside or outside of Germany, and scrupulously avoided all political, social, and religious questions.

IV. *Ability to perceive the similarities and dissimilarities between particular aspects of different texts.*

The following descriptions of the structure of various histories assume that each of the works involved can be divided on the basis of content into an *introduction* (ranging in length from one sentence to several chapters) and a *narrative* proper. For each item blacken answer space—

A. if the description applies accurately to Herodotus' history.

B. if the description applies accurately to Thucydides' history.

C. if the description applies accurately to Gibbon's history.

D. if the description does not apply accurately to any one of these three.

(NOTE. Blacken only one answer space for any one item.)

Item 5. The *introduction* describes the temporary organization of a state in terms of the character and function of its principal parts; the incidents of the *narrative,* in consequence, are the various reorganizations of the state (as it departs from its former condition) and the causes underlying these changes.

Item 6. In the *introduction,* the historian, while admitting that the traditions of antiquity are rather fictions of poetry than genuine records of history, yet maintains that a conception of the past may be formed which will suffice to show a decline in the manners, morals, and general happiness of the great nation in question, and thus to show also what men should choose or avoid; the *narrative* is told in the fullest detail of which tradition permits.

Item 7. In the *introduction,* the historian discriminates between the kinds of causes operating in the action he relates, arguing the connection of each with this action; the *narrative* directs attention to the elements which lead political groups to choose one policy rather than another, and then presents the resulting military and political operations by which their choices may be evaluated.

Item 8. The *introduction* states the topics of the history in terms of the historian's multiple aims; the course of the *narrative* is frequently interrupted by discussions, necessary for achieving the aims of the history, concerning the origin and general character of agents and events.

. . . Only the first of the examples given above (item 1) can be called a "mere memory" item—one to which the answer can be determined by anyone who stumbles on the explicit statement in the text which fixes the answer. A fact which is stated in a single sentence, of course, may be very important or very unimportant. *Knowing what facts must be mastered as a part of understanding a work is, in fact, one of the special arts* which the course seeks to develop. In any historical work the separate names and dates and events possess significance only as the historian makes them significant parts of his account, and they are to be remembered with the significance thus given to them. Take the sample question from Gibbon (item 1) as an illustration. Gibbon treats the religious policy of the emperors as one of the wisely chosen devices by which the Empire was held together in a political equilibrium; as such it is proper for the student to remember what kind of policy it was which had this effect. In a rhetorical work, the corresponding facts would be those which bear most directly on the central problem of the work, i.e., the task of persuasion. The main arguments and all the complex factors which define the speaker and his audience in their relation to each other and to the object of persuasion would be appropriate matters for examination questions. *In general, the kinds of facts which must be mastered and given order to are suggested by the questions raised* (in the syllabus) *as appropriate to the analysis of the different kinds of literary constructions. In other words, a student's analysis of a work provides the form for his memory of its contents, but the memory is necessary as the matter in which the form inheres. Neither can exist as a distinct thing without the other.*

Obviously, it follows that none of the other items given by way of illustration is independent of memory. For example, the inferences concerning the opinions of the British Parliament that item 2 investigates cannot be made by one who has never encountered the *Areopagitica*; the student's memory of particular references in the the text to the institutions of the Roman Catholic Church must provide the premises from which he may infer the facts that justify his rejecting answers A and C. And it is obvious that the succeeding sample questions (items 3 to 8) require the recall of increasingly large units of the student's reading experience—units, moreover, which have been subjected to various kinds of analytical interpretation. *It is important, then, that a student recognize that no interpretation of any work can be demonstrated as a plausible one unless certain particulars in the work are brought forward as evidence; nor is it likely that a reader will reach a tenable interpretation unless he keeps in mind a large number of the facts presented in the work. A test, therefore, of a student's ability to interpret an assigned work will of necessity involve that student's knowledge of those facts. . . ."*

In short, knowledge of specific works is necessary before a student can demonstrate his skill in interpreting and analyzing those works, whether studied in class or outside. But the knowledge is of a highly selected character. It is *not* the accumulation of a mass of details only more or less related.

Substantially the same kind of argument holds for other aspects of thinking. To apply facts and principles, the student must first *know* the facts and principles (or in some instances, be given them). Similarly, to evaluate any idea or work, the student must possess a good fund of appropriate information which provides his premises for reasoning. Memory, of some kind of information, is indeed necessary and important in the demonstration of an intellectual ability.

## USING CONTENT TO STRUCTURE TEST SITUATIONS

### Permitting the use of reference materials

One of the most significant ways of structuring test situations is to permit the use of reference materials, such as textbooks, technical handbooks, and dictionaries. This privilege frees students from the burden of remembering minute details, and hence tends to put everyone on an equal footing with respect to basic information.

There is a large element of realism behind the open-book examination, as it is often termed. In virtually every field, so rapid has been the growth of knowledge that it is no longer reasonable to expect students to remember every useful bit of information. Instead, it is considered more desirable for them to concentrate on developing skills, and to learn to draw upon reference materials for whatever information they need when applying their skills. The out-of-school situation, moreover, is one in which reference materials are at the practitioner's finger tips where he may draw upon them as the need arises. Hence, he may as well learn to perform in that way from the start.

The use of reference materials is certainly consistent with many educational goals, but especially for the following abilities:

1. To interpret, analyze, and evaluate materials in a given field.
2. To apply knowledge to problem situations not previously discussed in class.
3. To organize ideas drawn from a variety of sources.

For certain purposes, it may be necessary to duplicate special materials or to distribute reprints. In a course on the social sciences, one instructor collected a set of brief selections from several documents dealing with the issue of social planning. He deliberately chose documents containing a variety of approaches to this problem and a variety of methods of treatment. He duplicated and distributed these materials to students several days before the examination, instructing the students to read the different selections beforehand so that they might answer questions on them later. At the examination, he allowed students to refer to the selections and to any notes they may have made on them.

3. What educational values do you see in the open-book type of examination?
4. When testing minimum reading proficiency in a foreign language, would it be desirable to allow students to make use of a dictionary? Explain.
5. Are there any purposes in your field or activity for which you can use an open-book examination?

## Providing background information

At times it is desirable to provide necessary background information right along with the problems or questions. This saves time that might otherwise be spent in looking for the information in references. We shall consider here two important purposes for which this is good practice.

### To minimize knowledge of details

In the illustration below, consider how the provision of certain basic information serves to focus each item. The net effect is to eliminate this information as a potential irrelevant factor.

The following list is a partial activity series: magnesium, aluminum, zinc, iron, hydrogen, copper, mercury, silver.

Which of the following pairs of metals will produce the highest voltage when used as electrodes in suitable cells?

(This item was designed to test the understanding that the metals constitute an electromotive series: the farther apart any two metals in the series, the greater the voltage they will produce.)

A. Magnesium and aluminum
B. Magnesium and zinc
C. Aluminum and zinc
D. Mercury and silver
E. All will produce the same voltage.

Of those elements listed above, hydrogen will be liberated from hydrochloric acid by—

(This item was designed to test the understanding that in chemical reactions a metal will replace metals below it in the series, but will be replaced by metals above it.)

A. the first four metals.
B. the last three metals.
C. magnesium only.
D. silver only.
E. all seven metals.

It is clear that, to answer the two questions, the student must know (or have available as here) the partial activity series as given. But it should be equally clear that to answer these two questions, he must *know more than* the order of the metals in the series. He must also know the important properties of the series. It is these further understandings that the instructor wishes to test. The background information serves to put all students on an equal footing—specifically, to insure that the forgetting of a few details about the make-up of the activity series *will not prevent the student from showing the higher-order understandings.*

This practice is thoroughly defensible, and indeed highly desirable, for many purposes. Particularly is this true when the emphasis is upon the demonstration of understanding, or of proficiency in some skill. It is then often legitimate to provide the student with background information on physical constants such as $\pi$, atomic weights, involved formulas which are too intricate to remember, and definitions of terms or principles which must be understood for the solution of a problem but which may be beyond the experience of a sizable fraction of the intended group.

### To control differences in knowledge about a topic

A frequent problem in testing written composition is to control knowledge about the topic. The assumption is that individuals write better on those topics on which they are well informed (or at least, that they bring in many more pertinent ideas, which influence favorably appraisals of their compositions apart from skill in expression). Each of these possibilities is real.

To control this factor of knowledge, instructors of English sometimes allow students to choose from among several topics. The thought is partly that the student will write better on familiar topics, partly that he will write better on topics which interest him. There is a kernel of truth in both of these assumptions. However, the difficulty arises at the point of evaluating the compositions for any group. It is difficult to make comparable evaluations when students write on different topics.

There is another solution that enjoys acceptance among expert examiners in English. Students write on the same topic, but based on a set of common reading materials which they receive before the test. These materials are brief—just enough detail to supply a minimum background or to point up basic issues and contrasting viewpoints. A few reading passages may suffice; at times it is advantageous to gather several excerpts into a booklet or to distribute reprints of an article. Not only do such materials help to minimize differences in knowledge about a topic; they also help to stimulate thinking. (For evidence of these effects, recall the Traxler-Anderson experiment discussed on page 118).

6. The exercise below was designed to test the ability of tenth-grade students to analyze a situation and to formulate a course of action, with the help of given information (**8**, p. 109).

   a) Does the exercise emphasize application of facts and principles, or reading comprehension?
   b) If a similar situation and question were to be used with advanced high school students or with college students, would it be desirable to supply the background information? Explain.

*Information*

The United States produces 48 per cent of the world's corn. At the present time, corn crops cover more ground than any other crop in America. Three-fourths of our corn is consumed by pigs, cattle, horses, and poultry. Corn is a "soil-mining" crop, removing nitrogen from the soil.

Nitrogen may be put into the soil by means of farm fertilizers, commercial fertilizers, and "green manure." "Green manure" refers to crops such as beans, peas, alfalfa, or clover. On the roots of these plants live bacteria which are able to convert the nitrogen of the air—which cannot be used by plants—into a form in which plants can use it.

Plant roots hold soil in place and keep it spongy rather than compact. Spongy soil can absorb more water than compact soil. The more compact the soil is, the more likely is it that heavy rains will wash away the top layers. Heavy rains may also wash out the mineral matter in the soil. With too little rainfall, the soil may become so dry that it is easily blown away.

*Situation*

An Iowa farmer limited himself to growing corn on his acres, and had good crops—sometimes excellent—during most of the years from 1912 to 1927. After this he had much less success and was unable to make his farm pay. Conditions went from bad to worse, until in 1937 the farm looked like a desert, and the farmer abandoned it.

*Question*

What could the farmer whose plight is described have done to save his farm? Show how each suggestion you make is based upon information in the section above.[2]

## Including irrelevant data

Another way of using content is to supply more data than is necessary. This forces the individual to sift the relevant from the irrelevant, as in the simple accounting problem below.

[2] Reproduced by permission of *Science Education*.

Samuel Smith operates a trucking service between two cities. His equipment consists of one truck which he has leased at a monthly rental of $100. He rents garage and warehouse space for $50 per month. During the month of January, Smith's cash receipts and cash disbursements were as follows:

Cash receipts:
1. From customers for trucking services                                          $550
2. Borrowed from bank on last day of month                               300
3. Received a cash dividend on his life insurance policy          20

Cash disbursements:
1. For rental of truck                                                                        $100
2. For rental of garage and warehouse                                           50
3. Dentist's bill for his child                                                             12
4. Gasoline, oil, and supplies for his truck                                   122
5. Grocery bill                                                                                   135

Compute the net profit of the trucking service for the month of January.

Two assumptions behind the practice of including irrelevant data are that—

1. Life situations do not ordinarily contain *only* the data we need to solve problems; it is rather more common to find a variety of data present, only some of which is relevant to a given problem.
2. Evaluation situations which contain only the data needed to solve problems are not wholly realistic, and to that extent yield incomplete evidence of problem-solving ability.

These assumptions seem plausible, especially the first. We have, however, precious little experimental data bearing on the validity of the second. A study by Ebel is the only one with which this writer is familiar (6). Ebel tried to determine the effects of irrelevant data in physics problems. He administered, among other things, a set of problems in standard form and a parallel set in which each problem contained a piece of irrelevant numerical data. He found that—

1. Scores on the two types of problems did not differ significantly. ($r = .92$)
2. The introduction of irrelevant data into the problems produced a small average increase in difficulty without producing any significant average change in discriminating power.
3. The irrelevant data had widely varying effects from problem to problem. It was not possible to find a rational basis for these variations in the characteristics of either the original problems or the irrelevant data used.

These results do not necessarily disprove the value of irrelevant data. They do indicate that the choice of irrelevant data for any problem must be guided by actual tryout. The irrelevant data must be of a kind which some individuals do include in their solutions.

### Using unfamiliar content

Another and very important way of structuring situations is to use unfamiliar content. The function of unfamiliar content is to give the student an opportunity to demonstrate specific kinds of thinking independently of his memory of any particular organization of content. Unfamiliar content serves to control what, for this purpose, would amount to an irrelevant factor, namely, memory of previous judgments. If we are to get evidence of any intellectual ability, we must use situations in which a person cannot recall from previous experience the required solutions or judgments.

### Need for curricular relevance

But while such content must be new in particulars, it should contain familiar elements and relationships. It should be *similar but not identical with* that content (problems, reading selections, musical compositions, etc.) used for instructional purposes. *The crucial elements and relationships, however, should be those which were at the focus of instruction,* rather than concepts, principles, and relationships which were already a part of the student's general information and comprehension. Otherwise the content will lack curricular relevance.

Moreover, the mental operations to be done with the content must also be consistent with the instructional goals. Otherwise they, too, will lack curricular relevance. It is unreasonable to expect students to perform sophisticated mental operations if they have not had instruction along those lines. Take, as an illustration, skill in judging interpretations of data.[3] It is possible to include interpretations not definitely true or false according to the data, but which may be considered probably true or probably false. Such interpretations are in the nature of qualified inferences. They are inferences that go beyond the data but are suggested as probably true or probably false according to conditions, trends, or other

---

[3] As measured by the P. E. A. Interpretation of Data Test discussed in Smith and Tyler, *op. cit.*, 38–76. Other illustrations are in the *Taxonomy*, (1, 91–104).

extensions of the data. Now the distinction between "true" and "probably true," and between "false" and "probably false," is a subtle one and requires a nice sense of judgment to make. Students who have not had instruction on processes, such as interpolation and extrapolation, and on elementary notions of sampling, such as predictions from part to whole and from whole to part, are likely to have trouble with such inferences. Some may even use "probably true" and "probably false" to express doubt about their own answers, rather than doubt about the sufficiency of the data (1, p. 92).

### Selecting and adapting content

A few suggestions may be offered as guides to the selection of unfamiliar content. The following apply rather generally:

1. *The content should be relatively novel yet meaningful to the group.* Students should not be able to answer questions based upon the selection without having first studied it. But the material should be within their grasp, and it should be intrinsically interesting.

2. *The content should be sufficiently complex to permit a reasonable sampling of the instructional objectives.* If the selection is too simple, it prevents the student from demonstrating complex thinking. If it is too narrow in scope, it prevents him from demonstrating a variety of mental operations. This standard of complexity is again a matter of curricular relevance, just as was the preceding.

3. *The selection should be relatively short.* This is primarily a matter of economy. Students should be able to study the selection in a relatively short period of time. The exception to this requirement is, of course, the open-book examination, in which the selection(s) may be of such length as to take several hours of outside study. Short reading passages, tables of data, and the like, can be sufficiently complex to present a significant task. However, it is often necessary to adapt selections so as to make them short enough for the time available. Usually this involves eliminating unnecessary parts and revising others.

4. *The number of questions should be proportional to the length and complexity of the selection.* The student should not be required to spend a great deal of time on a selection which will yield only a few scorable points.

Beyond these general criteria, you would need to take other things into account. The nature of these additional criteria will depend upon the specific use to be made of the content. For other possible criteria, consult the three references annotated below.

*Appraising and Recording Student Progress* (**14**). At several places in Chapter 2, on aspects of thinking, you will find a discussion of criteria for selecting content. The discussions relative to interpretation of data and to application of principles of science are fairly complete. It is important to recognize that two sorts of content are discussed: (1) the facts, relationships, and principles which are at the heart of the objective, and (2) the types of content on which the student is to show his skill. This second aspect is our main concern here.

*General Education:* Explorations in Evaluation (**3**). Pages 45 and 46 contain a discussion of criteria for selection of problem materials in the social sciences. Of special note is the suggestion that problem situations be emotion-provoking rather than purely academic. Pages 183–185 contain, first, specifications for problem situations to be included in a general test of critical thinking, and, second, an analysis of several important areas from which problems might be drawn.

*Science Reasoning and Understanding* (**4**). Pages 25 to 35 contain a reprint of an article on photosynthesis, followed by a three-page condensed version. The ensuing discussion shows how the latter may be used for purposes of teaching and evaluation. Page 178 contains a bibliography of additional problem-type articles.

### A sample exercise

We shall reproduce a sample selection of content, with which it is assumed you are unfamiliar. Immediately after, there are two essay questions which you should try to answer.

This selection was originally condensed from longer technical accounts. It was intended for a test of educational progress which would not be tied in closely with a particular course of study or particular instructional materials (**18**). The exercise itself is appropriate for superior high school students or for college freshmen, provided that they do not have an intimate knowledge of the topic under consideration.

Though you may not be well-informed on this topic, this should not deter you from answering the questions. You will not be unduly handicapped if you have a broad general education—and strong motivation! To get the most out of this chapter, you should really answer these questions. Later, you will be asked to refer to your answers for other purposes.

In a very large group of patients suffering from conditions which had in common a delay in clotting time, the delay was shown to be due to a deficiency of prothrombin in the blood. Among these individuals were represented a wide range of ages, economic status, and racial background, as well as both sexes. An investigator interested in discovering the cause of the prothrombin deficiency made a few preliminary observations. He found that the patients could be divided into three main categories: (1) those suffering from obstructive jaundice (bile was not being emptied into the intestine) who had an adequate diet; (2) those allergic to a variety of foods including leafy vegetables and cereals, or who for one reason or another omitted these types of foods from their regular diet, but whose digestion and absorption were otherwise normal; and (3) those showing symptoms of "sprue" (a condition associated with defective absorption of fats and calcium but in whom bile secretion is normal), who had an adequate diet. Careful analysis of the blood of all types of patients showed two consistent differences in plasma composition between normal individuals and the patients: the abnormally low quantity of prothrombin and a corresponding deficient quantity of a fat-soluble vitamin known as K.

A. On the basis of these facts, formulate as few or as many hypotheses as you think necessary to help explain the *direct causal connection* between the amount of vitamin K and prothrombin in the blood. (By "direct causal connection" is meant a situation in which X causes Y. By "indirect causal connection" is meant a situation in which X causes Y and Y causes Z; X is then the indirect cause of Z.)

B. Then outline in general terms the smallest possible number of procedures necessary to test the hypothesis or hypotheses which you have formulated. Each procedure you describe should *not* run longer than 50 words.

### Controlling content in choice-type items

Thus far we have considered several important ways of using content to structure situations. These methods deal with the particular content around which an exercise, problem, or question may be built. Furthermore, they apply equally to supply or choice exercises. If we decide to cast our problems or questions in choice form, we would find additional ways of manipulating content to good effect. In multiple-choice items these inhere in the alternatives offered; in classification exercises, they inhere in both the categories used and the particular items to be classified.

#### Multiple-choice

Through the use of appropriate alternatives it is possible to improve the usefulness of a single item or a series of related items.

First, *it is possible partly to control the difficulty of an item by making the alternatives more or less similar.* In general, the more similar the alternatives, the more difficult the item becomes. The two versions below illustrate this point.

| | |
|---|---|
| Which of the following pupil behavior problems would mental hygienists generally regard as most serious? | Which of the following pupil behavior problems would mental hygienists generally regard as most serious? |
| 1. obscene notes and talk | 1. cruelty, bullying |
| 2. disobedience | 2. sensitiveness |
| 3. unsocialness | 3. unsocialness |
| 4. tattling | 4. nervousness |

In the left-hand version, the incorrect alternatives represent minor behavior problems, certainly not indicative of serious emotional disturbance. In the right-hand version, the behavior problems are all considered relatively serious from the standpoint of good adjustment. It requires more precise knowledge or more careful discrimination to decide which of these is most serious. Which version to use would depend primarily on the group and the precision of knowledge sought.

By making the alternatives close in meaning or in degree of precision, or in otherwise requiring fine distinctions, we thus may make an item harder. And by doing the opposite we may make it easier. Each of these adjustments is possible with many items but by no means all. With some items, the problem or question so restricts the alternatives which are suitable that the possibility of varying them is slight. It is important, then, to recognize that this method has limitations.

Second, *it may be possible to improve an item by basing the incorrect alternatives on students' written responses.* Compare these two versions of the same problem (11, pp. 131, 136):

| *Incorrect alternatives conceived by the test constructor* | *Incorrect alternatives based upon students' written responses* |
|---|---|
| It is not advisable to use cathartics and laxatives because they— | It is not advisable to use cathartics and laxatives regularly because they— |
| 1. weaken the muscle tone of the intestine. | 1. weaken the muscle tone of the intestines. |
| 2. destroy the enzymes of digestion. | 2. cause appendicitis. |
| 3. do not allow the food to digest sufficiently. | 3. are a habit-forming drug. |
| 4. make the person thin. | 4. injure the stomach and other organs of the body. |

In the left-hand version, the test constructor used his own judgment in framing the incorrect options. When the same question was given in short-answer form to a large sample of students, none of the incorrect alternatives were represented in the students' answers (11, p. 38). However, it did seem reasonable that some students would be able to read into alternatives 3 and 4 the misconceptions they revealed on the short-answer form. On the short-answer form the group tended to reveal misconceptions of the following sorts about the use of cathartics:

1. Cathartics injure organs of the body, particularly the stomach.
2. Cathartics cause appendicitis or other bodily ailments.
3. Cathartics are habit-forming in the sense that a drug such as cocaine is habit-forming.

The above misconceptions were then incorporated in the revised version. This latter version thus has more diagnostic value, in that an instructor can determine more fully the misconceptions held by students.

It is sometimes possible to inprove an item by changing the specificity of the alternatives as well as by including misconceptions. Notice the change in these two versions (11, pp. 52–53):

| *Incorrect alternatives conceived by the test constructor* | *Incorrect alternatives based upon students' written responses* |
|---|---|
| A good remedy in the case of a snake bite is— | A good remedy in the case of a snake bite is to— |
| 1. whisky taken internally. | 1. tie constricting band above the cut, make small cross-cut incisions, and apply suction. |
| 2. a bandage placed immediately on the wound. | 2. cut poisoned area, and apply tourniquet above the cut to prevent excessive bleeding. |
| 3. the promotion of free bleeding. | 3. wash, apply iodine or strong antiseptic, bandage, and get patient to doctor as quickly as possible. |
| 4. spirits of ammonia taken internally. | 4. give the patient a liquid to drink that will fight the venom. |

The original version was defective in two respects:

1. The alternatives were not at an appropriate level of specificity. Option 3, the correct answer, was especially at fault. Several students chose this option although their responses on the short-answer form revealed a misconception—that of gashing the wound.
2. It did not include the misconception of applying an antiseptic.

The preceding two illustrations may now have convinced you of two things: (1) that an instructor cannot conceive good distractors (incorrect alternatives) without having first tried out the questions in short-answer form, and (2) that basing the distractors on student errors always improves the item.

Neither of these interpretations is warranted, according to an intensive study by Loree (11). What he did was to adapt portions of three different tests—arithmetic problems, health knowledge, and word meaning—and administer each in three forms to a large sample of ninth-graders:

Form A—Original multiple-choice version; distractors conceived by examiner.
Form B—Short-answer test; students wrote out their responses to the same questions in Form A.
Form C—Revised multiple-choice version; distractors based upon students' responses to Form B.

Loree's findings indicate that the technique employed in Form C cannot be judged on the basis of a single aspect of test validity. We need to judge its contribution on the basis of more than one aspect of validity, of which Loree lists four (11, pp. 2–4):

1. *Discriminating* aspect—how well does the item or test spread out the scores of individuals?
2. *Curriculum* aspect—how well does the item or test sample the subject-matter content of the curriculum?
3. *Purpose* aspect—how well does the item or test meet the purpose for which intended? [This overlaps, in part, with the others.]
4. *Mental process* aspect—how well does the item or test reveal the individual's mental processes?

His data bear largely on the first and fourth of these aspects of validity. To his findings we turn now for further insight into the possibilities and limitations of this technique of selecting distractors.

With respect to discrimination, Form C did not improve upon Form A.[4] That is, the test based upon student responses as revealed in the short-answer form did not spread out the total scores any better. Nor did it correlate much better with results on the short-answer form than did the original.

---

[4] This held only if correct responses were taken into account in scoring Form C. However, there were indications that the discriminating aspect of validity will be improved if scoring takes into account the correct choices, the correct alternatives placed as second choices, and the crude errors (gross misconceptions) (11, p. 104).

Thus, if your confidence sagged earlier, it should now get a lift:

It would appear then that the test constructor in most instances is capable of "conceiving" misconceptions that serve the purpose of discriminating in competency of students and that the test constructor has to misjudge very badly what constitutes the misconceptions of students before the discriminating validity of an item is impaired (11, p. 108).

Moreover, basing the distractors on student misconceptions actually decreased the discriminating validity of some items (11, p. 104). This tended to happen when the distractors represented a smaller psychological distance from the correct response and when only the correct responses of students were taken into consideration. To illustrate this possibility, let us review the results on a word meaning item (11, p. 86):

|                                                          |             |                                                        |             |
| -------------------------------------------------------- | ----------- | ------------------------------------------------------ | ----------- |
| *Incorrect alternatives conceived by the test constructor* | | *Incorrect alternatives based upon students' written responses* | |
| epitaph                                                  |             | epitaph                                                |             |
| 1. reply                                                 | 2. verse    | 1. story                                               | 2. event    |
| 3. sermon                                                | 4. message  | 3. statement                                           | 4. memorial |
| 5. inscription                                           |             | 5. inscription                                         |             |

The 2 × 2 contingency tables for this item were as follows (11, p. 86):

|          |       | FORM B |      |          |       | FORM B |      |
| -------- | ----- | ------ | ---- | -------- | ----- | ------ | ---- |
|          |       | *Fail* | *Pass* |        |       | *Fail* | *Pass* |
| FORM A   | *Pass* | 50     | 23   | FORM C   | *Pass* | 27     | 12   |
|          | *Fail* | 65     | 1    |          | *Fail* | 88     | 12   |

Each table classifies the sample of 139 students into four groups according to performance on the two indicated forms of the item. Thus, of the 24 students who passed Form B of the item, all but one also passed the Form A version but only 12 of this subgroup also passed the Form C version. In this respect Form A of the item was superior because it functioned in much the same way as did the short-answer version (which was taken as the criterion). In another respect, however, Form A was not as effective as Form C. It did not discriminate well between those students who were unsuccessful on Form B, for it allowed a large percentage of them to succeed. In contrast, Form C did a better job in picking out those who were unsuccessful on Form B. This pattern, incidentally, Loree found to be typical. Thus, there was a general "tendency of more students, successful on Form B, to succeed on Form A than on Form C; and more students unsuccessful on Form B, to fail on Form C than on Form A" (11, pp. 106–107). The reverse of this pattern occurred on only one item. These comparative results indicate that *an item may be superior for doing one kind of job, but inferior for doing another.*

Closer study will show why the two versions above did work out differently. By eliminating students common to like cells in the two tables, we now have two contingency tables as follows (11, p. 87):

|  | FORM B | |  |  | FORM B · | |
|---|---|---|---|---|---|---|
|  | *Fail* | *Pass* |  |  | *Fail* | *Pass* |
| FORM A — *Pass* | 30 | 12 | FORM C — *Pass* | | 7 | 1 |
| FORM A — *Fail* | 7 | 1 | FORM C — *Fail* | | 30 | 12 |

An inspection of the responses of the twelve students successful on Forms A and B but unsuccessful on Form C showed that all of these students chose "memorial" as the right answer. All of the twelve, however, chose "inscription" as their second choice. Thus, the presence of the distractor "memorial," which is much closer to the correct meaning of the word than any of the other distractors in either multiple-choice form, decreased the discriminating validity of the item. This effect would have been reduced if the students' second choices were taken into account as eleven of the twelve students would have received credit for their second choice.

So much for the discrimination aspect of validity. Now for other aspects on which it happens that Form C proved superior to Form A. One of these is level of competency, which is related to the mental process aspect of validity. Table 5 shows that in average total scores Form C approximated Form B much more closely than did Form A (11, p. 105).

Table 5

Comparison of mean scores

| Test | Total Possible Score | Mean Scores | | |
|---|---|---|---|---|
| | | FORM A | FORM B | FORM C |
| Arithmetic problems ................ | 20 | 11.03 | 8.39 | 9.57 |
| Health knowledge .................. | 24 | 14.84 | 8.17 | 10.57 |
| Word meaning ..................... | 40 | 28.03 | 14.56 | 19.24 |

The remaining aspect of validity also deals with mental process. This is the extent to which the multiple-choice item provides an opportunity for the student to duplicate the kinds of errors he would make had he written out his answers. On each of the tests the errors made on Form B were duplicated on more occasions on Form C than on Form A. However, there was this qualification:

. . . the fact that a student was given an opportunity to duplicate an error did not insure that he would actually duplicate that error. More often than not the student either would make an entirely different error or would select the correct response on the multiple-choice item (11, p. 106).

To summarize Loree's findings, the basing of distractors on students' written responses has real merit. It does not, however, improve an item for all purposes. The study showed that students tended to make two kinds of wrong responses on the short-answer version: (1) responses lacking in specificity of meaning, and (2) responses that were misconceptions (11, p. 103). An item will serve more purposes if it includes distractors of both types, and if the scoring can be modified as indicated on page 225.

There is still a third major point to make about the framing of alternatives in multiple-choice items. *Sometimes it is possible to build a pattern of alternatives into a series of items or into an entire instrument.* The alternatives need not be the same from item to item, but only similar in type of content. As an illustration of this pattern design, the work of Porter and others is pertinent. Drawing upon his own materials and those of others, Porter assembled items of the following kind into a pretest for a short-term training program in client-centered counseling (12, p. 23):

Man—age 41

"I've been married four times and each time I've thought, 'Boy, this is the real thing!'But none of them has ever been like this girl. She's the most beautiful girl you ever saw—And dance! And she dresses like a million dollars. She's out of this world!"

1. You're really enthusiastic about her.
2. How does she compare with your other wives? How did you feel about them before you married?
3. If she's anything like you seem to feel she is, she must be quite a catch. Maybe this time you'll stick.
4. Doesn't it strike you as odd that every time you've felt the same way?
5. Just stop and analyze what you've said. The points which you mention as her good points are rather superficial. You are still a bit immature, I'm afraid.

Each item in the series followed the same pattern: an expression by a client concerning an aspect of a situation he faces, together with five possible responses which a counselor might make. The task for the would-be counselor was to select the one response which he felt was the most apt to make in reply. For each item the alternatives were so framed that five basically different counselor attitudes were represented, as follows (12, p. 201):

E—*Evaluative.* A response which indicates the counselor has made a judgment of relative goodness, appropriateness, effectiveness, rightness. He has in some way implied what the client *might or ought to do:* grossly or subtly.

I—*Interpretive.* A response which indicates the counselor's intent is to teach, to impart meaning to the client, to show him. He has in some way implied what the client might or *ought to think:* grossly or subtly.

S—*Supportive.* A response which indicates the counselor's intent is to reassure, to reduce the client's intensity of feeling, to pacify. He has in some way implied that client *need not feel as he does.*

P—*Probing.* A response which indicates the counselor's intent is to seek further information, provoke further discussion along a certain line, to query. He has in some way implied that the client *ought or might profitably develop or discuss a point further.*

U—*Understanding.* A response which indicates the counselor's intent is to so respond as in effect to ask the client whether the counselor understands correctly what the client is "saying," how the client "feels" about it, how it "strikes" the the client, how the client "sees" it.[5]

(Use this key to classify the alternatives in the sample item above.)

The advantage of the pattern approach is that it permits an analytic

[5] This key and the preceding item are reproduced by permission of the author and Houghton Mifflin Company.

profile of an individual's responses. Since each alternative is preclassified into one of the basic categories, summarization shows the distribution of the individual's choices over the categories. Thus, in this illustration, it is possible to see the extent to which the prospective counselor favors each of the five basic approaches. Valuable information would have been lost if the alternatives for each item were framed independently of those in the rest of the instrument. Likewise, scoring this instrument in terms of a single key (e.g., the *understanding*, or client-centered, viewpoint) would have reduced considerably its value as a diagnostic tool.[6]

### Classification

The unique problems in devising a classification exercise are to outline an appropriate set of categories and to frame an appropriate set of items to go with the categories.

A classification exercise, if it is to test specific objectives, should reflect careful choice of content. To appreciate this, you should really work through a well-built exercise and see for yourself. Such an opportunity will now be given you. At this point we will reproduce a classification exercise based upon the material on page 222. Since you have already answered essay questions on this material, you should have a flying start again (!).

DIRECTIONS: For each of the following statements, *blacken* answer space—
 A. if it is a hypothesis which is possible and deals directly with the causal connection between the amount of vitamin K and prothrombin in the blood.
 B. if it is a hypothesis which is possible but deals with other relationships than the direct causal connection between the amount of vitamin K and pro-thrombin in the blood.
 C. if it is a hypothesis explaining in whole or in part the sequence of events leading to prothrombin deficiency, but is untenable.
 D. if it is a hypothesis but is irrelevant to the explanation of the sequence of events leading to prothrombin deficiency.
 E. if it is not a hypothesis, but a restatement of facts given, a generally accepted biological fact, etc.

 1. Patients who are suffering from obstructive jaundice generally have a deficiency of both prothrombin and vitamin K.

[6] A more recent illustration is the inventory, *Problems in Human Relations*, Form I, available from Educational Testing Service, Princeton, N. J. This contains a series of problem situations, the proposed solutions of which regularly fall into four categories: democratic, autocratic, laissez-faire, and resort-to-expert. The democratic score is regarded as the principal one; the other three as only supplementary and suggestive.

2. Variations in amounts of prothrombin in the blood would be followed by corresponding variations in vitamin K content of the blood and vice versa (mutual causation).
3. The observed correspondence in amounts of vitamin K and prothrombin in the blood is probably coincidental.
4. Variation in the vitamin K content of the blood may be the cause of the corresponding variation in the prothrombin content of the blood.
5. Jaundice may lead to a prothrombin deficiency through its effect on the absorption of fat-soluble vitamins.
6. A deficiency in vitamin K in the diet may result in a decrease in formation of nondigestive materials of the bile (bile pigments) by the liver.
7. Allergy to leafy vegetables and cereals probably leads to prothrombin deficiency because the diet of these individuals does not contain vitamin K.
8. Elevation to the normal level of the vitamin K content of the blood of any of the patients would result in an elevation of prothrombin content to the normal level.
9. The injection of fat and calcium into the blood stream of sprue patients might correct the prothrombin deficiency.
10. Bile salts are essential for the normal digestion of fats.
11. The common factor leading to prothrombin deficiency in the blood in all three types of patients may be a disturbance in the bile secretory activity of the liver.
12. The common factor leading to prothrombin deficiency in all three types of patients may be a disturbance in vitamin K absorption from the intestines.
13. Variation of the quantity of some unknown factor in the blood will be followed by variations in the quantities of both vitamin K and prothrombin in the blood.
14. A deficiency of prothrombin in the blood of these patients may result in decreased production of fibrinogen by the liver.
15. Prothrombin deficiency will probably be found only in individuals who lack adequate vitamin K in their diet.

DIRECTIONS: For each of the following procedures, *blacken* answer space—
   A. if the procedure *should be included* in the list of the smallest possible number of procedures necessary to determine the causal connection existing between the amounts of vitamin K and prothrombin in the blood.
   B. if the procedure *need not be* included in the list.

16. Select a great number of widely varied substances and inject each into a large group of experimental subjects in nonharmful concentrations and observe the effect on the concentrations of vitamin K and prothrombin in the blood.
17. Vary artificially (by injection into the blood) the amount of prothrombin in the blood of a group of experimental subjects and observe the effect on the concentration of vitamin K in the blood.

18. Feed bile (in amounts corresponding to those normally present in the intestines) to a group of jaundice patients and observe the effect on the content of vitamin K and prothrombin in the blood.
19. Add vitamin K to the diet of patients who have been omitting leafy vegetables and cereals from their diet and observe the effect on the content of vitamin K and prothrombin in the blood.
20. Vary artificially (by injection into the blood) the amount of vitamin K in the blood of a group of experimental subjects and observe the effect on the concentration of prothrombin in the blood.

Now that you have so quickly disposed of this exercise, suppose you go on to do some further thinking. Consider the questions below in light of your experience with the two forms. The value of this experience will be further enhanced to the extent that you think through these questions.

1. *Objectives implicit in the exercise.*
   1.1 State the specific objectives implicit in each part (items 1–15 on hypotheses; 16–20 on experimental procedures). For the first part, list these objectives in a logical order—i.e., in the order implied by the types of judgments called for in the categories.
   1.2 Are these objectives identical with those on the essay? Explain.
2. *Relationship between the items and the objectives.*
   2.1 In the first part, why is it desirable to include categories D and E in the exercise?
   2.2 In the same part, are the items distributed fairly evenly over the categories? (The validity of your answer here will depend, of course, upon your having correctly keyed the items. See end of chapter.)
   2.3 In what *specific ways* does the examiner relate the second part to the first?
   2.4 In what sense or senses is it proper to say that this exercise, in its choice form, represents a *pattern of content*?
3. *Comparison of essay and choice forms.*
   3.1 In your case, which form—essay or choice—gave a more representative sample of evidence on the objectives outlined under 1.1?
   3.2 Would the lack of errors and misconceptions on the essay be good evidence that an individual would recognize these on a choice-type exercise?
   3.3 What difficulties would arise in evaluating such essays on a group of individuals?
   3.4 It is often argued that the choice form of test is more efficient than the essay or short-answer. What meanings are intended by the term "efficient" in this context?
   3.5 For what purposes would the essay be superior to the choice form here, though not necessarily so efficient? (Disregard the area of written composition.)

## REFERENCES ON THE TESTING OF PARTICULAR OBJECTIVES

As with any art, the art of constructing exercises and questions for evaluation has its finer points of technique. One who wishes to learn these finer points should certainly be able to profit from the experience of others, and especially from a careful study of materials which they have produced.

Fortunately, the literature on evaluation does contain models worth imitating. Some of these appear in books, others in bulletins, and still others in journal articles. Not all subject fields nor all important types of objectives are well represented. But there are some general references from which most instructors can profit, and some references that deal with special subject fields. It is our purpose in this section to list and annotate those books and bulletins which discuss important types of objectives *and* illustrate ways of testing for them. We omit reference to the many articles on the topic; these are too numerous to include.

Among the references of general significance, we include the following sources:

*Taxonomy of Educational Objectives* (1).

This handbook is one of the best general references available. Groups objectives into six main categories: knowledge, comprehension, application, analysis, synthesis, and evaluation. Includes for each category a discussion of problems involved in testing, together with a representative sample of annotated exercises and questions.

*Specimen Objective Test Items:* A Guide to Achievement Test Construction (7).

The heart of this valuable reference consists of eleven chapters of specimen items for measuring various educational outcomes, including appreciations, attitudes, and interests. Another part of the book reclassifies the 227 varieties by form, type, and variety; and then again by subject and educational level—elementary, secondary, college, and professional. Instructors will find especially helpful the accompanying references on source materials, mainly journal articles, for testing in specific subject fields.

*The Measurement of Understanding* (19).

This is also an excellent general reference. Discusses the problem of appraising understanding in a variety of subject fields at both the elementary and secondary levels. Contains sample exercises designed to test specific objectives in each field.

*Appraising and Recording Student Progress* (14).

Includes analyses of effective thinking, social sensitivity, appreciation of literary and art works, interest, and personal-social adjustment, together with a discussion of techniques for appraising them. Of special interest here are the sections on interpretation of data (pp. 38–76), application of principles of science (77–111), application of principles of logical reasoning (111–126), the nature of proof (126–154), and the ability to apply social facts and generalizations (168–203).

*The Construction and Use of Achievement Examinations* (9).

Though now relatively old, this book is still a valuable reference. Chapters 4 through 8 deal, respectively, with examinations in the social studies, natural sciences, foreign languages, mathematics, and English.

*Educational Measurement* (10).

A section in Chapter 7 deals with the "interpretive" test exercise: examples, characteristics, and suggestions for writing.

*General Education:* Explorations in Evaluation (3).

This is the final report of the Cooperative Study of Evaluation in General Education. Instructors interested in the evaluation of critical thinking will find this book extremely helpful. Chapters on social science, communications, science, and humanities each contain an analysis of critical thinking abilities which seem important in the area, together with representative test items. Two additional chapters deal with the pervasive objectives, critical thinking and attitudes, respectively. All of the instruments developed in the study may be purchased from Educational Testing Service, 20 Nassau Street, Princeton, N. J.

In addition to such general references, specialized bulletins and folios are beginning to appear. We may look for more and more emphasis upon the publication of source materials as the following:

*Objective Examinations in Professional Accounting:* Samples and Comment (13).

The author, a professor of accounting, argues cogently that objective exercises in accounting need not test "merely factual matter." He discusses types of accounting skills for which choice-type exercises are appropriate and then follows with excellent illustrations.

*Science Reasoning and Understanding:* A Handbook for College Teachers (4).

Contains a variety of science content, chiefly articles from periodicals, and shows how such materials can be used in teaching and evaluating for those science objectives enunciated in the cooperative study referred to earlier. There is also an annotated bibliography of recently published materials on college science in general education, including references on evaluation.

*Problems and Questions in Science:* Test Item Folio No. 1 (5).

This folio contains over thirteen thousand items organized under the major categories of the biological and physical sciences. The questions, predominantly of the choice-type, form a pool which science teachers at the advanced secondary and college levels may draw upon and adapt to their own purposes.

*Critical Thinking in Social Science:* A Handbook of Suggestions for Evaluation and Teaching (2).

Although this booklet duplicates, in part, material found in the *General Education* volume, it presents additional material worth consulting. Of particular interest is the chapter on written and oral methods of evaluation, which carries through the theme that critical thinking exercises can be used for both teaching and evaluation. There is a short appendix of illustrative test items and exercises.

The next five bulletins are put out by the National Council for the Social Studies, 1201 Sixteenth Street, N.W., Washington, D. C.

*Selected Test Items in Economics.* Bull. No. 11 (1939). By H. R. Anderson and E. F. Lindquist. Contains over 650 test items, mostly multiple-choice.

*Selected Test Items in American Government.* Bull. No. 13 (rev. ed., 1950). By H. R. Anderson, E. F. Lindquist, and H. D. Berg. Contains over 750 test items covering a range of topics common in civics and government courses. Most of the items are of the multiple-choice variety.

*Selected Test Items in American History.* Bull. No. 6 (2nd rev. ed., 1947). By H. R. Anderson, E. F. Lindquist, and H. D. Berg. Contains over 950 multiple-choice items covering a range of topics arranged roughly in chronological order.

*Selected Test Items in World History.* Bull. No. 9 (rev. ed., 1947). By H. R. Anderson, E. F. Lindquist, and F. H. Stutz. Contains over 650 items, most of which are multiple-choice.

*Selected Items for the Testing of Study Skills.* Bull. No. 15 (rev. ed., 1949). By H. T. Morse and G. H. McCune. Contains over 500 items sampling a variety of skills such as evaluating sources of information, distinguishing between fact and opinion, judging references, and interpreting data.

## RECORDING QUESTIONS

In writing questions or constructing items, it is a good idea to use a uniform system of recording these. For most types of single questions, a 5 × 8 inch card will serve well. Each question may be written or typed onto a separate card. Toward the left of the upper edge, one may enter the subject with which the question deals; and toward the right, the type of objective which it is designed to test.

A form other than a 5 × 8 inch card may also be useful. For recording brief essay questions and single statements such as true-false items, a 3 × 5 inch card is sufficient. For longer exercises, of course, it may be desirable to use a regular 8½ × 11 inch sheet of paper rather than the smaller cards. If one needs to obtain fairly extensive critical comments from others, as is sometimes necessary in larger projects, the use of 8½ × 11 inch sheets may be desirable even for single questions such as multiple-choice items. In that case, the draft of the item may be put near the top of the sheet so as to allow the space below for the comments.

A uniform system of recording questions on separate cards or sheets of paper has definite advantages. It makes the job of assembling questions into a single instrument much easier than otherwise. It also enables one to build a file of questions, which may be classified both by subject and objective. Finally, it makes possible the periodic recording of comments and statistical data concerning the usefulness of a question.

## REFERENCES

1. Bloom, B. S., Engelhart, M. D., Furst, E. J., Hill, W. H., and Krathwohl, D. R. *Taxonomy of educational objectives, handbook I:* cognitive domain. New York: Longmans Green, 1956.
2. Dressel, P. L., and Mayhew, L. B. *Critical think in social science:* a handbook of suggestions for evaluation and teaching. Dubuque:. Wm. C. Brown, Co., 1954.

3. Dressel, P. L., and Mayhew, L. B. *General education:* explorations in evaluation. Washington: Amer. Coun. on Educ., 1954.

4. Dressel, P. L., and Mayhew, L. B. *Science reasoning and understanding.* Dubuque: Wm. C. Brown Co., 1954.

5. Dressel, P. L., and Nelson, C. H. *Questions and problems in science:* Test item folio no. 1. Princeton: Educ. Test. Serv., 1956.

6. Ebel, R. L. Some effects of irrelevant data in physics-test problems. *Sch. Sci. and Math,* 1937, **37**, 327–330.

7. Gerberich, J. R. *Specimen objective test items:* a guide to achievement test construction. New York: Longmans Green, 1956.

8. Grant, Charlotte L., and Meder, Elsa Marie. Some evaluation instruments for biology students. *Sci. Educ.,* 1944, **28**, 106–110.

9. Hawkes, H. E., Lindquist, E. F., and Mann C. R. *The construction and use of achievement examinations.* Boston: Houghton Mifflin Co., 1936.

10. Lindquist, E. F. (Ed.). *Educational measurement.* Washington: Amer. Coun. on Educ., 1951.

11. Loree, M. R. A study of a technique for improving tests. Unpublished doctor's dissertation, Univer. of Chicago, 1948.

12. Porter, E. H. *An introduction to therapeutic counseling.* Boston: Houghton Mifflin Co., 1950.

13. Schmidt, L. A. *Objective examinations in professional accounting:* samples and comment. New York: The Amer. Inst. of Accountants, 1947.

14. Smith, E. R., Tyler, R. W., and others. *Appraising and recording student progress.* New York: McGraw-Hill, 1942.

15. *Comprehensive examinations in a program of general education.* East Lansing: Mich. State Univer., 1950.

16. *Concerning examinations in humanities 2.* The College, University of Chicago. (Lithoprinted.)

17. *The development of tests for evaluating research proficiency in physics and chemistry.* Pittsburgh: Amer. Inst. for Res., 1951.

18. *Test of educational progress in biological sciences.* Chicago: Study of Educ. Prog., Univer. of Chicago, 1945. (Lithoprinted.)

19. *The measurement of understanding. Forty-fifth Yearb.,* Natl. Soc. Stud. Educ., Part I. Chicago: Univer. of Chicago Press, 1946. Copyright 1946 by the University of Chicago.

Key for exercise on pages 230–32:

| | | | | |
|---|---|---|---|---|
| 1—E | 5—B | 9—B | 13—B | 17—A |
| 2—A | 6—D | 10—E | 14—D | 18—B |
| 3—C | 7—B | 11—C | 15—C | 19—B |
| 4—A | 8—A | 12—C | 16—B | 20—A |

# CHAPTER 9

# *Constructing Supply-type Questions*

EXTENDED-ANSWER QUESTIONS

Forms and Uses
Special Advantages and Limitations
Suggestions for Preparing
Questions for Criticism

SHORT-ANSWER QUESTIONS

Forms and Uses
Special Advantages and Limitations
Suggestions for Writing
Items for Criticism

This chapter deals with those types of questions, problems, and exercises for which the person must *supply* the required answers, solutions, and so on. Hence, the scope goes beyond that usually covered under the heading of essay examination.

The breakdown into extended- and short-answer questions seems both useful and meaningful. As this terminology suggests, the distinction rests on the scope of response called for. The distinction between these questions will, of course, not always be easy to make.

## EXTENDED-ANSWER QUESTIONS

### Forms and uses

The forms of questions, problems, and exercises that require extended responses are much too numerous to attempt to review. They include the conventional essay examination, written assignments calling for the integration of outside readings, the formulation of mathematical proofs, the translation of foreign language passages, the rationalization of procedures employed in the solution of problems, and, in general, any type of exercise which requires the individual to compose at least a paragraph of discussion. Illustrations of such forms may be found in the *Taxonomy* and in certain of the other references mentioned in the previous chapter.

Such illustrations, together with pertinent discussions in Chapters 4, 7, and 8, should indicate the more common uses of extended-answer materials. Quite frequently, as was previously mentioned, free-response situations do yield incidental data concerning attitudes. A subtle example of this comes from an essay written by a bright ninth-grade girl in response to the civics question on page 160. She began:

> Well, Mr. Russian Citizen, you've asked about our laws and I will do the best I can to tell you about them. Actually the basis for our laws was the Bill of Rights . . .

She then launched into an extended discussion of the origin and content of the Bill of Rights, finally closing her essay with this statement:

> There you are Mr. Russian Citizen. I hope you have learned something about the democracy of the United States and profited by it.

The tone of this response is clearly matter-of-fact and implies an attitude of superiority and ethnocentrism. In effect, this girl was saying: "Take it or leave it; hope you've learned your lesson." Certainly this lack of tact is no way to win friends and influence people, foreign or otherwise! [1]

1. The essay written by the ninth-grade girl suggests that she, and probably the rest of the class, failed to attain one of the major purposes of the assignment. What was this shortcoming? If the civics teacher was serious about this purpose, how could he follow up his evaluations of the essays?
2. As previously noted, free-response questions can contribute to the development and validation of choice-type items. Summarize how this can be done.
3. Should essay questions be used to test for memory of specific factual information? Would this represent the most appropriate use of the essay?
4. The task set by an essay question ". . . is practically the only writing situation in life in which a person writes to prove to someone who already knows the answer that the writer knows it too. In all other writing we attempt to convey something to someone who knows less about the specific point than we do" (1, p. 12).

   a) To what extent does your own experience support this observation?
   b) What implication does this comment have for the proper use of the essay question on examinations?

---

[1] We must not be too critical of this adolescent, though, for in a way she was only expressing an attitude (and an approach) widely prevalent in our society.

## Special advantages and limitations

The special advantages and limitations of extended-answer questions, in comparison to choice-type items, have already been brought out. In most respects, these differences also distinguish between extended-answer questions, on the one hand, and short-answer, on the other. There is, however, one important issue that comes to the fore when comparing these two forms. This is the issue of whether it is better to have one long, comprehensive question or to divide this into a series of shorter, more restricted questions. We will not discuss this issue here, but will invite you to come to grips with it in the thought question below.

5. It is sometimes suggested that the essay examination be improved by increasing the number of questions and reducing the amount of discussion required on each.

   a) How might these changes improve an essay examination?
   b) Can you think of specific purposes for which these changes would not improve an essay examination but might even destroy its advantages?

## Suggestions for preparing

In this chapter and the next, the discussion of principles will be pointed toward each of the major types of questions or problems. It is true that there are certain general principles that apply to all types, and that these could be repeated in each case. This will not be done insomuch as earlier parts of this book have already made these general principles evident. It should be understood that a test situation should focus on an important rather than a trivial outcome; should sample the specific objective and content for which intended; should be interesting; should be free of irrelevant factors; and should be at the appropriate level of difficulty.

In a few instances, we will find it desirable to repeat a general principle because of its frequent violation. The first suggestion to be made for preparing extended-answer questions is of this nature:

1. *Frame each question so that it tests for a particular objective.* A common weakness of essay questions is that they are too vague and general; they are not sharply focused on a particular objective. This criticism fits the question below:

*Poor:* Discuss the stability of the American economy today as compared to twenty-five years ago.

While the instructor may have had a particular aim in mind, it is not evident from the question. Some students might interpret this task to mean: "Compare the stability of the economy at these two points, without going into underlying causes." Legitimate as it may seem, such an interpretation may lead the instructor to comment: "But I want more than matter-of-fact description; I want some solid explanation along with it." Now, if his aim was explanation of differences in our economy, he would better have framed the question to make this explicit, somewhat as follows:

*Better:* It is now widely held that our present-day economy is less subject to the violent cyclical fluctuations of past decades, and that this relative stability arises in large measure from certain built-in features of our economic and social order. List the major factors present in modern America which make for greater economic stability and explain how each factor operates to bring it about.

2. *Give definite instructions regarding the form and scope of answer desired.* This is of course desirable when the questions themselves do not make too clear what is required.

One device for indicating the form and scope of answer desired is the model answer. As an example of this we draw upon a history examination which stressed comparison and contrast of different movements, periods, and the like.

*Model.* Compare and contrast the policies of the Jacobins in the French Revolution with those of the Bolsheviki in the Russian Revolution.

The Jacobins were a party of democratic republicans who dominated the policy of the First French Republic from the fall of the monarchy in 1792 until the Thermidor reaction in 1794. The Bolsheviki were a faction of the Social Democratic Party which seized power in Russia late in 1917 (the October Revolution) and are still in office under the name of the Communist Party. Both parties were radical, of the extreme left, and both used a reign of terror, directed against all political adversaries, to keep themselves in power. Both had to face the test of war, and emerged victorious over foreign armies and internal rebellions.

Yet there were differences. The Jacobins, while destroying rank and feudal privilege, affirmed the right of private property; only a few extremists, such as Babeuf, were collectivists. The Jacobins claimed to speak for the people as a whole, the Bolsheviki to speak only for the proletariat, a class. The Jacobins were soon set aside by Napoleon Bonaparte's dictatorship, which merged into the First Empire. The Bolsheviki retained their class and party dictatorship under their own leaders, Lenin and Stalin.

Still another way to structure the task is to let students know the bases upon which their work will be judged. This has been done below in the directions for a three-hour writing assignment designed to test general skill in English composition. (The assignment permitted students to take a stand on the question of whether women should receive the same education as men.)

Your paper will be evaluated impartially without regard to the position you take on this question. Such criteria as the following will form the basis of judgment by the readers:

1. Your paper must evidence a total plan. In other words it must have a beginning and an end, with consistent internal organization.
2. The arguments advanced to support your purpose must be reasonable and must not contradict each other. Generalizations should be supported by example or evidence.
3. Avoid mechanical errors. You may use your dictionary.

3. *Use optional questions only when justifiable.* Some instructors allow students some choice of questions to write on. Ten questions may be presented from which each student is to choose five. This practice is usually justified on grounds that it is fairer to the student; and that since the ability to organize knowledge is the important thing, rather than recall of facts on a particular topic, any of several topics will provide an opportunity to demonstrate it.

There are two serious objections to this practice from a measurement standpoint. First, it does not provide a representative sample of the student's competence since he will tend to choose topics on which he can do best. Second, it destroys the basis for making precise comparisons of different students' work. The fact that students will tend to choose different patterns of questions introduces another source of variation into an already complicated task of grading.

Yet it would seem that optional questions can be justified under some conditions. This would seem to be so if a course of instruction has encouraged the intensive pursuit of individual interests; or if in a class there are two or more well-defined subgroups which have had instruction differentiated along the lines of their special interests. It seems only fair that techniques of evaluation should be consistent with such differentiated goals and experiences. It is noteworthy that at least one large-scale testing program makes use of optional questions. The Advanced Placement Tests, designed to reward superior students for doing college-level work in high school, follow this practice (2).

6. If students are told the bases on which their work will be judged, as was done in the writing assignment on page 242, would this tend to encourage habitual performance or ability on demand? What can you assume regarding the point of view taken by the instructors who defined this particular writing assignment?

7. Frame an essay question and try it out on a sample of individuals. Try to determine from the responses whether the individuals interpreted the question as you had intended.

### Questions for criticism

In order to give you an opportunity to apply some of the principles for preparing extended-answer questions, we will present materials for your criticism. Try to decide in each instance whether or not the question or exercise is satisfactory, and, if you find it unsatisfactory, suggest how it might be improved. Some of the questions will require close study, for the features worth commenting about may be subtle.

1. Our first example is this question: "Write all you know about the freedom of the press in the United States." This particular *type* of question occurs in a variety of subject fields.

2. The next series of questions was constructed by a beginning high school teacher of American history. He hoped to appraise the ability of high school seniors "to relate and show the significance of past events to those of the present day." We include here both the questions and the kind of answers he was looking for.

I. How has the Machine Age influenced our present-day mode of living? (It has forced us to change our concepts and personal attitudes; created inequality of wealth initially.)

II. What reason can be attributed to the failure of the United States to enter the League of Nations, and how was this remedied to enable us to enter the United Nations? (Party politics prevented the United States from entering; this was remedied by establishing bi-partisan policies.)

III. Is there any connection between the controversy of Federal aid to education and the action taken by the Northern states with respect to the schools after the Civil War? Explain your answer. (Yes, there is a connection. Joint schools were set up by the North in the South after the Civil War; the South was bitter and vowed never to have joint schools, and then set up a dual school system. The legislators from the South have fought Federal aid because changes would have to be made in school systems.)

3. Our third sample consists of the major portion of a writing exercise designed for entering freshmen in a state university. The English composi-

tion staff sought direct evidence of writing ability which could be considered along with various objective measures of scholastic aptitude and language proficiency. The general purpose was to screen out those students whose writing was of such a high quality as to exempt them from the first semester of the one-year course. The staff thought that students should have a choice of the topic on which they were to write, and so it listed eight different topics. We include four of these topics below, together with the directions to the students.

## *ESSAY*

Write an essay of 400–600 words on one of the following topics. The suggestions and questions provided with each are intended to stimulate your thinking, *not* to give you an outline. Be sure that your composition has a beginning (in which you state clearly what limits you put upon your subject and what your purpose is), a middle (in which you give evidence, illustrations, explanations, arguments, etc.), and an end (in which you present a summary, or state conclusions).

II Modern Art

What makes modern painting, or sculpture, or music "modern"? Describe and discuss the techniques and effects of some modern artist with whom you are familiar in such a way as to bring out the force of the definition with which you began.

III A Sports Term

Define fully and accurately some technical expression frequently used by sports writers (double wing back formation, zone defense, fielder's choice, slice into the rough, etc.), so that a person entirely unacquainted with the game will understand it.

IV Votes for Eighteen-year Olds

What benefits would the individual and the nation enjoy if the voting age was fixed at 18? What harm might result? Is there any necessary connection between draft age and voting age? Are you eager to vote? Why?

VI Machinery and Science

Describe the operation of a machine or of some scientific process with which you are quite familiar.

## SHORT-ANSWER QUESTIONS

### Forms and uses

As mentioned in Chapter 7, the classification of problems and question types adopted in this book is of the simplest sort. Consequently, the heading above includes quite a variety of subtypes, a few of which are sometimes classified in a category other than this. The heading does not include any choice types, however, because the latter do not require the subject to supply the answers directly.

By definition, a short-answer question or problem is one which calls for a word, phrase, sentence or two, numerical answer, short sketch, or some similarly restricted response. The most familiar of the forms is the simple *direct question*:

What is the chemical symbol for mercury?

Who was the author of *Les Miserables*?

If a merchant wishes to realize a 25 per cent profit on the selling price of an item, by how much must he mark up the cost price?

Certain other forms are so very nearly direct questions that for all practical purposes they may be considered the equivalent:

Name the capitals of the following states:
California ————
Nevada ————
Oregon ————

Give an example of rationalization as a defense mechanism.

Given $\frac{1}{x} = \frac{1}{a} + \frac{1}{b}$. Solve for $x$.

State a proposition concerning some relationship between the two things in each pair below. Your statement should be based on material covered in this course. You are not to give definitions, comparisons, or distinctions.
1. Social class : occupation

————————————————————————————————
————————————————————————————————
————————————————————————————————
————————————————————————————————

Another common form is the *completion* or *fill-in* item. This requires the subject to fill in a blank or blanks in an incomplete statement or expression. Some of the above illustrations may be changed into this form with ease:

The chemical symbol for mercury is ————.
If a merchant wishes to realize a 25 per cent profit on the selling price of an item, he should mark up the cost by ————.

If $\frac{1}{x} = \frac{1}{a} + \frac{1}{b}$, then $x$ equals ————.

Additional examples of completion items include:

*mean* is to *central tendency* as *standard deviation* is to _____.
atom : molecule :: element : _____

An extreme form of the completion item is the so-called *sentence completion* test. Designed originally for personality study, it has possibilities for classroom use. With elementary school children, it may be used to determine the pupil's adjustment to school. With adolescents and adults, it may yield valuable information along the same lines—provided the papers are filled out anonymously, however. A portion of such a test might run as follows (with enough space for writing answers):

DIRECTIONS: Below is a series of words or incomplete statements. Please complete each of these into a meaningful sentence. You may write anything that comes to your mind.
1. This course _____
2. Other students _____
3. Somehow _____
4. What I _____
5. One thing that concerns me _____
6. Breaking into small groups _____
7. The instructor _____

This brief review of common short-answer forms has also illustrated some possible uses. These forms are well suited for testing knowledge of specific facts, terminology, and principles; ability to solve numerical problems; skill in manipulating mathematical symbols and expressions; ability to complete chemical equations; ability to interpret data; and in general, a wide variety of cognitive outcomes ranging from knowledge on one end to synthesis and evaluation on the other. In addition, they are useful for collecting expressions of opinion and attitude. These remarks cover short-answer questions and problems as a class. A specific variety, the completion item, is of course more limited in its usefulness.

### Special advantages and limitations

Vis-à-vis extended-answer questions, short-answer forms enjoy many of the advantages possessed by such forms as multiple-choice. But like the previous category, they too have the disadvantage of rather laborious scoring. In addition, short-answer questions have certain limitations of their own.

1. It is difficult to frame many short-answer questions in which one and only one specific answer is acceptable. This arises because acceptable alternate ways of expressing the answer or near-equivalents in meaning are possible. (In this connection, recall the illustration on page 158.) The result is that, because of the subjective judgments required, it may not be possible to have clerks do the scoring routinely.

2. The short-answer form may encourage instructors to test for subject-matter details to the neglect of broad understandings, application, and sustained reasoning. This is not an inherent weakness but rather an inviting possibility.

### Suggestions for writing

The variety of short-answer forms and the variety of purposes which they serve make it virtually impossible to lay down rules which will apply under all conditions. There are a few maxims that are widely applicable and that do need emphasis. But occasionally, for some special testing purpose, they too may be set aside.

1. *Word the question in such a way that it calls for a definite short answer, such as a word, number, symbol, phrase, or sentence.*

*Poor:* Trees which shed their leaves annually are (deciduous).
*Better:* Trees which shed their leaves annually are called (deciduous).

The original statement above could logically be completed by many words or phrases, as for example: "common," "seed-bearing," "the oak and maple." In its present form it resembles the incomplete sentences technique frequently used to elicit expressions of opinion and attitude. The statement is much too open and needs to be structured as in the revision.

It is not always possible, however, to pin down a statement so that it does call for a single definite answer. In the following incomplete statements, other expressions than indicated could qualify as acceptable answers.

One of the best means of preserving foods is by (freezing).
California's perishable foods are shipped to all parts of the country in (refrigerated cars).

An item such as the first may be expanded somewhat: "Name the two most common commercial methods of preserving foods." The second may perhaps be changed to call for an explanation: "How are California's perishable foods kept from spoiling when they are shipped to all parts of the country?" This revision is more in keeping with the modern emphasis on understanding rather than rote memory.

2. *In completion items, omit only key words.* The omission of too many words may change the task into a general intelligence test or a puzzle. Compare the two versions below in this respect.

*Poor:* The _____ was originally adopted primarily as a method of raising _____, but this purpose has been discarded in favor of _____ from foreign _____.

*Better:* The tariff was originally adopted primarily as a method of raising (revenue), but this has been discarded in favor of (protection) from foreign (competition).

### Items for criticism

Additional suggestions could be offered but instead a list of items will be presented for criticism. It is recommended that you go over these carefully with a view toward identifying weaknesses and suggesting improvements. Some of the items illustrate poor format. Consider also whether a change in form, as to a direct question, will overcome an awkward construction. In cases where you detect a possible weakness, try to frame a maxim to cover it.

The war in 1814 changed, for the Canadians, from defensive to offensive as a result of (the defeat of Napoleon) in Europe.

Pickling metal is done with (weak acid). Aluminum should be (soft) for ease in shaping.

An (isthmus) is a narrow body of land connecting two larger bodies.

What is the volume of a cone having an altitude of 40 inches and a base diameter of 24 inches?

What is UNESCO?

The long sway of (1) _____ sea power in the nineteenth century rested as much upon her far-flung naval bases as upon the number of her warships. The Atlantic Ocean is roughly an S shaped sea. At its four corners stand British naval bases. At the northeast corner is (2) _____, in the Orkney Islands, in which the British Home Fleet was based in both world wars. Almost directly across the Atlantic, at its northwest corner, is (3) _____ in Nova Scotia. Lying approximately 250 miles east of Cape Horn, guarding that passage between the Atlantic and Pacific, are the (4) _____ Islands. There the British have the naval base of (5) _____. The chief port in South Africa is (6) _____, situated on Table Bay. The naval base protecting this port is (7) _____.

## REFERENCES

1. Findley, W. G. The ultimate goals of education. *Sch. Rev.*, 1956, **64**, 10–17.
2. College Entrance Examination Board. *Advanced placement program.* New York: CEEB, 1956.

## FURTHER READINGS

Lindgren, H. C. The incomplete sentences test as a means of course evaluation. *Educ. psychol. Measmt,* 1952, **12**, 217–225.

Sims, V. M. The essay examination is a projective technique. *Educ. psychol. Measmt,* 1948, **8**, 15–31.

Stalnaker, J. M. The essay type of examination. In E. F. Lindquist (Ed.), *Educational measurement.* Washington: Amer. Coun. on Educ., 1951. Pp. 495–530.

# Constructing Choice-type Items

The concern of this chapter is with those types of problems and questions which call for a choice from among given alternatives. As in the previous chapter, the breakdown will be broad and simple. Major emphasis will be placed on the art of item writing.

## MULTIPLE-CHOICE ITEMS

### Forms and uses

A multiple-choice item consists of two parts: a *stem* or *lead,* and a *list of suggested alternatives*, one of which is correct or clearly best. The alternatives are also called "answers," "options," or "choices." Those alternatives which are incorrect or not clearly best are variously called "distractors," "decoys" or "foils."

The stem, or lead, may take a variety of forms, but two cover most uses: the direct question (as shown on page 254) and the incomplete statement (as shown on page 252). The direct-question form is easier to write, whereas the incomplete-statement form takes a greater degree of skill. If skillfully framed, the latter form results in a more concise and pointed lead. Sometimes, as shown below, the lead consists of a word or a few words preceded by explicit directions on what to do. In such instances the directions must be considered part of the lead.

Select the best synonym for the word on the left and *blacken* the corresponding answer space.

| 1. charlatan | A. lizard | B. pretender | C. acrobat | D. songbird |
| 2. pungent | A. poisonous | B. loud | C. hard | D. sharp |

The alternatives also may take a variety of forms—letters, numbers, single words, formulas, phrases, clauses, sentences, diagrams or parts thereof, pictures, and so on. In short, they may take just about any form that will satisfy the logical requirements of the question posed.

Typically, a multiple-choice item will contain four or five options, although occasionally only two or three are logically possible. A four- or five-option item is generally more satisfactory than a three-option item, except for testing children in the primary and intermediate grades.

The uses of the multiple-choice item are many—too many to catalogue here. References such as those annotated in Chapter 8 demonstrate this well. Contrary to the opinion of some instructors, the multiple-choice item can test complex thinking as well as knowledge. It is the complexity of the problem situation that makes this possible. One must not *confuse* the end point—the recording of a choice—with the sequence of thinking that preceded it. Nor must one assume that a simple process necessarily goes with a simple format. How well a multiple-choice item tests complex thinking depends to a great extent on the ingenuity of the examiner. Yet there are limits to what even an ingenious examiner can do. It is unlikely that multiple-choice items can be designed to test ability to organize and present ideas, ability to produce original works of any sort, or most other educational objectives that fall in the synthesis category.

### Special advantages

The multiple-choice item shares certain advantages (and limitations) possessed by choice-type items as a class. These are features that set the latter apart from supply-type questions. It is not our intention here to repeat the advantages mentioned in Chapter 7. It is our intention, however, to note those advantages which the multiple-choice item holds over the other major class of choice-type items.

1. First and foremost, the multiple-choice item is extremely adaptable. It lends itself to an unusually wide range of uses.

2. The multiple-choice item appears to be relatively free of response sets, as was pointed out on pages 113–14.

3. It generally provides greater test reliability per item than does the true-false type of test.

4. It generally can provide more analytic data than the true-false test. If carefully formulated, the several alternatives on a multiple-choice item can provide the instructor with some basis for assessing errors in thinking, whereas judgments of truth and falsity leave him in the dark on the bases upon which the judgments were made.

### Suggestions for writing

For those who wish to cultivate the art of writing choice-type items, there is now available a body of recommended rules. In recent years a number of formulations have appeared in the technical literature (3). These rules or maxims have, for the most part, grown out of firsthand experience. Many have been formulated after a study of the way examinees have responded to individual items. Defects in items have become evident through such studies. Comparatively few maxims have been tested through rigorous experiment, however. Perhaps in most cases this is unnecessary, for the maxims reflect what most of us would regard as ordinary principles of logic or common sense.

The rules or maxims which we are about to survey constitute a minimum list. We include here only the most important—exclusive of other principles that have been developed in earlier parts of this book. In the latter category we include such principles as devising the item to test an important, rather than a trivial, outcome, keeping the language clear and precise so that it will not interfere with validity, and so on. It seems to the author that these principles should now be understood and recognized by the reader as basic to what follows.

1. *Present a single, definite problem in the lead.* The item below, drawn from a technical field, clearly shows a violation of this maxim.

If a tooth is sensitive to percussion it means that—
 a) the patient always needs an occlusal adjustment.
 b) there is a periapical pathology present which will be discernible in an X ray.
 c) the pulp is dead.
 d) an inflammation is present in the periodontal membrane.
 e) a root canal must be done.

Here the instructor probably had a particular problem in mind, but he did not focus it sharply. The expression "it means that" is thoroughly vague. The lack of focus shows up in the alternatives, which deal with two different problems: (1) *conditions or symptoms* possibly associated with sensitiveness to percussion (b, c, d), and (2) *type of dental treatment* to be given (a, e). Notice too that the word "always" makes alternative (a) suspect.

After this basic defect had been pointed out, the instructor then wrote *two* items in place of the one above:

If a tooth is sensitive to percussion, one will generally find—

   a) an inflammation in the periodontal membrane.
   b) periapical pathology present which will be evident in an X ray.
   c) an incipient carious lesion in the interproximal area.
   d) the pulp dead.

What should be done if a tooth is found to be sensitive to percussion?

   a) Perform an occlusal adjustment routinely.
   b) Do a root canal.
   c) Extract the tooth.
   d) Remove caries present and remove tooth from premature occlusion.

Stating a single, definite problem in the lead helps the student. He can grasp the problem quickly, and then go on to consider the various alternatives.

This practice also tends to sharpen the instructor's approach to item writing. It encourages him to specify the particular objective he wishes to test, and then to devise a single item which will test this objective.

Sometimes it is possible for the lead to be so clear that a student can answer the question without reading the alternatives. This is a worthy goal, but, of course, it is not possible for most best-answer items. There, in the very nature of the task, the student *must* read all the alternatives before he can judge which one is best. In such items the lead sets the general problem but the specific problem inheres in the item as a whole.

There is a difference, however, between a well-framed best-answer item and an item which is nothing more than a collection of true-false statements. Items beginning, "Which of the following statements is true?" and similar variations, are not likely to deal with a single definite problem. While sometimes appropriate, this type of item should generally be avoided.

2. *Include as much of the item as possible in the lead.* This practice cuts down on the reading and often on the space as well.

*Poor:* Which of the liberal ideas of the eighteenth century found its/their way into the Declaration of Independence?

    a) Theory of the natural rights of man, right of revolution, and social contract theory of the origin of the state.
    b) Only the theory of the natural rights of man and the right of revolution.
    c) Only the theory of the natural rights of man and the social contract theory of the origin of the state.
    d) Only the right of revolution and the social contract theory of the origin of the state.
    e) Only the right of revolution.

*Better:* Which of these liberal ideas of the eighteenth century found its/their way into the Declaration of Independence?
    1. Theory of the natural rights of man
    2. Right of revolution
    3. Social contract theory of the origin of the state

a) 1, 2, and 3      b) Only 1 and 2      c) Only 1 and 3
d) Only 2 and 3      e) Only 1

Here the improvement was brought about by listing the ideas and coding them. This improved version illustrates an item type which is useful whenever the task involves judgments about various *combinations* of elements. The elements may be possible conclusions from given data, possible assumptions in an argument, possible characteristics of a historical period, and so on. Notice here the more compact way of placing the options across the page rather than down.

3. *State the lead in positive terms, as a general rule.* Negative statements such as those below tend to confuse the reader since most items usually ask for choice of the *correct* or *best* answer.

Which of the following is *not* a reason . . . ?
Which of the following is *not* an advantage of . . . ?
With which of the following would John Dewey *not* agree?

There is also the possibility that the lead itself may not raise a question of any educational significance if it is stated in negative terms. However, some instructors argue, and with good reason, that *the ability to reject certain untruths is educationally significant and in many cases does differentiate the better from the poorer student* (2).

If a negative statement must be used, it is advisable to underline or capitalize words such as *not* and *never,* and prefixes such as *in* in *in*appropriate and *un* in *un*desirable. Sometimes a statement such as the following brings out the emphasis:

All but one of the following are advantages of buying on a cash basis. Which one is *not?*

4. *Make the alternatives consistent with the lead.* The options should be logically and grammatically consistent with the lead. Look at the following item.

A man leaves an estate of $70,000. Of this, 40% is willed to his wife; 55% of the remainder is left to his son. What percentage of the estate does the son receive?

1. 5%
2. 22%
3. 33%
4. 55%
5. $38,500

The fifth alternative is expressed as dollars, not percentage, and hence is inconsistent with the question. True, it does reflect a possible error, but fundamentally it seems intended to trick the unwary student. While at some levels of education it is appropriate to test the student's understanding of what *percentage* means, this item was not intended to do that. Inexperienced writers often let grammatical inconsistencies slip by:

*Poor:* Circumstances which historically were least favorable to the growth of nationalism were—

a) revolutionary democratic movements.
b) mercantilist policies in international trade.
c) the commercial revolution.
d) the mores of the Roman Catholic Church.

*Better:* Circumstances which historically were least favorable to the growth of nationalism were—

a) revolutionary democratic movements.
b) mercantilist policies in international trade.
c) the forces shaping the commercial revolution.
d) the mores of the Roman Catholic Church.

Option (c) in the original version was singular and did not agree with the antecedent "circumstances." Students learn to eliminate such alternatives and to narrow their discrimination down to the remaining. This type of error is most serious when only the correct alternative is grammatically consistent with the lead.

5. *Make the alternatives reasonably similar.* They should be similar in content, grammatical form, degree of precision and length. The item below illustrates a few subtle weaknesses:

*Poor:* It has been said that in the twentieth century in the United States owners of industry no longer control the businesses which they own. Which of the following is the *best* explanation?

a) This is generally true because of the increasing encroachment of government on the rights once exercised by property owners.

b) This is generally true because of the increasing encroachment of strong labor unions on the rights which have generally been exercised by owners of property.

c) This is generally true because the increasing concentration of ownership has resulted in a destruction of the people's rights.

d) This is generally true because the diffusion of ownership associated with corporate development has made it impracticable for most of the owners to have any control over the policies of the corporations which they own.

*Better:* It has been said that in the twentieth century in the United States owners of industry no longer control the businesses which they own. Which of the following is the *best* explanation?

a) Government has increasingly encroached on the rights of the owners.

b) Strong labor unions have increasingly encroached on the rights of the owners.

c) The growth of the enterprises has forced owners to delegate much authority to executives.

d) The diffusion of ownership has made control impracticable for most of the owners.

Although the original item contains a number of weaknesses, perhaps the most serious is the length of the correct alternative (d). This alternative goes into more detail in its explanation, and hence is longer than any of the others—a cue which the alert student will readily detect. Another subtlety is the fact that (c) and (d) deal with opposite tendencies—concentration versus diffusion. Again, the alert student might reason that the choice really lies between these two since they are opposite sides of the same point. To remove this possibility and to get away from a few other weaknesses in (c), this alternative was rewritten. Undoubtedly, the revised alternative makes the discrimination required of the student more difficult. Thus, (c) is true and quite plausible. However, it does not necessarily overlap with (d), for it need not imply diffusion of ownership nor loss of control of general policies, as (d) explicitly states.

The original item violates another maxim.

6. *Make the alternatives as brief as possible.* There really was no need to repeat the expression, "This is generally true." The lead and the remaining parts of the alternatives imply that the statement is true, or should be so regarded. If the item were to be used with a well-informed student group, the instructor might shorten the alternatives still further:

a) Increasing regulation by government
b) Encroachment by strong labor unions
c) Delegation of management to professional executives
d) Diffusion of ownership

It would then be desirable to rephrase the question: "Which of the following factors *best* explains this condition?"

7. *Make the foils plausible and attractive.* Unless they are so, the item will not differentiate between those who have the understanding and those who have not. Two of the foils in the item below are not likely to prove plausible and attractive to many students.

*Poor:* Organizations such as Consumers Union and Consumer's Research try to help the consumer chiefly by—

a) lobbying for special legislation.
b) organizing consumers into cooperatives for quantity buying.
c) advocating the establishment of a socialistic order.
d) publishing buying guides.

*Better:* Organizations such as Consumers Union and Consumer's Research try to help the consumer chiefly by—

a) working for special legislation.
b) organizing consumers into cooperatives for quantity buying.
c) uncovering fraudulent products and selling practices.
d) publishing buying guides.

In option (a) of the original, the word "lobbying," because of its negative connotation, would probably not seem plausible to some examinees who would otherwise choose it. Lobbying is a good word for what the instructor had in mind, but not in this setting. More serious, though, is option (c) because it suggests an aim which runs counter to present-day American mores. Indeed, this option almost carries the flavor, "advocating the overthrow of the private enterprise system." Few students would believe that any organization could espouse so radical a cause in times such as these. For this reason, the content of (c) was revised in a neutral direction. Notice that in content, (c) is now more like the other options.

Stereotypes or near-stereotypes tend to make foils less attractive. Sometimes these are very subtle:

*Poor:* A universal psychological aspect of nationalism is—
a) the innate tendency to prefer people of one's own racial stock.
b) habituation in identifying one's own interests with the interests and honor of one's country.
c) selfishness of the ruling class in all countries.
d) the dominance of selfish individual motives over idealism and altruism.

*Better:* A universal psychological aspect of nationalism is—
a) the glorification of the military.
b) habituation in identifying one's own interests with the interests and honor of one's country.
c) selfishness of the ruling class in all countries.
d) the dominance of selfish individual motives over idealism and altruism.

In the above context, and in many others, the expression "innate tendency" amounts to a near-stereotype. Educators and popular writers have done much to debunk beliefs about the inheritance of social traits, so much so that many segments of the population regard such beliefs with suspicion. Hence, option (a) in the original is not likely to prove attractive to a sophisticated group. With groups which have not been exposed to such teaching, the original version might well prove satisfactory—provided the ideas are expressed in simpler words.

8. *Use with discretion such options as "none of the above."* In certain items, particularly those involving numerical or mathematical solutions, a good case can be made for offering "none of the above" as a possible answer. The argument is that the use of this option helps to overcome some of the limitations of the multiple-choice form. An item such as that on page 116, for example, can be solved through a mechanical substitution process in which the examinee tries one suggested answer after another until he finds the number which satisfies the equation. It is argued that the use of "none of the foregoing" in such items forces the examinee to work the problems out rather than rely upon guessing or a substitution process. Unfortunately, as should be evident from the illustration, the use of this option does not make the item over into a free-response form. But it would seem to improve the item somewhat.

If this option is offered in an examination, it should, of course, appear as the correct answer in a proper fraction of the items.

### Items for criticism

The preceding list of suggestions, together with the examples, should now have given you some of the fundamentals of item writing. The list itself was not exhaustive; scores of additional, but often minor, points could have been made. Such a presentation cannot, of course, impart any skill in the art of writing. Practice is essential. As a beginning, it would seem desirable for you to try your hand at criticizing several items and revising them to the extent that you are able. Each of the miscellaneous collection of items below contains one or more defects, however subtle. Try to identify these defects. Indicate which of the previous maxims the item violates. If none of the maxims cover the violation, formulate a maxim that will. Then suggest how the item might be revised to make it more acceptable. If possible, rewrite it.

"Ladies and gentlemen—I hesitate to articulate for fear that the consequences of my utterances in this amphitheater will be misconstrued." The chief difficulty with the preceding excerpt is its use of—

a) barbarisms.
b) the historical present.
c) hackneyed phrases.
d) long words.
e) trite phrases of speech.

Before American armed forces could attack another country—

a) Congress must declare war.
b) the President must order the attack.
c) the National Security Council must approve the plan.
d) the Joint Chiefs of Staff must advise the Congress.

The Rh blood factor problem—

a) occurs primarily when women are having their first babies.
b) results whenever an Rh negative mother conceives by an Rh positive father.
c) results whenever an Rh positive mother conceives by an Rh negative father.
d) is not worth worrying about because doctors know how to handle it.
e) should be a consideration in choosing a marriage partner.

In many sections of the mountains in the southern United States, as is also true in other parts of the world where farmers till steep slopes in small areas, the farmers carry on practices which are harmful to the land. The economic reason which is most plausible for this misuse of the land is—

a) land is overcapitalized.
b) scale of farm is too small to be successful.
c) too much labor is needed.
d) mechanization is not possible.

In Argentina, horses raised in the mountains are required by the rules of the racing association to be kept for a month or more on the plains before they may be raced with horses raised on the plains. The reason for this is that—

a) unless acclimated to the plains, the horses from the mountains would have a physiological advantage.
b) unless acclimated to the plains, the horses from the mountains would have a smaller vital capacity.
c) unless acclimated to the plains, the horses from the mountains would have brittle feet.
d) the horses from the mountains are quarantined because of disease.
e) the horses from the mountains require at least a month's training.

Individuals with assured dollar incomes would probably approve of—

a) an increase in the price level.
b) a decrease in the price level.
c) the continuation of the present price level.
d) none of the above.

One of the outstanding characteristics of social planning by the Tennessee Valley Authority has been—

a) the dominance of politicians in the Authority.
b) the high cost of electricity produced.
c) planning with people of the valley, not merely for them.
d) the discouragement of private enterprise in the area.

Is the comparative immaturity of the social sciences a valid reason for putting off the responsibilities of social planning?

a) Yes, because planning can be no better than the knowledge that it is based upon.
b) Yes, because, as Alexander Pope said, a little knowledge can be a dangerous thing.
c) Yes, because history has conclusively demonstrated that man is not competent to plan his own future.
d) No, because planning itself may contribute to the maturity of the social sciences.
e) No, because the social sciences are not immature.

DIRECTIONS: Circle the number of the one statement you feel is the most accurate of the five statements concerning the particular field of conservation.

*Man's use of water*

a) Man has little control over water, therefore he should not be particularly concerned with water as an important natural resource.
b) Pollution of water is man's only abuse of the use of water.
c) Man should be concerned only with the way in which water can benefit him and not worry about elimination of water pollution, provision of additional supplies of water in the future, and flood control.
d) Water provides man with many benefits, such as food and power. These benefits do not, however, outweigh the damage and destruction water has brought upon man.
e) Man should become aware of the abuses and problems of the use of water and should be concerned with remedies to these problems for future control and beneficial use of water.

When you look at a red object through blue glass, it appears to be—

a) black.
b) red.
c) white.
d) blue.

An explanation for the previous question is that—

a) red objects reflect all colors except red, but the blue glass only allows blue to pass through it.
b) red objects reflect all colors and these pass through the blue glass.
c) red objects reflect only red rays, and these pass through the blue glass.
d) red objects reflect only red rays and blue glass only allows blue rays to pass through it.

## CLASSIFICATION EXERCISES

### Forms and uses

Whenever two or more multiple-choice items make use of the same set of alternatives, it is possible to recast them into a classification exercise. This possibility exists in the items below.

1. A brick can be pulled along a fairly smooth surface by means of a string; the string would break, however, if pulled sharply. Which *one*, if any, of the principles below is most directly useful in explaining this fact?
   A. Force is equal to mass times acceleration.
   B. Friction exists between any two bodies in contact with each other.
   C. Conservation of momentum.
   D. Conservation of energy.
   E. None of the foregoing.

2. A given door to be opened slowly requires a small force; to be opened quickly it requires a much greater force. Which *one*, if any, of the principles below is most directly useful in explaining this fact?
   A. Force is equal to mass times acceleration.
   B. Friction exists between any two bodies in contact with each other.
   C. Conservation of momentum.
   D. Conservation of energy.
   E. None of the foregoing.

If there are only a few such items, perhaps no more than six or so, one way is to place the leads on the left, the common alternatives on the right, and the common directions above, as has been done below.

DIRECTIONS. For each statement of fact on the left, *blacken* the answer space corresponding to the *one* explanatory principle on the right which is most directly useful in explaining the fact. If none of the principles applies, *blacken* answer space E.

1. A brick can be pulled along a fairly smooth surface by means of a string; the string would break, however, if jerked sharply.

A. Force is equal to mass times acceleration
B. Friction exists between any two bodies in contact with each other
C. Conservation of momentum
D. Conservation of energy
E. None of the foregoing

2. A given door to be opened slowly requires a small force; to be opened quickly it requires a much greater force.

In this form, the items comprise a kind of matching exercise. Each statement is to be matched with the appropriate category on the right. But despite the rearrangement, each item is essentially multiple-choice.

A further rearrangement is to place the categories above the statements:

DIRECTIONS: For each statement of fact below, *blacken* the answer space corresponding to the *one* explanatory principle, from the list preceding the statements, which is most directly useful in explaining the fact. If none of the principles applies, *blacken* answer space E.

Explanatory Principles

A. Force is equal to mass times acceleration.
B. Friction exists between any two bodies in contact with each other.
C. Conservation of momentum.
D. Conservation of energy.
E. None of the foregoing.

1. A brick can be pulled along a fairly smooth surface by means of a string; the string would break, however, if pulled sharply.

2. A given door to be opened slowly requires a small force; to be opened quickly it requires a much greater force.
3. The velocity of a body moving along a curve cannot be constant.

And so on.

This second rearrangement is the usual way in which classification exercises are set up. Further statements or items to be classified may be added as desired.

To summarize to this point: A classification exercise is simply a list of statements or other items which are to be classified according to a common set of categories. In this respect, it is a matching exercise. But since each item involves a choice from among given alternatives, a classification exercise is also a variation of the multiple-choice form. The terms "key list" and "master list" are also used to designate this type of exercise.

There is a great variety of classification exercises, and the uses are greater yet because many basic types fit testing needs in all content fields. The reader is doubtless already familiar with the simpler forms: true-false, right-wrong, correct-incorrect, yes-no, and similar variants. As commonly used, these two-category forms call for factual judgments of rightness or wrongness when applied to a list of items. The items may be (or purport to be) facts, generalizations, words correctly and incorrectly spelled, and so on. These simpler forms also lend themselves to the testing of outcomes other than knowledge, e.g., interpretation of reading passages or data.

Since the varieties of classification exercises and their uses are probably not well known, we might go into more detail than we did with multiple-choice forms. The examples can be grouped into two broad areas of application: testing of knowledge and testing of intellectual skills and abilities.

### Testing of knowledge

Classification exercises can test efficiently knowledge of the characteristics of particular or typical literary, artistic, musical, historical, philosophical and scientific works; the characteristics of particular historical periods; the characteristics of plant and animal groups; the properties of chemicals; the provisions of laws and treaties, and the like.

A common form suitable for content, such as the foregoing, is this exercise on functions of federal and state governments:

DIRECTIONS: For each of the following items, indicate the government or governments in the United States to which the individual or group would turn at present for protection or assistance. Record your answer for each item below by *blackening* the proper answer space according to the following key.

1. *Federal government* but not state
2. *State government* but not federal
3. *Either* the federal or the state government or both
4. *Neither* the federal nor the state government

1. A Georgia farmer desires to negotiate a loan for improvements on his farm but the collateral he has to offer is not liquid enough to meet the demands of commercial banks.

2. Mr. A, a resident of Houston, decides to build a home, provided he can find some way to finance 60 per cent of the value of the property.

3. Mr. B, whose business enterprise is confined to the state of Minnesota, alleges that his trademark has been trespassed by a firm operating only in Ohio.

4. An Iowa farmer discovers that his corn crop is being endangered by the spread of corn rust.

5. The condition of U. S. Highway No. 212 is such that the safety of one of Mr. C's farm buildings is endangered.

And so on.

Notice that this exercise permits a *comparison and contrast of two things,* bringing out characteristics held in common and characteristics held independently.

If more than two things were likewise to be *compared and contrasted* over a range of features, a more complicated design would be necessary— too complicated to fit the usual type of answer sheet. A compromise is to list the several things, followed by descriptive statements that apply to *only* one of the things:

DIRECTIONS: *Blacken* the answer space corresponding to the play to which each statement best applies.

A. *Macbeth*
B. *Taming of the Shrew*
C. *The Tempest*
D. *Emperor Jones*
E. *Arms and the Man*

1. The play has a single line of action which is not complicated by any supplementary action. The problem is shown clearly at the beginning of the play, and each division of action clearly moves toward a solution of the problem, which occurs with the end of the action.

2. The play has two definite lines of action which are closely related and interdependent. The minor action starts first but seems dependent for its solution upon a step in the major action. Both lines of action are concluded by the energy and initiative of the characters involved rather than by fortunate circumstances.

And so on.

Knowledge of chronology is an important outcome for which this technique is suitable. The advantage of the exercise below is that it requires substantial knowledge of historical events without holding the student to memory of many specific dates.

DIRECTIONS: Five chronological periods are listed below. Under each period are grouped several descriptive statements. For each statement, *blacken* answer space—

A. if it correctly applies to the period named.
B. if it does *not* apply to that period but to an *earlier one*.
C. if it does *not* apply to that period but to a *later one*.
D. if it does not apply correctly to *any* period of American history.

*Period:* 1760–1800

1. The English obtained Canada from the French.
2. Manufacturing became a dominant occupation in New England.
3. Representative institutions arose in the colonies.
4. The debts of the states, acquired in the Revolution, were assumed by the federal government.
5. Provision was made for induction into the Union of states in territory occupied by present states of Michigan, Illinois, Wisconsin, etc.
6. Most of the area between the Mississippi River and the Rocky Mountains was added to the United States.

(Twenty-six additional items distributed over four other periods— 1801–1828, 1829–1866, 1867–1900, 1901–1933—complete this exercise.)

Similar exercises can cover phylogenetic development—the relative order in which given biological characters evolved—and the characteristics of geological periods.

In addition, key-list exercises are useful for testing knowledge of cause and effect relationships between paired phenomena; knowledge of whether correlation existing between paired variables is positive, negative, or zero; and knowledge of the relative magnitude of paired phenomena.

### Testing of intellectual skills and abilities

With ingenuity, key-list exercises can be devised to test reflective thinking. They meet well certain evaluation needs in general education. It is in this area that the more complex and tailor-made varieties have had their origin.

The exercise on pages 230–32 is a good example of one designed to test reflective thinking. Further examples of exercises testing intellectual skills and abilities may be found in the *Taxonomy* (1). This reference includes key-list exercises in five of its six major categories. The exception is synthesis, a category in which multiple-choice exercises are least useful. Illustrations abound in the chapters on comprehension and application.

### Special advantages and limitations

Among the unique advantages of classification exercises we should certainly include these:

1. *They are compact.* Because the same set of categories may be used with a whole series of statements, key-list exercises are economical of space. A given exercise can yield a large number of scorable units in a relatively small amount of space.

2. *They test comparison and contrast efficiently.* In their very nature, key-list exercises emphasize discriminative thinking, that is, the ability to make valid differentiations among similar things as well as to recognize their essential similarities. Such outcomes are important in education.

3. *They sometimes permit an analytic pattern of scores.* The form discussed on page 173 is a good example. Thus, it is possible to build into an exercise a variety of statements, each of which permits the student to make one or more types of error. Scoring can then sort out each student's judgments, showing the number of times he makes each type of error. This is helpful in assessing habits of thought.

4. *It is sometimes possible to duplicate an exercise just by changing the content.* This possibility is most likely for exercises testing intellectual skills and abilities. Once an exercise such as that on pages 230–32 has been devised, it is easier thereafter to develop one like it which will test similar discriminations. This economy of effort is an aid to the busy instructor. It also encourages the development of parallel exercises for purposes of assessing progress.

Key-list exercises, however, are not without their limitations. In particular, they are subject to the following:

1. *Many judgment categories invite response sets which interfere with the validity of the results.* In this connection, review the list on pages 113 and 114. Items 2 and 4 in that list are especially pertinent here.

2. *Not all categories may function for each statement to be judged.* Thus, even though there may be five categories, only two or three of these

may be pertinent for many statements in the exercise. Such items increase the student's chances of guessing correctly, and hence cut down on the reliability of the scores. For informal uses of test results, this effect is ordinarily not serious.

3. *Key-list exercises may overweight a test.* This possibility stems from their compactness. Because each statement usually takes little space and constitutes a scorable unit, a key-list exercise can contribute two or three times as much to a total score as a series of multiple-choice items using the same amount of space. However, if each judgment called for is important, then there is no real cause for concern.

4. *Key-list exercises may encourage the testing of superficial outcomes.* This is not inevitable, nor is it peculiar to this form. But there seems to be a tendency for some instructors to overdo a technique simply because the form suits a variety of content and they can compose a series of items in short order. Thus, there is a tendency for certain of the forms, such as true-false, to crowd out important outcomes which are harder to test, and more appropriately tested, by other means. The nature of the outcome rather than the convenience of the form should determine the technique.

### Suggestions for writing

Again, what was said on page 252 with reference to multiple-choice items applies here too. Our approach here will be to suggest some maxims for the writing of key-list exercises in general, and then to follow with some special suggestions for true-false items.

1. *Use a small number of not too complex categories.* It would be quite arbitrary to set a given number as the limit, or even the optimum. But when the number of categories begins to reach, or exceed, seven, the task becomes unwieldy or the discriminations much too fine. If the exercise is to be machine scored, the limit allowed by the usual answer sheets is five answer categories.

If the categories are too complicated, of course, one runs the risk of throwing unnecessary language barriers in the student's way.

2. *Make sure that the categories in the key list are related but mutually exclusive.* This is like saying that for any item there should be only one correct or best answer. It is also like saying that the alternatives should be drawn from the same domain but that they should not overlap. A subtle disregard of this maxim appears in the following exercise.

Three biological situations are listed below. In each situation, a *specific phenomenon* is *underlined*. After each situation is a numbered list of statements, each of which may or may not be directly related to the specific phenomenon.

DIRECTIONS: For each numbered statement *blacken* the answer space, in accordance with the series of choices given below, which best characterizes the statement.

*Blacken* answer space—
   A. if the statement helps to *explain* the cause of the phenomenon.
   B. if it *merely describes* the phenomenon.
   C. if it describes a *consequence* of the phenomenon.
   D. if the statement is *true,* but does not directly relate to the phenomenon.
   E. if the statement is *false.*

Situation I: A child injures his finger. *A red, hot, swollen area* develops.

11. Local metabolites from the injured area effect a dilation of arterioles and capillaries.
12. An oxygen deficit in the blood stream serves as a direct stimulus for increased red blood cell manufacture.
13. Bacteria and their products are diluted by fluids from the blood.
   (Seven additional items complete the remainder of the exercise.)

As it stands, the exercise is acceptable for testing knowledge about the phenomena in question. However, the main emphasis is upon 1) the ability to distinguish statements of cause, consequence, and mere description. Categories D and E are really not related to the first three, for they test two additional types of judgments: 2) truth or falsity of statement; and 3) relevance of statement to phenomenon.

The trouble with this exercise, it would seem, is that the instructor is trying to bring in too many *different* types of judgments. At the least, he could have dropped category E and omitted false statements. Category D has some value in exercises of this sort, both to minimize the possibilities for guessing correctly and to require the student to show his knowledge by rejecting statements which do not apply.

   3. *Avoid an even matching of categories and items.* By this we mean an exercise in which there are as many items as categories and each item fits only one category. This condition increases the student's chance of guessing correctly. Most likely, the exercise is not sampling the particular outcomes comprehensively enough. Yet there are occasions when an exercise might justifiably contain fewer items than categories, should the time be limited or only a few important points worth testing.

The preceding suggestions deal primarily with the categories. Because of the wide variety of content with which such exercises can deal, it is hard to single out a general list of rules for writing the items themselves. Perhaps a compromise is to list rules for writing true-false items on the assumption that some of these rules will apply generally to key-list exercises. In any case, the true-false form is used widely enough to justify separate treatment. Moreover, because the categories are themselves simple, the crucial problems are overwhelmingly those of framing good statements. Once again we will not try to detail all the possible maxims, but will remind the reader of points covered in Part I, especially page 112.

1. *Avoid taking statements directly from textbooks and other instructional materials.* Consider this old standby from books on educational and psychological measurement:

T   F   Validity is the degree to which a test measures what it is intended to measure.

Many students can repeat statements like this without having much understanding of the concept of test validity. The practice of taking such statements directly from textbooks, or changing a word or two to make them false, tends to encourage rote learning. The example above also illustrates a verbal stereotype, the expression "what it is intended to measure." This expression, which is widely used in discussions of test validity, helps to cue the right response from the rote learner.

2. *Use statements that are unequivocally true or false.* The following statement, keyed by an instructor as true, can be challenged:

T   F   Nearsightedness is hereditary in origin.

While geneticists and eye specialists generally agree that nearsightedness has its origins in hereditary factors, the evidence is not yet conclusive. What they agree upon is that the *predisposition* to nearsightedness is hereditary, *but that precipitating factors must operate before an individual will develop this condition.* A bright student will so reason, and hence reject the statement above as not absolutely true. This item might better read:

T   F   Geneticists and eye specialists believe that the predisposition to nearsightedness is hereditary.

The standard laid down by this maximum is rigorous and consequently difficult to apply. There are relatively few important statements in any field that can meet a standard of absolute truth. Because the nature of reality is such that there are exceptions to most generalizations, true-false items often contain an element of unrealism. This is their basic weakness.

3. *Avoid sweeping generalizations, as well as guarded statements.* As discused on page 112, statements which are either strongly worded or carefully qualified tend to give away the answer. Notice the emphatic quality in these statements, which are false:

T   F   Two people living in the same area necessarily have the same environment.
T   F   Diffusion of all culture traits goes on at approximately the same rate.

And the guardedness in these, which are true:

T   F   The rate of juvenile delinquency may, but will not necessarily, be higher in the older neighborhoods of a city.
T   F   Generally, commercial apples are propagated from cuttings or grafts rather than from seed.

Because they often are carefully qualified and restricted, true statements tend to be longer than false ones. This is a tendency which the instructor must try to forestall.

4. *Include only one idea in each statement.* If one proposition is true and the other false, the judgment called for would seem to be rather unfair and confusing to the student. For example:

T   F   Water will boil at a higher temperature if the atmospheric pressure on its surface is increased and more heat is applied to the container.
        (First part true; second part false)

It seems preferable to divide such an item into two parts.

A common practice is to include in one item a proposition, together with a *possible explanation or supporting statement:*

T   F   During the last twenty years the general tendency has been to liberalize credit because it is an effective competitive device.
        (First part true; reason false)

Although this type of item violates the rule here, under certain conditions it may be acceptable. This would seem to be the case if, in a series of such items, the propositions are generally true and the judgments deal only with the truth or falsity of the reasons. Certainly few of us would question the importance of testing the student's understanding of causal factors.

Very often, the way out of this difficulty is to use a finer set of judgment categories than just true and false:

DIRECTIONS: For each of the following items, *blacken one* lettered space to designate that the statement is—
  A. true, and its truth is supported by the reason given.
  B. true, but its truth is not supported by the reason given.
  C. false.
1. During the last twenty years the general tendency has been to liberalize credit because it is an effective competitive device. (B)

And so on.

DIRECTIONS: In items 11–20 *blacken one* answer space for each item according to the following key:
  A. if *both* parts of the statement are true.
  B. if the *first* part is *true,* and the *second* part *false.*
  C. if the *first* part is *false,* and the *second* part *true.*
  D. if *both* parts are *false.*
11. Tempo and meter are synonymous terms—for both refer to the temporal aspect of music.
12. Motion (variation in pitch) is the single essential ingredient of melody for rhythm, being a separate and independent element of music, is not closely bound up with melody.

And so on.

5. *Try to balance the number of true and false statements.* There should not be a disproportionate number of either kind. Otherwise, students "catch on" to the pattern and make their judgments accordingly.

### Exercises for criticism

1. Evaluate the exercise below. (We shall keep the directions for this task unstructured, so that you may have the fullest opportunity to apply what you now know about the art of test development.)

In the following questions indicate by appropriate numbers—

  1. if the statement in the left-hand column is false and the statement in the right-hand column supporting it is false.
  2. if the statement in the left-hand column is false and the statement supporting it indicates that the statement is false.
  3. if the statement in the left-hand column is true and the statement supporting it is true.

4. if the statement in the left-hand column is true but the statement supporting it is false.

5. if the statement in the left-hand column is true and the statement supporting it is true but irrelevant.

_____ 1. Philadelphia was long under the heel of the corrupt Philadelphia Gas Ring.

Winston Churchill, the American novelist, once described Philadelphia as "the whitened sepulchre."

_____ 2. Tammany Hall is the name of the corrupt Republican party organization which has repeatedly controlled city government in Boston.

Fiorello LaGuardia was one man who was able to wage a successful campaign against this entrenched group.

_____ 3. Chicago had very little corruption when its major city offices were held by members of the Republican party.

Big Bill Thompson ran an anti-British platform for mayor of Chicago in the early twenties.

_____ 4. Appointment to rank and file city offices through civil service examination now applies in the majority of cities.

This has virtually eliminated opportunity for corruption in city politics in these cities.

_____ 5. Fraudulent elections have been an important factor in gaining control of city government in many cities.

In Kansas City during the Pendergast regime one thousand "voters" registered as residents of a vacant lot.

_____ 6. According to Marx, the laborer "sinks deeper and deeper below the conditions of existence of his own class."

The American laborer has a higher standard of living than at any previous time in history.

_____ 7. The "world of furnished rooms," described by Zorbaugh, Trotter and Wolfe, may be described chiefly as the anonymous world of college students in a great city.

The young men and women from the hinterland who seek employment in our great industrial centers often lead a lonely life in their rooming house lodgings.

_____ 8. Urban life has contributed to the decline in unity of interest among family members.

Many members of the same family are employed at different kinds of work.

2. An English composition staff devised a placement test, a portion of which is reproduced here. Read this and do the items before answering the discussion questions below.

DIRECTIONS: This is a test of your ability to detect misspelled words and also words which are misused. After each item number on the answer sheet, *blacken* space—

A if the corresponding word is *correctly spelled or used.*

B if the corresponding word is *misspelled or misused.*

Regretfully predominate among Americans is the belief that the principal
    1              2          3                                                    4
function of a college is to train young people for jobs, or, in other words, to
make its graduates financialy sucessful. Also common are the beliefs that an
                    5          6
early choice of vocation is indispensable and that studies which do not specificly
                           7                                                      8
prepare one for that vocation are irrelevant and thus to be avoided. Because
                                  9
these views have led to unwise parential counsel I wish to voice a protest.
                              10       11
For the student who trys to limit his education in strict accordance to these
                   12                              13            14
principles may leave college a narrower person than when he arrived and may
15
even fail to obtain his vocational goal. . . .
            16

a) What difficulties might a student have in applying these judgment categories?
b) How might the judgment categories be revised to minimize or overcome these
   difficulties?
c) What difficulties might arise in interpreting scores made on this test?
d) Do you think the attempt to test both spelling and diction on the same test
   is sound? Why or why not?
e) Is it necessary to test spelling in context? diction in context?

3. Examine each of the following true-false statements to determine if it
contains a defect. Revise the item if this seems possible. If the statement
contains a defect for which we have not listed a rule, frame one that will
cover the defect.

1. There is conclusive evidence that war is part of the universal culture pattern.
2. A child talented along mental lines will almost never be talented in athletics.
3. It is an established fact that daily bathing is a health essential.
4. Pure DDT does not cause irritations of the skin in either animals or man, nor
   is there definite evidence of a sensitizing effect or of the production of other
   allergic reactions, such as asthma.
5. If rabbits gnaw all tissues of a tree down to the sap wood, it is not unlikely
   that the tree will die.
6. Automobile accidents occur more frequently late in the day than early.

## REFERENCES

1. Bloom, B. S., and others. *Taxonomy of educational objectives, handbook I: cognitive domain.* New York: Longmans Green, 1956.
2. Nedelsky, L. Ability to avoid gross error as a measure of achievement. *Educ. psychol. Measmt,* 1954, **14,** 459–472.
3. Trump, J. B., and Haggerty, Helen R. *Basic principles in achievement test item construction.* Personnel Research Section, Pers. Res. and Procedures Branch, The Adjutant General's Ofc., Dep. of the Army (PRS Rpt. 979), 1952.

## FURTHER READINGS

Ebel, R. L. Writing the test item. In Lindquist, E. F. (Ed.), *Educational measurement.* Washington: Amer. Coun. on Educ., 1951. Pp. 185–249.
Gerberich, J. R. *Specimen objective test items:* a guide to achievement test construction. New York: Longmans Green, 1957.

# CHAPTER 11

# Review, Assembly, and Reproduction

REVIEW OF TEST MATERIALS

ASSEMBLY OF MATERIALS INTO A SINGLE INSTRUMENT

    Ways of Grouping Questions
        By subject matter. By objective. By form.
        By degree of difficulty.
    Layout and Format

REPRODUCTION OF MATERIALS

Having developed a good pool of questions, one may now breathe a well-deserved sigh of relief. Lighter tasks lie ahead. But they should not be taken lightly. The review of questions, their assembly into a single instrument, the reproduction of the test, and certain other tasks also require careful attention. The concern of this chapter is with those further tasks which precede administration, scoring, and analysis.

## REVIEW OF TEST MATERIALS

No matter how good his grasp of the subject or how skillful his technique, an instructor can generally profit from a review of his test materials. When one has worked on the same materials for some time, he tends to lose some of the freshness with which he began the task. As a result, he may fail to detect ambiguities and other technical defects that have crept in. What seems clear to him may prove confusing to the examinees. Moreover, his conceptions of what is worth testing and his skill in translating these into test situations may be limited. Thus, even if the situations are free of ambiguities and other technical defects, they may still be inappropriate for the intended objective and content.

For the reasons indicated, it is good practice to submit the materials to one or more associates for their critical review. A less desirable but minimum procedure is to lay aside the materials for a day or longer and then review them oneself.

Reviewers should be asked to work through the questions, independently recording their choices or outlining their answers. This experience should permit them to judge the appropriateness of each item or question as well as to spot defects. One defect in multiple-choice items which reviewers should especially look for is the lack of any thoroughly adequate answer. While one of the choices may have been keyed as the best of those presented, it may not be a thoroughly adequate answer as judged by competent subject-matter specialists. In fact, it may even be incorrect.

When the sample of questions has been tentatively chosen, it is important to make additional checks as follows:

1. *Check the intended answers, or key, against the answers recorded by the independent judges.* Eliminate those questions on which agreement cannot be obtained even after revision.

2. *Check for overlapping items.* These are items in which the information in one gives away the answer to another. Revise or eliminate such items which overlap or duplicate one another.

3. *In choice-type tests, check the distribution of best answers.* It should be as nearly random as possible so that there are no identifiable patterns in the sequence. The use of a table of random numbers will help to bring this about (2).

The scope of any such review is, of course, greater than that implied here. Actually it may cover many of the points discussed in previous chapters. The final chapter in this book goes into more elaborate procedures for analyzing tests. Some of these procedures could also be applied at this point in test development.

## ASSEMBLY OF MATERIALS INTO A SINGLE INSTRUMENT

### Ways of grouping questions

After the questions have been written and reviewed, they must be put together in some meaningful way. There are four important groupings of questions or items: according to (1) subject matter, (2) objective, (3) form, and (4) difficulty. No one of these is inherently better than the others. Several considerations must usually be taken into account before deciding on a scheme, and then the decision will most likely be a compromise anyway. Research is needed on the merits and limitations of different schemes of organization.

### By subject matter

Certainly one of the most meaningful ways of grouping questions is according to the subject matter with which they deal. It is easy to accomplish. It makes the examinee's task easier in that he can concentrate on one area at a time. And it is convenient for purposes of scoring, summarizing, and interpreting performance.

A special case is the type of exercise built around common background materials, such as reading passages, statistical data, and charts. Here it is of course necessary to keep the questions together, and then often in a certain logical order of development.

If an examination covers two or more large segments of subject matter, it is possible to make these the primary basis of grouping. Within each block one may then scramble the questions or arrange them according to objective, difficulty, or even form and similarity of directions.

### By objective

Grouping according to educational goal is less common than the preceding, yet for some purposes it is quite meaningful. Thus, one group of questions in an examination may deal with knowledge of basic facts, terminology, and principles, while a second may deal with application of these to problem situations.

One advantage of this is that it makes the examinee's task at any time fairly uniform; that is, it demands of him essentially the same kind of operation over a whole series of items. Another advantage is that it encourages the instructor to build his examination around explicit objectives. This, in turn, serves to impress upon students the importance of those very objectives.

A possible disadvantage is that this arrangement, if followed slavishly, would split up blocks of questions that deal with a topic at different levels and are best left together. For some purposes it is most meaningful and less arbitrary to organize questions by topic.

Another possible disadvantage is the monotony and fatigue that may be induced by running in succession several blocks of similar exercises.

It may be better to utilize some cyclical arrangement so that there is variation in the nature of the task.

## By form

A third common arrangement is to group the questions by form—for example, all essay questions together, all completion questions together, all key-list exercises together, and so on.

This has certain practical advantages. With short-answer and choice-type items at least, it permits the use of common directions and format for recording answers. These features tend to make the student's task more uniform and apparently easier. In addition, they facilitate scoring and summarization.

Of course, there is the possible disadvantage of this uniformity becoming monotonous to the student; and also it may not be so useful an organization as one by subject matter or objectives.

## By degree of difficulty

Many standardized tests have their items arranged in an increasing order of difficulty—from very easy to moderately difficult to very difficult. This is the common sequence when items are grouped according to difficulty. The advantages are that—

1. The easy items which come early give the student a chance to warm up and to build up confidence rather than to experience discouragement at the outset.

2. It paces the tasks so that the student can work steadily to the limit of his ability rather than get stalled early on hard items. This makes for increased test reliability since the functioning sample of items for each student tends to reach a maximum in the time available.

3. It gives a greater spread of scores than would a jumbled order or an inverse order of difficulty.

The disadvantages of this arrangement are that—

1. It may not provide as comfortable, meaningful, or useful a grouping as one by subject matter, type of objective, or form. Thus, it may be fatiguing for the student to have to shift continually from one topic to a different one rather than to concentrate on related material.

2. The very difficult items come at the end of the test when the student reaches the point of greatest fatigue. Actually it might be better for students to encounter these hard items after an early warm-up period; or to

work alternately on easy and hard items so as to have a chance to relax between periods of intense concentration.

3. It requires knowing the true order of difficulty before tryout—and this information is usually not available. However, an experienced teacher can judge the difficulty of items with some degree of accuracy, particularly the extremes. Pooling the judgments of subject matter experts is a still better method and may give a sufficiently accurate estimate (1, 4).

### Layout and format

After a sequence has been decided upon, one must get the items into a legible, attractive, and economical format. This is an important step. Matters of format affect not only the attractiveness and acceptance of a test but also the validity of its results. The time devoted to such matters will be small indeed in relation to that spent in composing the questions.

A rather thorough discussion of layout and format may be found in *Educational Measurement* (3), and it is not necessary to duplicate that here. However, comments will be made on the placing of items and on provision for response.

For economy of space, it is ordinarily best to arrange multiple-choice items in two columns as shown on page 223. If the items must have long alternatives, then it may be more desirable to run these across the page. In any case, practice varies and it is acceptable to use both arrangements in the same booklet. Whichever layout is used, it is best not to split items at the bottom of a column or page.

In the case of true-false and other key-list exercises, it is generally better to run the statements across the page. Practice is more likely to vary with respect to key-list exercises. If the categories and statements are short, it is more economical to run the exercise in a double column, often right along with multiple-choice items.

Whenever background material and the accompanying questions take more than one page, it is desirable to put them on facing pages. This arrangement saves students from continually turning pages back and forth.

Whenever choices are to be recorded or answers written out on the booklet, this poses an additional problem. With essay questions, the main thing is to allow space consistent with the scope of answer desired. This space must allow for the fact that some students will have unusually large handwriting. With short-answer or choice-type items, the most important thing is to arrange the spaces in column form along one of the margins, preferably the right. This facilitates scoring.

## REPRODUCTION OF MATERIALS

Of the general reproduction processes available, two kinds will meet the needs of the usual small-scale test development project. These are: (1) duplication by office-type machines, such as the Mimeograph and Dittomaster; and (2) printing by the photo-offset method.

Duplication by office-type machines requires that each page be typed on a special stencil or master sheet. Drawings may also be made on the stencil. This process reproduces copies each of which is exactly the same size as on the stencil or master sheet. Generally it is not worth while to try to ditto more than a few hundred or to mimeograph more than several hundred copies.

The photo-offset method also requires that each page be typed on a master sheet, unless there are maps, drawings, pictures, and so on, to be reproduced. Since the photo-offset method makes use of a photographic process, anything that can be photographed lends itself to this method. It is possible to alter the size of the original copy, either reducing or enlarging it in the process. Generally it does not pay to use photo-offset for only one or two hundred copies, unless one has drawings and the like which cannot be reproduced clearly by office machines. It is possible to run off several thousand copies by this method.

Offset reproductions of prints and photographs for examination purposes are not altogether satisfactory (5, p. 116). In the process they may take on a washed-out appearance. This is particularly upsetting if the reproduction has obscured in a print the detail about which one has framed certain test items. Then it is unreasonable to expect students to make the fine judgments called for. Better but more expensive methods involve half-tone printing or the use of special color prints distributed in packets to individual students.

## REFERENCES

1. Lorge, I., and Kruglov, Lorraine. A suggested technique for the improvement of difficulty prediction of test items. *Educ. psychol. Measmt,* 1952, **12**, 554–561.
2. Mosier, C. I., Myers, M. C., and Price, Helen G. Suggestions for the construction of multiple choice test items. *Educ. psychol. Measmt,* 1945, **5**, 261–271.

3. Spaulding, Geraldine. Reproducing the test. In E. F. Lindquist (Ed.), *Educational measurement*. Washington: Amer. Coun. on Educ., 1951. Pp. 417–454.

4. Tinkelman, S. *Difficulty prediction of test items*. New York: Bur. Publ., Teach. Coll., Columbia Univer., 1947.

5. *Comprehensive examinations in a program of general education*. East Lansing: Mich. State Univer., 1949.

## FURTHER READING

Spaulding, Geraldine. Reproducing the test. In E. F. Lindquist (Ed.), *Educational measurement*. Washington: Amer. Coun. on Educ., 1951. Pp. 417–454.

# Administration and Scoring

After a representative sample of situations has been assembled in final form, some further work remains to be done—work that is preliminary to the administration of the test. This work deals mainly with the preparation of accessory materials such as special answer sheets and directions. And of course there may be the job of making arrangements for physical facilities such as rooms and equipment, if these are special for the occasion. Then comes the actual tryout or administration of the test, followed by the job of scoring or otherwise summarizing the test results. This cluster of essentially administrative tasks will be our concern in this chapter.

## FURTHER PRELIMINARY WORK

### Devising a separate answer sheet

In the use of choice-type tests, it is common to have examinees record their answers on a special answer sheet. If the papers are to be scored on an IBM test-scoring machine, a special answer sheet from among the variety of forms is available. However, if the tests are to be hand-scored, it is much cheaper and just as satisfactory to devise a homemade answer sheet. Three or four columns as the following may be put on a Dittomaster or Mimeograph stencil:

> 1. a   b   c   d   e
> 2. a   b   c   d   e
> 3. a   b   c   d   e
>       etc.

Directions should tell the student to cross out the letter corresponding to the alternative in each item which he considers the correct or best answer. It is better to have students cross out rather than encircle the best answer inasmuch as a cross can be seen more easily through a hole in a stencil key.

When examinees must sit so closely together that copying of answers becomes a problem, the common practice is to use alternate test forms with a standard answer sheet. However, it is believed to be more economical and just as satisfactory to use a single test form but to provide two or more forms of answer sheets as illustrated below (4, p. 102).

| *Form A* | *Form B* | *Form C* |
|---|---|---|
| 1. B D E A C | 1. D C B E A | 1. A C D E B |
| 2. E B C A D | 2. B C A E D | 2. C D E A B |

Notice that the options for each item are presented in a scrambled order, and that the sequence differs for the corresponding items on each form. Hence, it is believed unlikely that adjacent examinees would be able to copy easily from each other.

### Outlining directions for recording answers

The recording of answers is not usually a critical problem of test administration. There is one situation, however, in which it is: i.e., when answers are to be recorded on a special IBM answer sheet by means of a special pencil. It is then highly desirable to impress upon the group certain precautions which they must observe when filling out such an answer sheet. These precautions, or special directions, may be printed on the cover page of the booklet, as shown below.

1. Mark your answers only on the special answer sheet. To do this, you must use the *special pencil* provided.
2. Do not fold or crease your answer sheet.
3. Note the *item number* of the question you are answering, and find the *row* on the answer sheet that has the same number.
4. In this row find the pair of dotted lines (lettered, numbered) the same as the answer which you consider correct for that question, and *blacken* this answer space, i.e., draw a heavy vertical line between these two dotted lines, as in the example below. *Misplaced answers are counted as wrong answers.*

5. Go over each mark two or three times and press firmly on your pencil. This will make a solid black mark as in the example.
6. Make your marks as long as the pair of dotted lines.
7. If you change your answer, erase your first mark completely. Do not cross it out. The machine will count partially erased answers as wrong answers.
8. Make no unnecessary marks in and around the dotted lines; the machine cannot distinguish between intended answers and stray pencil marks. Do not rest your pencil on an answer space while deciding which space to mark.
9. Keep your answer sheet on a hard surface while marking your answers.
10. Make one and only one mark after each answer sheet number. Your score will be reduced by an amount equal to the number of extra marks on your answer sheet.

### Deciding what to do about guessing

On every multiple-choice test, the examinee will run into some items on which he is not sure of the right answer. This uncertainty may range from a slight lack of confidence to almost complete ignorance. His problem is to decide whether to omit the item or to record a judgment anyway. If there are no explicit directions on this matter, the decision is up to him. Chances are that he will guess if he stands to increase his score.

If the score is the number right, those who guess will tend to raise their scores. This would happen if their guesses were made on a purely chance basis. But there are few items on which such guesses are purely chance. On most such items the examinee already has some knowledge, and he may at the least be able to reject the worst alternatives and narrow his choice to the remaining. To this extent he improves his chances of guessing correctly. Moreover, individual differences in tendency to guess will, under these conditions of scoring, favor the guesser over the nonguesser. Hence, some penalty for wrong answers (i.e., correction for guessing) would be necessary to prevent serious distortion in relative standing.

In view of these conditions, what directions should be given to examinees? As with other decisions of this kind, no hard and fast rule can be laid down for all purposes. Indeed, any of the four main possibilities listed below has its merits and would be preferred by some test specialists over the remaining.

1. Instruct the individuals *not* to guess. Such instructions are difficult to comply with fully. For some judgments, the distinction between guessing and not guessing is a subtle one to make. Nor will such instructions discourage all individuals from guessing freely. There will be some who will guess despite the directions, and there will be others who will be overly cautious. For either extreme, "do not guess" instructions will lead to invalid scores. Nevertheless, so far as statistical considerations of reliability and validity are concerned, the experimental evidence favors "do not guess" directions (1, pp. 90–91). For the group as a whole, these directions seem to give the most useful results.

2. Instruct the individuals to try all the items, to guess even when not sure. The intent of such directions is to eliminate individual differences in tendency to gamble. Such directions are appropriate for untimed or liberally timed power tests, in which everyone does have an opportunity to try practically all the items. They are not appropriate for highly speeded tests, where it is not expected that all individuals will do all the items.

If all individuals comply fully with these directions, there will be no need to substract a penalty for wrong answers. It can be proved mathematically that if everyone in the group answers *all* the items, the correlation between uncorrected scores (number of right answers) and corrected scores will be perfect. The numerical values of the corrected and uncorrected scores will not be the same, but the relative ranks of individuals in the group will.

Since these directions encourage guessing, they tend to introduce large chance errors into scores. This is one objection to the procedure. Another and probably more serious objection is educational in nature. Many educators object to such directions on grounds that they foster careless habits of thinking. The objection may have validity, but unfortunately we lack evidence on it.

If one need not be concerned about the possibility of large chance errors and the encouragement of guessing, this procedure is as good as any. It is economical of time since it does not require a correction for guessing. To forestall any misunderstandings on the part of students, however, it is desirable to explain to them *why* they are to answer all the items even when not completely sure.

3. Instruct the individuals to guess when not completely sure but to avoid wild guessing. Such directions are a compromise between "guess" and "do not guess" instructions. Educational Testing Service, for example, uses the following statement on the cover page of its Cooperative Achievement Tests:

. . . You may answer questions even when you are not perfectly sure that your answers are correct, but you should avoid *wild* guessing, since wrong answers will result in a subtraction from the number of your correct answers. . . .

An additional example comes from an unpublished scholarship test for college applicants:

. . . You should not guess wildly, but it is to your advantage to answer each question. In the questions for which you have difficulty arriving at an answer, it is suggested that you eliminate the alternatives you consider wrong and select an answer from the remaining alternatives. Do not spend too much time on any one question.

4. Inform the individuals that a correction formula will be used but give no specific directions as to whether they should guess or not. However, before the test begins explain the reason for using the correction formula.

These instructions leave it up to the individual to decide whether he should guess on doubtful items. Hence, their intent is not to try to eliminate individual differences in tendency to gamble, but to try to control their effects on the scores.

1. Guessing is less serious a problem when items are at the right level of difficulty for a group. Explain why this is so.
2. Using the following symbols, derive a formula for correcting for chance success, and explain why you expressed the formula as you did. $S = $ corrected score, $R = $ number right, $W = $ number wrong, and $n = $ number of alternatives in each item. Assume that no items were omitted.
3. Prove that the rank order of corrected and uncorrected scores will be the same when all individuals answer all items on a test.

### Giving advance instructions

The preliminary work so far described does not directly involve those who will be most concerned—the individuals who will take the test. One of the issues that arises prior to the giving of a test is whether or not to give advance instructions about what to expect or about what special preparation to make.

Large-scale testing agencies, such as the College Entrance Examination Board and Educational Testing Service, go to great lengths to explain and illustrate the tests to be administered in their particular programs and the conditions under which the tests will be given. These agencies print and distribute well in advance of any test administration special booklets furnishing such information to examinees. Any person who plans to take one of these tests thus has a pretty good idea of what to expect before he actually sees the test.

In the case of classroom tests, there are similar advantages to be gained by giving students detailed information on what to expect and what special preparation to make *for a particular test*. But there is also merit in giving students at the outset of a course a detailed statement concerning examinations and other methods of evaluation to be used *throughout the course*. Such general instructions will make it unnecessary to repeat the same suggestions for each test. As an example, take the writing of essays and similar extended answers. If this technique is to be utilized frequently in a course, students can profit from special tips on how to prepare for and answer such questions. As a start, an instructor may pass along special advice on the art of writing essay examinations. A list such as that below may be distributed and discussed with students very early in a course (after Edmiston, 3, pp. 137–38).

### IMPORTANT CONSIDERATIONS IN TAKING EXAMINATIONS

1. Enter your name on the first or last sheet of the examination, if sheets are securely bound. On each loose sheet enter your name inconspicuously, preferably on the back where it will not be seen by the reader.
2. Write legibly. If your answer can't be read, it can't be judged right. Be sure your pen or pencil (if allowed) does not produce blurred writing.
3. Use terms or a vocabulary suited to the subject. Do not use a word unless its meaning is clear to you; repeat a word rather than use another which may not have exactly the same desired meaning.
4. Use the back of sheets, an extra sheet, or the margins for—
   a) computations.
   b) the drafting of answers, not padded but furnishing quality rather than quantity.
   c) the hasty jotting down of points as they occur to you.

5. Consider fully the statement of each question. Carelessness not only penalizes you but it also lowers the dependability of the grade or evaluation obtained by the instructor.

6. Follow carefully the directions telling how to answer the questions. Underscore the important points in the directions.

7. In essay questions, underscore the part of the statement that contains the direct question asked. Then underscore any parts of the statement that provide data for the answer. Number each part so that you will not omit anything from your answer.

8. Work directly through the examination without dwelling on unfamiliar points or difficult questions. After you complete the parts which you were able to answer readily, return to the more difficult questions.

9. If, after thorough consideration, you do not understand some direction or question other than because of your ignorance of the subject matter, call the attention of the person in charge with as little disturbance as possible so that he may come to your seat or allow you to come to him as conditions may determine.

10. Reread each answer before passing to the next question and the completed examination before turning it in to the instructor. Is the meaning clear and the writing legible?

Perhaps still other general points could be added to this list. One such point is in the nature of a caution: When the task is to draw generalizations from given data, do not merely restate the data.

In time, as students did the above operations habitually, an instructor could concentrate on getting across finer points of technique. The latter, in all likelihood, would correspond closely to the instructional objectives of his course—as they surely must if evaluation and instruction are consistent with one another.

4. List several important advantages of the practice of giving students advance instructions concerning a particular course examination.

5. What values might there be in distributing to students at the start of a course copies of previous examinations or sample problems and questions? If this is done, what cautions must be impressed upon students?

6. For a course that you will teach, prepare a general statement concerning examinations and other methods of evaluation to be used in that course. Before you begin, list the purposes you expect to accomplish through such a statement. (In this connection, review the portion of the statement on pages 210–13).

### Dividing the session into phases

Almost every test administration has certain phases: a preliminary orientation period during which directions are given and materials distributed, the test proper, and, finally, the collection of materials. Beyond this rather commonplace division, it is possible to see other ways of dividing a test administration into phases. The more important of these will follow quite naturally efforts to meet such conditions or purposes as the following:

1. To minimize fatigue by dividing a long test into parts.
2. To separate the testing of different functions which require somewhat different materials and conditions of administration.
3. To break down a large, comprehensive problem into two or more phases and to work in feedback or additional information along the way.
4. To provide reference materials for study, to be followed by an exercise based on these.
5. To provide a short practice session before the test proper.
6. To make a preliminary screening of the group and then to follow this with differential testing of individuals.
7. To follow the test with an inquiry of some sort.
8. To obtain an estimate of test reliability.

The possibility of an informal classroom test being overly long is perhaps slight below the college and university level, for below this level tests are rarely planned for longer than a class period. The possibility is real in the case of comprehensive examinations in colleges and universities. There, examinations may run to three or four hours in one session and may prove too fatiguing. Instructors must consider the need for providing short intermissions or rest breaks, or even giving the test in two separate sessions on different days.

At other times, it is not so much the sheer length of a test that justifies a division but the fact that different functions are being sampled. One section may be testing vocabulary of a foreign language; another, reading comprehension of that language; a third, oral comprehension. Speed may be an important component of one skill, requiring a rigorously timed subtest; but a related skill may be tested immediatley afterward under untimed conditions. Or one part may be in multiple-choice form, to be followed by an essay section. At the extreme, one test may be in written form and another essentially a laboratory or practical test requiring manipulation of special equipment.

With perhaps one or two exceptions, the remaining possibilities in the above list are not common in classroom testing. The sixth represents a much-neglected approach in educational and psychological testing, although we do have some precedents for it. All too commonly we administer the same situations to all individuals in the group, rather than adapt the sample to the individual's level of functioning (competency). A short screening test could sort out a group into several levels of over-all competency, after which these several subgroups could be tested more intensively with problems at their particular levels.

Following a test with an inquiry phase is well worth the effort if the administration amounts to a tryout of the situations. The inquiry may take various forms. One may simply ask the group to write down critical comments on the test, to indicate whether the directions were clear, to list items which were ambiguous or too difficult, and so forth. At the other extreme, one may interview individuals in order to ascertain how they had arrived at their answers; or, if their responses are in written form, to find out what they had meant by particular statements; or to "test the limits" by asking further questions to probe their understanding.

At this stage of test planning and development, then, it is a good idea to examine closely the plans for administration. It is entirely possible that the purposes could be served best by dividing the total administration into phases, or that some additional advantages could be gained by adding other phases. Better coordination of the separate phases should also result from such preliminary work.

7. One further task is to make some decision concerning time limits for the test or its parts.

   a) What factors should be considered in deciding on time limits?
   b) What practice would you recommend for the usual informal school achievement test?

8. What advantages might there be in making a test long enough so that few, if any, persons will finish before the end of the test period? What possible disadvantages? (For further treatment of this topic, see the articles by Ebel suggested at the end of this chapter.)

### Readying the materials

The efficient handling of test materials can do much to make the session go off smoothly. Steps to facilitate this can begin before administration.

One useful practice is to number the booklets beforehand. (If there is reason to believe that during the test administration some individuals will forget to enter their identification numbers on their answer sheets, both the answer sheets and the booklets may be numbered before the session and the answer sheets inserted in the corresponding booklets. An inexpensive serial numbering device speeds this operation.) Another practice that generally pays is to set aside extra materials—booklets, answer sheets, pencils, scratch paper—to meet shortages likely to arise for one cause or another.

## ADMINISTERING THE TEST

The goal of test administration is to establish the conditions which are most consistent with the purposes of the test. In the case of an achievement test, this will mean establishing those conditions which will insure the most efficient work by the individuals taking the test.

Test administration can become a complex activity—as it does in large-scale testing programs—so that the administrator must make a painstaking preparation. Our brief treatment of test administration in this book is not intended for this kind of person, but for the classroom instructor who ordinarily deals with a small-scale operation. We leave to a book such as *Educational Measurement* (6) the many fine points of technique so essential to the large-scale programs.

### Providing the right conditions

One must see to it, first of all, that the physical conditions are conducive to good work. There should be adequate light and ventilation, a comfortable temperature, sufficient quiet that outside noises do not distract the group, a comfortable seating arrangement, and adequate working space so that individuals may spread out their materials. If the size of the group necessitates the use of an auditorium, the acoustics should be satisfactory and a public address system should be utilized.

Not to be overlooked are the more subtle psychological conditions, of which proper motivation is paramount. The establishment of these conditions will depend a great deal on one's rapport with the group, and on the specific directions conveyed before and during the administration.

### Carrying out the procedure

From this point on, the administration of the test should proceed according to plan. All of the details of procedure so carefully worked out in advance should now be carried out with precision. This is especially necessary if the test is to be given on separate occasions to two or more groups. For the results to be truly comparable, the test must be given in the same way to all.

To avoid distraction and confusion, test materials should be distributed and collected according to a plan. As a general rule, special materials, such as electrographic pencils and answer sheets, should be distributed before test booklets. If the booklets are numbered, it is an easy matter to count the number required for each row and then to pass out that quantity and no more. To insure control of the materials, individuals should be instructed to record the number of the booklet in a designated space on the answer sheet. At the time of collecting materials, special pencils should be called for first, followed by booklets and answer sheets in that order. If the booklets have been passed out in numerical order, they can easily be collected in the original order and checked to see that all have been turned in.

9. During an examination, individuals sometimes raise questions about procedure or about the interpretation of the materials. How would you respond to the following?

a) A request for clarification of the directions.
b) A request for definition of a concept that appears in one of the options in a multiple-choice item. The concept itself is not the point being tested. Though not discussed in class, it has appeared several times in the instructional materials.
c) An individual asks whether he should work right through the test cr skip the hard questions and return to them later.

## SCORING CHOICE-TYPE TESTS

In Chapter 6 we emphasized that both evaluation and counting are involved in scoring a choice test. Our discussion should have made this point clear. To maintain the proper perspective, however, it would be a good idea to review pages 152–74 at this time.

Our interest now is on the more mechanical operations involved in arriving at a raw score for each individual. First will come a consideration of hand and machine methods of scoring, including their comparative advantages and limitations; then, a discussion of the problem of applying a "correction" for guessing.

### Hand scoring

Before scoring can be done, one must have a convenient key with which to work. If there are relatively few—10 to 20—test booklets, a blank test with the correct answers marked on may serve as the scoring key. Scoring then consists of counting the answers which agree with the key. When a marked booklet is used as the scoring key, it may be easier to score the same page for all individuals consecutively than to go through each individual's booklet at once.

Hand scoring of *booklets* goes quickest when the answers have been recorded down one side of each page. The key can then be lined up with the answers. Sometimes it is worth the effort to prepare a set of strip keys. This is done by cutting from each page of the key test the vertical strip of answers and mounting these strips on cardboard.

If special answer sheets have been used, one may punch out a stencil key. The IBM Corporation sells a special punch that can punch holes four and one-half inches inside the edge of the paper. This device works equally well for IBM or homemade forms. The scoring procedure involves placing the stencil over each answer sheet and counting the rights or wrongs. However, it is usually necessary to scan the answer sheets first in order to see whether any students have marked more than one answer to any of the items. Such items should be lined out and counted wrong.

10. What advantages might there be to students and teachers in having answers recorded in test booklets? How would these differ from the advantages realized in using special answer sheets?

11. It has been pointed out that the use of a separate answer sheet constitutes a simple coding test. For what types of individuals would it be inadvisable to use a special answer sheet?

### Machine scoring

As an alternative to hand scoring, machine scoring is now available in many school systems and colleges. At the present time, machine scoring is done largely on the IBM Test Scoring Machine (7). In the not too distant future, electronic devices may replace this type of machine.

The IBM machine operates on the fact that a graphite pencil mark will conduct electricity. When an answer sheet is inserted, it is pressed against a sensing unit containing 750 sets of contacts corresponding to the 750 answer spaces on the answer sheet (150 items $\times$ 5 spaces each). The machine distinguishes between right and wrong answers, and instantaneously shows the score on a meter. The operator reads the score from the meter and records it on the answer sheet.

Machine controls make it possible to obtain many types of scores, such as number right, number wrong, rights minus wrongs, and rights minus a fraction of the wrongs $\left( R - \dfrac{W}{n-1} \right)$. The three sets of controls make it possible to score, with one insertion of the answer sheet, three different parts of a test. The machine performs all steps of scoring in a single operation. Since all pencil marks on a sheet are sensed at the same time, speed is not affected by the number of questions in the test. A test with 150 items can be scored as quickly as one with 15 or 50 items. Scoring is done as rapidly as the operator can feed answer sheets into the machine and record scores. Average rates are 400 to 800 scores an hour.

### Hand scoring versus machine scoring

The use of special answer sheets, homemade or IBM, permits more rapid scoring than that possible when answers have been recorded in test booklets. It cannot be said, however, that machine scoring is always more efficient than hand scoring of special answer sheets (6, p. 408).

Both hand and machine scoring require scanning of answer sheets. But in addition to that, machine scoring requires other work and materials which make it more costly than most people realize. After scanning, clerks must erase all stray marks around the answer spaces, and they must either hand score or re-mark those sheets which are too lightly marked. Then there is the preparation of stencils and check sheets, followed by the testing of the machine's accuracy. These preliminary operations may take as much or more time than the scoring of the papers themselves. For this reason, machine scoring is not ordinarily economical with fewer than 100 answer sheets.

Machine scoring also requires the use of electrographic pencils and specially printed IBM answer sheets. The latter cost about two cents each and thus are relatively expensive. These additional paraphernalia, together with the administrative problems they create, offset some of the advantages of machine scoring.

In short, the decision to hand or machine score will rest largely on practical considerations. But regardless of which method is used, it is desirable to rescore the papers as a check. Human errors enter into both methods.

12. "The problems of machine scoring are not those of scoring alone; they are problems of administration as well" (6, p. 361). List the main points that support this statement.

### Applying a correction formula

As noted earlier, there are some situations in which it is desirable to use a formula to correct for guessing. The usual formula is—

$$S = R - \frac{W}{n - 1}$$

where the symbols are as defined on page 286. The underlying assumption is that all wrong answers plus a fraction of the right ones were made on a purely chance basis. Notice that the formula requires a separate count of right and wrong answers. (Omitted items are not counted as wrong answers.)

Opinion differs as to the value of applying a correction formula. Many specialists do not believe it is worth the trouble, especially when the test consists of four- or five-option items. Others, however, argue for it on educational grounds, even when the correction will not alter the standings of individuals in the group. They believe it unwise to give the student the impression he knows more than he actually does. One authority, F. B. Davis, even feels inclined to urge the correction for chance success "for almost all educational purposes." He illustrates his point dramatically through a rather unusual example:

. . . Recently the writer tested a group of 393 high school pupils with Form B of the Nelson-Denny Reading Test. The 47 pupils who obtained the lowest scores were then grouped together and told that they might have done better if they had marked an answer for every item whether they knew the answer or not. This is, of course, true since the Nelson-Denny test is rather highly speeded and is not scored with a correction for chance success. Form A of the test was then administered. The average score of the 47 pupils on the first test (Form B) was 25.53; on the second test (Form A) it was 46.32. According to the published norms, this difference amounted to a gain of 2.7 grades for the group. Yet, when scores on both forms were corrected for chance, the average gain was only 2 raw-score points (though the standard deviations of the distributions of scores were larger). This gain, attributable largely to regression to the population mean, is obviously a more meaningful and more readily interpreted indication of the real change that took place in the reading ability of the pupils between testings than is the gain represented by the difference in raw scores uncorrected for chance success . . . (2, p. 277).[1]

13. It has been argued that the "correction for guessing" is a misnomer. Do you agree? Explain your position.
14. If an item writer succeeds in making the wrong alternatives plausible, what effect will this have on corrected scores?
15. Is it more desirable to correct for guessing on a true-false or on a four-option multiple-choice test? Why?
16. Some instructors prefer to apply a heavy penalty for guessing through the use of a formula, such as rights minus twice the wrongs. Will this practice penalize more heavily those who guess more? Explain.
17. For which of the following achievement tests is the use of a correction formula desirable?

   a) The obtained scores of students are to be compared with the maximum possible.
   b) There is great variation among individuals in the number of items omitted.
   c) The relative standing of students is to be determined on an informal, liberally timed, multiple-choice test.

## GRADING WRITTEN RESPONSES

Free-response problems and questions do not lend themselves to the routine, mechanical operations described in the previous section. Written responses and the like call for personal judgment on the part of the reader. This process of judgment was reviewed in Chapter 6 under the heading of Evaluation. What was said there certainly applies here. The discussion in the following pages supplements that, but is intended to deal with the more restricted problem of grading written responses.

### Short-answer type

It is a fairly straightforward operation to grade short-answer items if one has worked out a satisfactory key. Then it is largely a matter of comparing each response with the key.

While it is possible to prepare a key before reading the actual responses, this does not always suffice. Such a key may not anticipate the variety of acceptable answers which are often possible. Therefore it is good prac-

[1] Reproduced by permission of the American Council on Education, Washington.

tice to pick up these acceptable variations in form and content of the best answer by reading a sample of responses first.

## Extended-answer type

### General suggestions

The task of evaluating extended answers or essays is a difficult one, no denying that. It is difficult to distinguish degrees of quality and to control personal biases. Nevertheless the task can be made easier and biases reduced if readers follow certain suggestions. These hold whether one wants to analyze an answer in detail or form an over-all impression of it.

1. *Determine in advance the qualities to be judged.* As discussed in Chapter 6, these qualities should relate to the educational objective(s) on which one is seeking evidence.

A common issue is whether to evaluate written expression in courses other than English. This is largely a matter of educational policy. Of course, it is desirable to provide the student with further evidence of his progress in written expression. Indeed, written work done outside the English class may well provide better evidence than papers written in it. Perhaps the main objection is that instructors in other classes do not have the time or inclination to concern themselves with qualities of written expression.

2. *Define quality levels in advance of grading.* This step serves to eliminate some of the guesswork and subjectivity. It can be facilitated by preparing a model paper or by reading a sample of papers. The latter procedure helps to peg the quality levels or numerical credits to the actual variation one may expect to find in the particular group.

3. *Grade one quality or one question at a time.* This permits one to concentrate on a single task and to avoid contaminating ratings of different things. It is easier to keep in mind the standards for different quality levels or the list of points which make up a model answer.

If, in an essay examination, one wants to evaluate organization of ideas as well as mastery of subject matter, it is best to make these evaluations separately. Then it is possible to interpret grades directly, without having to consider how much of an over-all grade is due to each factor.

4. *Grade the papers anonymously.* This can be facilitated by having each student use a code number on his paper in lieu of his name, or by having him write his name in an inconspicuous place. This is essential if

the reader is to judge a paper on its own merit, rather than on the basis of other impressions formed of the person.

5. *To obtain higher reliability of grading, reread the papers after a lapse of time; or better yet, enlist the help of other competent readers and average the ratings.* This is desirable only if the test is important enough to justify the additional effort.

### Analytical method

One general approach to the reading of answers is the analytical method (5, p. 522). According to this method, the reader analyzes each answer into a number of specific elements and assigns a weight or credit to each element. He may base his analysis and weighting on a model answer prepared by himself or upon a sample of student responses. Generally it is desirable to modify a model answer after reading such a sample.

Through the use of such an analytical method it is possible to achieve highly objective grading. However, there is evidence to suggest that the method will not work as well with extended answers and long English compositions (5, pp. 523–24). It is also very tedious for a reader to carry out on long compositions.

### Whole method

The other general approach to the reading of essay papers is the whole method (5, p. 522). Here the reader judges the merit of an answer or a paper as a whole, without breaking it down into constituent elements.

The use of sample answers or papers facilitates grading. One should read a sample of papers and select specimens representative of each quality level to be distinguished. These may then serve as standards against which to compare any individual's response.

An alternate but related procedure is to sort out the papers according to their merit. Usually three to five piles will suffice, with six being an upper limit. There is some value in reading through the papers quickly and making a rough preliminary sorting. Then one can reread the papers in each group and shift up or down those that seem out of place. If five piles are used, one may aim for a distribution as follows: 10 per cent, highest; 20 per cent, next highest; 40 per cent, middle or average; 20 per cent, next to lowest; 10 per cent, lowest. This is only a rough guide, and should not be followed slavishly without considering the ability level of the group.

When this alternate procedure is applied to single questions within an examination, it is desirable to shuffle the papers before going on to the next question. Otherwise one may not grade the answer to a question independently of the evaluation made on the preceding question or questions.

18. Why is it generally desirable to revise a model answer after reading a sample of student responses?

19. If you were to use the whole method to sort some specimens into quality levels, could you generally do this without making any analytical comparisons between specimens? Explain.

20. The tasks covered in this chapter are often treated lightly, so that neglect of these mechanical procedures frequently leads to invalid test results. Defend the proposition that "valid test results depend upon proper administration and scoring."

## REFERENCES

1. Cronbach, L. J. *Essentials of psychological testing.* New York: Harper, 1949.
2. Davis F. B. Item selection techniques. In E. F. Lindquist (Ed), *Educational measurement.* Washington: Amer. Coun. on Educ., 1951. Pp. 266–328.
3. Edmiston, R. W. Examine the examination. *J. educ Psychol.,* 1939, **30**, 126–138.
4. McKenna, F. S. A scrambled answer sheet. *Amer. Psychologist,* 1957, **12**, 102.
5. Stalnaker, J. M. The essay type of examination. In E. F. Lindquist (Ed.), *Educational measurement.* Washington: Amer. Coun. on Educ., 1951. Pp. 495–530.
6. Traxler, A. E. Administering and scoring the objective test. In E. F. Lindquist (Ed.), *Educational measurement.* Washington: Amer. Coun. on Educ., 1951. Pp. 329–416.
7. *IBM test scoring machine type 805:* principles of operation. New York: Internat. Bus. Mach. Corp., 1954.

## FURTHER READINGS

Diederich, P. B. Measurement of skill in writing. *Sch. Rev.,* 1946, **54**, 584–592.

Ebel, R. L. Maximizing test validity in fixed time limits. *Educ. psychol. Measmt,* 1953, **13**, 347–357.

Ebel, R. L. The characteristics and usefulness of rate scores on college aptitude tests. *Educ. psychol. Measmt,* 1954, **14**, 20–28.

Stalnaker, J. M. Weighting questions in the essay type examination. *J. educ. Psychol.,* 1938, **29**, 481–490.

Traxler, A. E. Administering and scoring the objective test. In E. F. Lindquist (Ed.), *Educational measurement.* Washington: Amer. Coun. on Educ., 1951. Pp. 329–416.

# Analysis and Revision

Having devoted many hours of time and careful thought to the development of a test, one may feel inclined to believe that it is adequate for the given purpose. Unfortunately, however, the adequacy of a test cannot be assumed from the amount and quality of workmanship that have gone into its development. Only a systematic analysis of the instrument and the results it produces can establish its adequacy.

It is the purpose of this chapter to review several procedures helpful in analyzing and improving a test. The first group of procedures to be considered deal with the property of relevance; a second group deal with the properties of discrimination and test reliability. Of the three major *technical* criteria for a satisfactory test—relevance, objectivity, and reliability—the first and the third come in for consideration here. It is assumed that procedures for determining and improving the second have been sufficiently covered in Chapter 6.

Not all of the procedures to be discussed are of value in analyzing classroom tests, particularly those that are short. But some of the procedures will be widely applicable and well worth trying even on short, informal tests. An understanding of the more technical of the procedures, such as item analysis, will at the least improve one's understanding of what makes a good test.

## LOGICAL ANALYSIS

One way to analyze a test is to study the individual items in an effort to understand what processes they sample and what content they deal with. This is known as "logical analysis."

Although the kind of analysis we have in mind here does not deal with test *results*, it is nonetheless helpful. If you have written the items for your test to fit specific objectives, and if you have a colleague who will consent to go through your test item by item, his analyses can help to show how well your items fit the objectives for which you had intended them. Or, if you had not initially used a set of specifications to prepare the test, you may want to work back from the items to the objectives they appear to sample. This will give you an indication of where the emphasis in your test falls, and whether you have achieved a fair balance among both types of objectives and content areas of the course.

Exactly the same procedure can be used in evaluating a published test or instrument. If you have a statement of what the author intends his instrument to test, then you can compare your analysis of the test against his statement. Or, if the author provides no specific statement of what he intends to cover, the analysis will throw light on what he apparently did cover.

## An illustration

To see how logical analysis works, let us turn to the exercise which begins on page 89. And for the sake of brevity, let us concentrate on item 2 and ask ourselves, "What processes must the student go through in order to cope successfully with the situation indicated?" It is suggested that the student must be able to do the following:

Read the entire problem situation, comprehend what is involved, and then do the same for the individual item.

Reject alternative (a) because this would not facilitate the discussion but would probably embarrass Tom and put him on the defensive.

Reject alternative (b) because this would represent a passive, "buck-passing" approach on his part.

Reject alternative (c) because, while this might satisfy *his* personal needs, it would not facilitate group discussion and airing of opinions.

Choose alternative (d) because, by expressing his opinion and giving reasons, he would have facilitated group discussion of the issue. He would also have shown his willingness to express his own opinion.

For this type of item, we assume that the student must read and weigh each alternative. This seems necessary because the task is to choose the best course of action from among four options, and hence implies some attention to all possibilities.

Viewing the situation portrayed in item 2 very broadly, we should agree on the following elements in our analysis:

That it is a miniature social situation on paper, and hence is not the real thing. It leaves out certain realities that would be very important in the actual situation: personal loyalties to others, control of emotions, etc.

That it calls for an intellectual judgment of alternative courses of action; and hence aims at whether the student *knows* the right act, rather than whether he would habitually act that way.

That while the item calls for an intellectual judgment, it also reflects through the alternatives certain attitudes.

We should also agree that this general analysis or description would hold for the other items in the exercise.

It so happens that we have a statement of what the teacher intended to test with these items (see page 88). A close study will show that her analysis is not as specific as we would like it to be. Thus, under the general heading, Ability to participate, she lists three specifics which might be restated as tolerance or fair-mindedness, group orientation, and co-operativeness. Apparently, ability to participate means to her the possession of certain attitudes and values which will predispose the individual to participate in group thinking. In this sense, it is a form of readiness or a pattern of enabling behaviors. The other heading, Development of social techniques, is not further defined. While we are somewhat handicapped by this inadequate analysis on her part, we do have a general idea of what she is aiming at and can therefore judge the relevance of the items.

To judge the relevance of a test item or exercise, we compare the processes and content involved in it with the processes and content implied by the objective. Returning to item 2, we see that it does present a social situation that involves the use of a social technique, but that this is at the level of knowledge or critical judgment rather than overt behavior. We see, too, that it indirectly gives the student a chance to express his acceptance of certain social values: thus, the rejection of alternatives (a, b, c) suggests a concern for the interests of the group rather than of one-self or any one person. Perhaps more directly it shows the presence of undesirable attitudes when the student chooses one of the incorrect alternatives. In summary, the item—and the entire exercise—seems directly relevant for showing the student's *ability* to select certain specific social techniques but not for indicating his *disposition* to do so in the real-life situation. It may be relevant for showing certain social attitudes such as those implied by the first objective, but such evidence would be quite indirect at best.

When recording logical analyses of problems or questions, a form such as the one below can be useful.

| *Behavior* | *Content and area* |
|---|---|
| All processes essential to answering correctly | Specific content involved as well as general area |

The advantage of this form is that it encourages us to focus on behavioral processes as well as on content elements. It is especially useful for making a systematic analysis of the items in an achievement test.

1. Two test construction agencies began work about the same time on an objective test to measure the clerical skills involved in alphabetical filing (10). Up to a certain point, the two agencies worked independently, each devising its own test. Agency 1 developed items like the first example below, and Agency 2, items like the second. Make a logical analysis of each of these items. Do you think that one item type is better than the other? If so, which one?

*Type of item constructed by Agency 1:*
Below are five names, in random order. If the names were placed in strict alphabetical order, which name would be third? (1) John Meeder; (2) James Medway; (3) Thomas Madow; (4) Catherine Meagan; (5) Eleanor Meehan.

*Type of item constructed by Agency 2:*
In the following items you have one name which is underlined and four other names in alphabetical order. If you were to put the underlined name into the alphabetical series, indicate by the appropriate letter where it would go:

<u>Robert Carstens</u>

A. ————
Richard Carreton
B. ————
Roland Casstar
C. ————
Jack Corson
D. ————
Edward Cranston
E. ————

2. Use the form on page 303 for making a logical analysis of several items that you have written.

### Classification of problems and questions

It is of course not usually necessary to go into so much detail in analyzing items. This is desirable for certain purposes, as we indicated earlier. But for ordinary purposes of test analysis, classifying the items according to type of objective and content area seems sufficient. The classification gives an indication of the distribution of the items according to these two aspects.

How one should classify the items is a further problem. Content poses less of a problem than does type of objective. Classification of content will usually follow the major areas of the course, although it is always possible to disregard this and use a different breakdown.

Classification by type of objective seems inherently more difficult, for reasons such as these: It is not always easy to know what processes an item will sample; a single item generally involves more than one process; there are many ways of classifying items; and items classified together will still differ in certain ways. Yet difficulties such as these should not deter us from realizing some of the benefits that derive from a classification of items.

Should you want to use some classification scheme other than your own, there are a few widely applicable schemes in existence. Two that the writer knows of are organized in terms of a hierarchy of complexity, such that each category takes in much of what goes before it but also goes somewhat beyond the preceding category.

The first of these is the *Taxonomy of Educational Objectives,* introduced on pages 37–38. This scheme has been used very extensively at the University of Chicago for developing comprehensive examinations, for reporting results to students, and for conducting research on thought processes in classroom instruction. It is also used in the folio, *Problems and Questions in Science,* for classifying items within each subject-matter division (2).

The other scheme is the one developed by Ebel at the State University of Iowa Examinations Service (after **3**, pp. 355–56). His system of categories is much coarser than the foregoing since it is not broken down any further than is shown below.

1. A *content detail* item deals chiefly with instructional materials rather than with the objectives of instruction, or has no significance outside a particular classroom, or can be answered correctly only in terms of a particular source of information.
2. A *vocabulary* item is one in which the principal basis for correct response is knowledge of the meaning of a single term.
3. A *fact* item is based upon some specific observation or some statement which is restricted in application.
4. A *generalization* item is based upon the summation of an extensive group of objects, events, observations, or experiments, or deals with a conclusion, a principle, a trend, or a general condition.
5. An *understanding* item calls for explanation of a condition or an action, for interpretation of a statement, for knowledge of purposes or determining factors.
6. An *application* item calls for originality on the part of the examinee in dealing with a specific situation, solving a problem, recommending a procedure, or making a judgment, an evaluation, or a prediction.

Ebel's outline has much to commend it, and certainly there are purposes for which such a crude classification will suffice. This outline was developed as an aid in analyzing instructors' classroom examinations, and so it had first of all to meet standards of utility.

The classification of items, through the use of schemes such as the two just shown, can be quite revealing—indeed, quite shocking—to instructors. It is not unusual to find that most of the items in an examination deal with content details, vocabulary, and facts, to the neglect of understandings and applications. This seems especially likely to happen in courses which do not emphasize the development of intellectual skills and abilities, but which should really be doing so—courses in the sciences and social studies, for instance, in programs of general education. Such an analysis can be a powerful stimulus not only to the improvement of examinations, but also to a thoughtful reconsideration of teaching aims and methods.

3. Read the first part of Chapter 3 in the *Taxonomy* (1) and then classify the sample test exercises on pages 54–59 of that chapter. Do the same for a sample of test items which you have developed.

### Some cautions

Both the logical analysis of test situations and their further classification have definite limitations. Neither procedure leads to neat, fixed characterizations.

We have noted already some limitations of the logical analysis of test items into processes and content. To begin with, the distinction between processes and content is always artificial. Nevertheless, it is a helpful distinction. More serious, though, is the fact that the analysis may not correspond closely to the actual processes that the item calls forth among the group for which intended. This is an ever-present possibility, and one for which we have ample experimental evidence to substantiate on both groups and individuals.

Regarding the further classification of items into categories, we must recognize that the categories of behavior or subject matter are not mutually exclusive. Many test items draw upon a variety of mental processes ranging from the relatively simple to the relatively complex. The classification serves to abstract what seem to be the most essential features. We must recognize, too, that the classification of a test item will depend upon the experiences the examinee has had, particularly those experiences that arise from instruction. With one student who has studied a problem situation involving the use of a principle, an item may be testing recall of information; with another who has not met that particular application in his instruction, the same item may be testing reasoning.

For reasons such as these, it is desirable to turn to other kinds of evidence which throw light on what processes test items actually call forth. It is especially desirable to supplement judgments of expert opinion with evidence derived from what we might term "process" or "behavior" studies.

## PROCESS STUDIES

Probably the most direct method we have of studying thought processes is to record a person's utterances as he goes about working problems or answering questions aloud. This method was illustrated in Chapter 2.

Up to the present, very little use has been made of thought-process studies in the development of achievement tests. It is more common to follow up tests with statistical analysis of the results than to obtain thought-process records for the purpose of validating the items. Occasional research studies have made use of the technique during the past thirty years, but primarily to study learning and problem-solving. Perhaps the first formal attempt to use this technique for validating test exercises was that of Lingenfelder (9). She obtained thought-process records on students, then submitted these protocols to experts to have them judge the degree of correspondence between the behavior as defined in the specifications and the behavior as evoked by the test situations. Their judgments were, of course, judgments of relevance. In lieu of such a direct approach, we may resort to less formal approaches. A compromise is to interview students after taking a test and to have them tell how they went about working particular problems. This may be done on either a group or an individual basis. The approach is better than no follow-up at all, but it falls short of what we can get from the processes as they take place. There is a tendency for people to forget many details of their thinking and to reconstruct it in a logical order, leaving out errors, false starts, backtracking, and so on.

Process studies are time-consuming, but they need not be carried out on so large a scale as to make them impractical. It is not necessary for an instructor to try to obtain information on all items in a test, nor protocols on all students in a class. It is usually sufficient to identify the more important and common types of problems in a subject, and to obtain protocols on a small sample of students—perhaps a few of the very able, a few of the average in the group, and a few of the less able. This procedure should give insight into the way the problems work out with students at different ability levels, especially into the difficulties students have, and so contribute to a better understanding of the requirements of both learning and instruction.

When students write out their solutions to problems or their answers to questions, we also have a source of evidence that is psychological in nature. Though not direct evidence of thought processes, such records do give some indication of thinking.

4. Ask a few friends to work aloud the two alphabetical filing items on page 304. If possible, record their utterances.
   a) What processes make for success on these items?
   b) What correspondence do you find between the processes shown and the criterion?
5. Choose a small sample of questions you have developed and administer these to a half dozen students—two good, two average, and two poor students. Have each student think out loud as he tries to answer the questions individually; obtain voice recordings if possible. Describe the processes used by students and compare these with what you had intended the questions to elicit. Determine the extent to which individuals at different ability levels use similar processes.

## CORRELATION WITH AN EXTERNAL CRITERION

Another fundamental way to study the relevance of a test is to correlate it with some external criterion. This may be done at the level of the individual test item or the total score, but the latter is more common. If we know what the criterion measures, we can then determine how closely the test agrees with it—i.e., measures essentially the same characteristic.

This approach should not seem new to you. You may recall that in Chapter 3 we emphasized the necessity of correlating results obtained with supposedly indirect techniques against those obtained with directly relevant techniques. Again, in Chapter 8 (pp. 223–28), we reviewed a test development project in which multiple-choice items were validated against their free-response counterparts.

It should be clear that in such comparisons the criterion is all-important. There is little point trying to determine the validity of an achievement test by correlating results on it with grades covering the same field, unless it can be shown that the grades provide directly valid evidence of achievement. This latter possibility is remote, since teachers' marks ordinarily are not valid and reliable enough to serve as a satisfactory criterion.

In test development, it is much more common to correlate aptitude than achievement tests with external criteria. There are basic reasons which account for this difference. An aptitude test *must* correlate with an external criterion if it is to be at all useful; that is, it must yield scores that are indicative of future performance in some defined activity. An achievement test need not be used for purposes of prediction, although it may. The validity of an achievement test is determined by showing the extent to which it samples the processes and content defined in the specifications.

6. The two agencies referred to on page 303 eventually got together and tried out their respective tests on the same sample of filing clerks. The tryout yielded the following data:

Reliability coefficient of Test 1 ................................. .81
Reliability coeffiicent of Test 2 ................................. .89
Coefficient of correlation between scores on Test 1 and supervisors'
    ratings of accuracy of filing materials ......................... .09
Coefficient of correlation between scores on Test 2 and supervisors'
    ratings of accuracy of filing materials ......................... .09
Coefficient of correlation between scores on Test 1 and scores on Test 2 .01
(The reliability coefficients were based on a Kuder-Richardson formula. It may be assumed that each test was sufficiently reliable.)

a) Draw out what seem to you to be the main conclusions that follow from the above data. In doing this, assume that the supervisors' ratings were moderately reliable and valid indicators of alphabetical filing ability.
b) Describe briefly what you would regard as a better criterion than the one used.
c) Compare the results of your analysis of the two items on page 304 with your description in (b) above.
d) Describe briefly another way of measuring alphabetical filing ability that would be different from what either of the two agencies developed and that would, in your judgment, yield relevant evidence.

## ITEM ANALYSIS

In the previous section, we were concerned with the *external* relations of a test—specifically, how the results correlated with an independent criterion. This is a form of statistical analysis, but it is so fundamentally different from the kinds of analysis we are about to consider that, for the sake of emphasis, we accorded it separate treatment. In the remaining sections we will focus on the test results themselves, without reference to their correlation with outside criteria. We will, in short, concern ourselves with the *internal* statistical properties of the test results—with such properties as difficulty level, discriminating power, and reliability.

When we prepare items for a test, we hope that each of them will be useful in certain statistical ways. That is, we hope that each item will turn out to be of the appropriate level of difficulty for the group, that proportionately more of the better students will get it right than the poorer, and that the incorrect alternatives will prove attractive to the students who cannot arrive at the right answer through their own ability. These are the specific properties we hope for, but of course we can never know whether our hopes have been realized until we turn to the actual results. It is at this point that item analysis procedures come into their own, for they can throw light on the effectiveness of the individual test item.

Basically, item analysis reduces to a sorting and counting operation. First we sort out a group of test papers or answer sheets into two or more subgroups; then we count the number of times each subgroup chose each item alternative. This gives the raw data from which we can make comparisons of subgroup performance, and eventually derive item statistics.

Item analysis works best, and indeed seems most justifiable, under the following conditions: (1) when the number of test papers is fairly large—say, 100 or more; (2) when the answers have been recorded on separate answer sheets; (3) when there is available an IBM test-scoring machine equipped with graphic item counter. Since the first and third of these conditions are not likely to be met in many school situations, item analysis becomes impractical under the circumstances.

Yet item analysis can be done even when these conditions are not met—if the information is worth getting and the instructor is willing to see that the job gets done. Fortunately, there are short-cut procedures that take some of the labor out of the job without sacrificing the essential information. We will note some of these short-cut procedures presently.

## Procedures

There are many item analysis procedures—too many, in fact, to try to cover here. Moreover, they tend toward the highly technical, which places many of them out of reach of most readers. For these reasons, it seems best to emphasize the basic steps in the process, to point out variations in method at each of these steps, and to indicate the types of data yielded. Later, we will want to consider uses and limitations of item analysis data.

Item analysis procedures break down into the following main steps:

1. Determine the basis of comparison.
2. Choose a representative sample of papers.
3. Sort the papers into comparison groups.
4. Obtain an item count for each group.
5. Convert the frequency data into the desired indexes.

1. *Determine the basis of comparison.* For the kinds of analyses we have in mind here, the usual basis for grouping the papers is the total test score. This is an internal criterion, in contrast to the use of some criterion external to the test itself. Although it is not appropriate for determining the validity of an item—as we shall eventually explain—it is a convenient criterion and does serve certain purposes. When we use the total test score in this way, we assume that those who get the high scores are the "best" students and that those who get the low scores are the "poor" students.

If a test is composed of two or more parts, or subtests, then it may be necessary to carry out an item analysis separately for each part rather than to sort the papers on the total score. If the part scores are highly intercorrelated and are thus measuring much the same thing, then it would not be necessary to carry out separate analyses.

2. *Choose a representative sample of papers.* While one can always work with all of the papers in the total group, it is often not necessary to do so. Only if there are fewer than 100 papers does this seem indicated. As in most statistical studies, a well-chosen sample will give results that agree closely with those that would be obtained with the total group. Depending upon the size of the total group, samples of the following sizes are especially convenient: 100, 185, and 370.

3. *Sort the papers into comparison groups.* Working only with the sample of answer sheets drawn from the total group, one now has to separate the sample itself into subgroups. The conventional procedure is to rank the answer sheets in order of total score and then to select the upper and lower 27 per cent. The remaining 46 per cent of the answer sheets, constituting the large middle group, is set aside and not used for purposes of item analysis. The choice of 27 rather than 25 per cent may seem arbitrary, but there are statistical arguments for this figure (7). It generally yields the optimum proportions with which to work. This figure explains why we recommended the sample sizes in the previous paragraph: 27 per cent of 185 is 50; of 370, 100.

Other common procedures are to sort the answer sheets into upper and lower quarters, or into thirds, or into upper and lower halves. It is especially convenient to use such proportions with a sample of 100 answer sheets, for it is then quite easy to convert frequency counts into percentages.

4. *Obtain an item count for each group.* The purpose of this step is to get a count of the number of individuals in each comparison group who

chose each alternative in each item. This would include the incorrect alternatives as well as those keyed as correct or best. If you are not interested in how attractive the incorrect options proved to be, you can omit getting a count on them. This would greatly shorten the task if you are doing the counting by hand, and it will still give you the most important information on each item.

At this point you would need to decide where to record the frequency data. There are three main possibilities: on the test booklet, on a separate card for each item, or on a worksheet. Any one of these will serve well. The first two have the advantage of recording the data next to the item where they can be directly studied. The worksheet itself can always be filed with a copy of the test booklet, although it is not too convenient to refer from one to the other when studying the data. If you want to make use of an item card or a worksheet, you can use some such form as that below.

| Item No. | Choices-High Group | | | | | | Choices-Low Group | | | | | | Item Indexes | | | |
|---|---|---|---|---|---|---|---|---|---|---|---|---|---|---|---|---|
| | A | B | C | D | E | O | A | B | C | D | E | O | $p$H | $p$L | $p$ | $r$ |
| 1 | 2 | 17 | 3 | 1 | 4 | 0 | 5 | 9 | 4 | 2 | 6 | 1 | .63 | .34 | .48 | .29 |
| 2 | 25 | 0 | 1 | 1 | 0 | 0 | 6 | 15 | 2 | 3 | 1 | 0 | .93 | .22 | .71 | .71 |
| 3 | 24 | 1 | 0 | 2 | – | 0 | 25 | 0 | 0 | 1 | – | 0 | .07 | .04 | .05 | .11 |

Fig. 12. Form for recording item analysis data.

This form provides spaces for recording the number of times each of five alternatives was chosen, the number of omissions (o) per item, and certain statistical indexes derived from the frequency data. The frequency count for each correct answer can be underlined as shown.

5. *Convert the frequency data into the desired indexes.* This is the point at which item analysis procedures can become highly technical, for there are a variety of complex statistics that might be derived.

If you follow the conventional procedure, you must first convert certain of the frequency counts into proportions. As a minimum, it is necessary to find the proportion of the high and low groups, respectively, that chose the right answer. To make this step easy, it is wise to prepare a table of cumulative proportions as shown below.

| Number Right | 27 | 26 | 25 | 24 | 23 |
|---|---|---|---|---|---|
| 1 | .04 | .04 | .04 | .04 | .04 |
| 2 | .07 | .08 | .08 | .08 | .09 |
| 3 | .11 | .11 | .12 | .13 | .13 |
| – | – | – | – | – | – |
| – | – | – | – | – | – |
| – | – | – | – | – | – |
| 25 | .93 | .95 | | | |
| 26 | .96 | | | | |

Fig. 13. Cumulative proportions for N's of different sizes.

In Figure 12, these proportions fall in the columns labelled $p_H$ and $p_L$. Thus, for item 1, 17 out of the 27 in the group chose the right answer; this corresponds to a proportion of .63. For the same item, 9 out of the 26 in the low group chose the right answer, or a proportion of .34. The remaining two statistical indexes may be read directly from the *Item Analysis Table* (4) by using the $p_H$ and $p_L$ values for each item. The value $p$ is an estimate of item difficulty—the proportion of the total sample (from which the high and low groups were drawn) getting the item right. Note that it will lie between the $p_H$ and $p_L$ values. The value $r$ is a discrimination index. Technically, it is the coefficient of "correlation between the criterion score, which forms the basis for the selection of the high and low 27-per-cent groups, and the continuous score assumed to underlie responses to the items" (4, p. 3). In short, if you have the $p_H$ and $p_L$ values for any item, you can go directly to the *Item Analysis Table* and find the corresponding item difficulty and discrimination values.

There are other methods of indexing item difficulty and item discrimination than those defined above, but they are not by far as common. Occasionally, you will run across articles defining difficulty as per cent failing rather than per cent passing an item. Among the variations in computing an index of discrimination, we need only mention a few simple forms. A method that gives a combined index of difficulty and discrimination is to subtract the number of correct responses in the lower group from the number of correct responses in the upper group. Thus, for the three items in Figure 12, the respective differences are 8, 19, and 1. Note that these values are roughly proportional to both the corresponding $p$ and $r$ values. Crude as it is, this combined index seems to serve well enough for the informal evaluation of achievement tests (3).[1] Indeed, it is believed to add precise and useful data from which even the statistically sophisticated test specialist can profit (5).

7. Compare the three items in Figure 12 with respect to attractiveness of the options, difficulty, and discrimination. To interpret the index of discrimination, use the following rough guide:

.50 and above—high positive
.30 to .49     —moderate positive
.20 to .29     —borderline positive
.00 to .19     —zero to low positive
—.01 and below—zero to negative

### Interpretation and uses of item analysis data

As mentioned previously, the three main types of item analysis data are, respectively, the attractiveness of the individual options, an index of difficulty, and an index of discrimination. The interpretation of these data is relatively easy.

Item analysis data are useful in improving an instrument, in providing a basis for defining levels of performance or competence on a test, and in improving curriculum and instruction. The second of these uses is highly technical, and for this reason will not be treated here.

### Improving the instrument

Item analysis contributes to the improvement of a test by providing data on the effectiveness of individual items. These data help to identify items that should be revised or eliminated entirely from the test. Generally, such an item will be defective in one or more of the following respects: it is too easy or too difficult for the group; it is ambiguous in some ways; it contains a stereotype or cliché in the best answer, so that better students tend to avoid choosing it; it contains irrelevant clues to the best answer; it contains elements of content that do not function.

As an example of a questionable item, consider that below. The data

[1] A simplified item-analysis procedure, based essentially upon upper-lower group differences, may be found in C. C. Ross and Julian C. Stanley, *Measurement in Today's Schools,* 3rd ed., pages 436–53. New York: Prentice-Hall, Inc., 1954.

to the right are frequencies for the high and low 27 papers out of a total of 100.

| | High 27% | Low 27% | |
|---|---|---|---|
| $C_6 H_{12} O_6$ is a: | | | |
| 1) fat | 0 | 0 | |
| *2) carbohydrate | 26 | 25 | |
| 3) protein | 1 | 2 | |
| 4) vitamin | 0 | 0 | $p = .95$ |
| | | | $r = .11$ |

An item so easy as this one does not contribute to individual differences in score. From the standpoint of discrimination, it is just so much dead-wood. It could be eliminated and replaced by one that would be more effective in this respect. If the instructor here is interested in the extent to which the group knows this specific point, then he has some justification for including it in the test. (The same sort of reasoning can be applied to an item which is technically sound but proves to be difficult for the group.) It is apparent, though, that this item is testing a bit of information that is quite elementary and may be assumed to be common knowledge in the group.

8. Another possible use of item analysis data is to help identify the *best* items in a test,

   a) Should the index of discrimination be used as the primary basis for choosing among the more discriminating items? Justify your position.
   b) What purposes do you think the index of discrimination can best serve?

9. Evaluate the following statement: "All item analysis is ultimately concerned with the selection of good test items."

10. Evaluate the item below on the basis of the data given. The figures to the right are frequencies for the high and low subgroups chosen from a total sample of 100 papers.
   When a muscle fiber is stimulated, it—

| | High 27% | Low 27% |
|---|---|---|
| 1. contracts in proportion to the strength of the stimulus. | 2 | 8 |
| *2. contracts completely or not at all. | 24 | 18 |
| 3. fails to contract. | 1 | 1 |
| 4. loses tone. | 0 | 0 |

$p_H = .89$        $p_L = .67$        $p = .79$        $r = .31$

On the basis of the above data and other considerations, would you approve the following revision of this item?

What is the relationship between strength of the stimulus and degree of muscle contraction?

   1. The muscle contracts in proportion to the strength of the stimulus.

\*2. The muscle contracts completely or not at all.

   3. There is no predictable relationship.

### Improving the curriculum and instruction

In passing, we should underscore the ways item-analysis data can help to improve the curriculum and instruction. By providing detailed information on student strengths and weaknesses, item analysis helps to—

1. Identify specific objectives that are especially easy for the group to attain and deserve much less emphasis than given, and to identify those that are especially difficult to attain and need much more emphasis.

2. Identify content that is intrinsically too difficult for the group and might well be simplified or omitted entirely. This often happens in general education courses when highly technical concepts and principles inappropriately find their way into courses.

3. Provide evidence of student misconceptions, or faulty thinking, which can stimulate improvements in teaching.

### Some cautions

1. *Internal consistency data do not indicate the validity of the individual item or of the test as a whole.* The index of discrimination merely shows the degree to which the item measures what the total score measures. To establish the validity of an item or of a test, one must either correlate results on it with an independent criterion, or show that the operations and content sampled correspond to those required by the specifications. It is possible for a test to contain items which have a high degree of internal consistency or homogeneity, and yet have little relevance for the intended purpose. To rely upon internal consistency data for sole evidence of the validity of an achievement test is to deceive oneself. Such reliance would be most unfortunate if the test were used not simply as a device for ranking or grading students, *but as a data-gathering device for helping to evaluate the effectiveness of curriculum and instruction.* On this point no one has argued more cogently than Ralph Tyler:

. . . for achievement testing to serve the purposes suggested the criterion of test validity must be evidence of the degree to which the students are attaining the objectives rather than the index of discrimination which is now so commonly used for many achievement test items. To use the index of discrimination as a criterion of validity assumes in advance that the total test score is both valid and comprehensive, so that when each item is correlated with the total score the resulting correlation indicates the validity of that individual item. Such an assumption is not a safe one to make when achievement tests are to be used for the analytical purposes previously indicated.

Validation by use of the index of discrimination assumes that the teaching, the content, and the learning is of such a nature that the students who are generally best are also more successful in connection with every important aspect of the test. This may not be the case, especially when there are inadequacies of teaching or of curriculum planning so that certain important matters are not dealt with in the course, or when there has not been adequate provision for their learning. In such cases it is possible for the so-called better student to do no better on the test item than a poorer student. If such items are automatically eliminated because of their low discrimination indices, then the test no longer serves the purpose of helping to improve the curriculum or instruction. We must develop validity checks that are based upon the concept of attaining objectives rather than upon the concept of homogeneity of learning outcomes (12, pp. 403–04).[2]

2. *The value of an item is not directly proportional to either its difficulty level or its index of discrimination.* Certainly test items may often be highly difficult not because they test complex ideas but because they require rare or minute information. Difficulty in itself is not a guarantee of complexity. Correspondingly, a test item with a high index of discrimination is not necessarily better than an item with a much lower index. Each may be testing an important concept or ability. The former may, in fact, be duplicating another item in the test so that it could justifiably be omitted. (Intercorrelation among any two items is an important consideration about which the index of discrimination tells nothing.) If we retain only items with high indexes of discrimination, we may narrow the scope of the instrument so much that it no longer gives a comprehensive sampling of the legitimate content and objectives.

3. *Item analysis data are always specific to the particular group and to the particular test on which obtained.* If the test is tried out with a group more or less able than the original, the item analysis data will tend to change. Moreover, even if it is tried out with a similar group, differences in educational experience will cause the item statistics to be different. As course content and instruction change, so too will the properties of test items that are carried over from previous use. The difficulty and

[2] Reproduced by permission of the University of Minnesota Press.

discriminating power of an item are also a function of the other items that happen to be in the test. Changing the composition of the test in any way will tend to alter the properties of the individual items. In view of these facts, it is unrealistic to regard item analysis data as stable properties.

4. *If a test is speeded, item analysis data may be misleading and cannot be taken at their face value.* What happens under such conditions is that relatively few individuals in the sample reach the later items in the test. The per cent of the total sample passing such items will thus be relatively low, and these items will appear more difficult than they actually are. Moreover, the discriminating power of the later items will come out spuriously high. This arises because the more proficient individuals tend to work faster, and hence are more likely to reach the later items than are the less proficient.

## DETERMINING AND IMPROVING RELIABILITY

### Methods of determining reliability

After tryout, it is also desirable to determine the degree of reliability and to decide whether this needs improvement. The problem of reliability is to estimate the degree to which the sample of behavior taken by the instrument is large and representative enough to yield results which are typical of the individuals concerned.

There are three important types of method which may be used to estimate reliability: equivalent forms, test-retest, and internal consistency. Each of these yields a coefficient of correlation, or reliability coefficient. The coefficients yielded by these different methods are by no means identical, although they often approximate each other in numerical value.

### Equivalent-forms method

Perhaps the ideal way to estimate reliability is to administer a second, equivalent form of the instrument and then to correlate the two sets of scores derived from both instruments. The coefficient of correlation gives an indication of the consistency with which the two instruments rank the individuals concerned. If the coefficient is high, we can say that either form yields a reliable set of scores.

Two difficulties make this method impracticable for all but commercial test development. One is the problem of developing two forms which will prove to be equivalent in the content and processes they sample, in difficulty, and in other respects. The other is the inconvenience of giving a second form.

### Test-retest method

If time is available, a relatively easy way to estimate reliability is to give the same instrument a second time to the group after an interval of a few or several days. Then one can calculate a coefficient of correlation between the two sets of scores.

This method has important limitations too. Repeating the test at too short an interval gives spuriously high coefficients because individuals tend to remember their responses on the first occasion. Repeating the test at too long an interval does not give a true estimate of reliability, for the test is in all likelihood assessing permanent changes in the individuals concerned. Moreover, by utilizing the *same* set of items, the method gives no true indication of the adequacy and representativeness of sampling from the possible tasks within the area.

### Internal-consistency methods

Because of the practical limitations of the equivalent-forms and test-retest methods, procedures have been devised for estimating reliability from a single administration of a test. There are several methods in wide use.

*Split-test methods.* A common method is to divide the items in a single test into halves, usually by pooling the odd-numbered items for one part score and the even-numbered for the other. The reasoning here is similar to that for the equivalent-forms method. It is assumed that the two two halves represent equivalent samples of the same area. The coefficient of correlation between the two sets of part scores gives an estimate of the reliability of *one half* the whole test. To estimate the reliability of the whole test, it is then necessary to use the Spearman-Brown prophecy formula:

$$\text{Reliability of lengthened test} = \frac{nr}{1 + (n-1)\,r}$$

where $n$ = number of times test is lengthened

$r$ = original reliability coefficient

Thus, if the half-score coefficient were .75, one would substitute in the formula $n = 2$ and $r = .75$:

$$r_n = \frac{2(.75)}{1 + (1).75} = \frac{1.50}{1.75} = .86$$

The split-half method will give misleading results unless the half tests are equivalent in certain respects. They must be as equivalent as possible in content and processes sampled, in average score, and in variability of scores. The Spearman-Brown formula applies only to the extent that these conditions are fulfilled.

There are two other split-test methods which do not require computing a coefficient of correlation directly or correcting by the Spearman-Brown formula. The first of these is Guttman's formula (6):

$$r = 2 \left( 1 - \frac{s_o^2 + s_e^2}{s_t^2} \right)$$

where $s_o$ = standard deviation of odd half
$\quad\quad s_e$ = standard deviation of even half
$\quad\quad s_t$ = standard deviation of total test

The second is Rulon's formula (11):

$$r = 1 - \frac{s_d^2}{s_t^2}$$

where $s_d$ = standard deviation of differences between half-test scores
$\quad\quad s_t$ = standard deviation of total test

This formula yields the same results as the previous.

*Kuder-Richardson formulas.* There are other internal-consistency methods which do not require splitting a test into halves, rescoring, and calculating a coefficient of correlation. The most widely used of these are the formulas derived by Kuder and Richardson (8).

Item analysis data are necessary for their formula 20:

$$r = \frac{n}{n-1} \cdot \frac{s_t^2 - \Sigma pq}{s_t^2}$$

where $n$ = number of items in the test
$\quad\quad s_t$ = standard deviation of the total test
$\quad\quad p$ = proportion of individuals passing each item
$\quad\quad q = 1 - p$, again for each item in turn
$\quad\quad \Sigma$ = take the sum over all items

The $pq$ products may be read from a special table found in some statistics textbooks. This formula assumes that the items in the test measure a single ability, that the correlations between the items are all equal, and that the items have equal variability. This formula tends to underestimate reliability if the test items sample a number of different abilities.

Formula 21 is simpler, and easier to apply since it does not require item analysis data:

$$r = \frac{n}{n-1} \cdot \frac{s_t^2 - n\,\bar{p}\,\bar{q}}{s_t^2}$$

where $n$ = number of items in the test

$s_t$ = the standard deviation of the total test scores

$$\bar{p} = \frac{\text{mean test score}}{n} = \frac{M_t}{n}$$

$$\bar{q} = 1 - \bar{p}$$

This formula involves the further assumption that all items are of the same difficulty. It underestimates the reliability if there is variation in difficulty among the items. If the test items do not vary much in difficulty, then this formula gives a useful estimate.

### Determining the reliability of essay examinations

Determining reliability is more complex with essay examinations than with instruments that yield a simple count of correct choices. The general procedure is straightforward enough: present a second sample of questions and correlate grades on this set with those on the first. However, serious complications arise. One is that the score or grade on an essay examination reflects variations arising from the unreliability of judges, as well as variations that arise from the particular sampling of questions. It is first necessary to control variation in grading (i.e., to assure objectivity) before one considers the further problem of whether the sample of questions is adequate and representative enough. Another complication is that writing is itself rather variable from occasion to occasion. Finally—and this is a practical limitation—the essay examination does not lend itself to the use of internal consistency procedures, such as the formulas which make use of score or item analysis statistics.

### Interpretation and uses of reliability coefficients

#### The meanings of reliability

The first step in interpreting a reliability coefficient is to make certain what the coefficient estimates. *What a reliability coefficient estimates depends upon the method used to calculate it.*

The several methods do not estimate quite the same things. Reliability is only a general term to cover at least three different characteristics of test results: equivalence, stability, and internal consistency. The equivalent-forms method estimates equivalence, unless the forms are given some time apart—in which case it estimates stability of performance to some extent also. The retest method estimates stability of performance; it tells nothing about the internal consistency of a test. The split-test methods and Kuder-Richardson formulas estimate internal consistency, or the homogeneity of the *parts* or *items* of a test for measurement purposes.

Regardless of method of estimation, a reliability coefficient indicates the consistency with which a test ranks the individuals concerned. Hence, it is a summary index of the discriminating power of the test as a whole.

*Reliability is a necessary, but not a sufficient, condition for a test to have validity.* For a test to yield valid results, it must measure something accurately, but that *something* must have relevance for the intended uses of the test. *A low reliability coefficient indicates a test of doubtful value, but a high reliability coefficient does not in itself establish the value of a test.*

### How high should a reliability coefficient be?

In general, the higher the coefficient, the greater the confidence one may place in the accuracy of the test results. Hence, the issue at stake is how much confidence one wants or needs for his purposes.

A most important consideration is the seriousness of the decisions to be made on the basis of the test scores. This can vary from one extreme to the other. If a student's performance in a course over an entire school year is to be graded on the basis of a final comprehensive examination, then one needs a high degree of confidence in the scores. The reliability coefficient should be correspondingly high. If one wants to analyze rather informally a student's strengths and weaknesses in a subject, particularly those of the very poor or very good student, one can normally tolerate a lower degree of confidence in the scores than in the first instance. The reliability coefficients of the several part scores can be correspondingly lower.

Another consideration is whether the decisions are to deal with group or individual performance. For an instrument of given reliability, one can have much more confidence in the accuracy of the mean score than of any individual's score. The justification for this statement comes from the facts of sampling. The mean score for a given group has much less error in it because of inadequacies of sampling than does any individual's score.

Apart from considerations such as the foregoing, it is very difficult to lay down rigid rules as to how high reliability coefficients should be. Much depends upon the purposes which the scores are to serve. Much depends upon the time available for testing. Much depends too upon the nature of the group taking the test. A good figure to shoot for on a relatively important final examination is .90, with .80 as a minimum.

### Lengthening or shortening the test

A reliability coefficient helps one decide whether a test should be lengthened. Lengthening a test *may* give a more representative sample of the individual's performance. Through the use of the Spearman-Brown formula, it is possible to estimate how much a test should be lengthened to achieve a given degree of reliability. The formula then becomes:

$$n = \frac{R(1-r)}{r(1-R)}$$

where $n$ = number of times test is to be lengthened
  $r$ = original reliability coefficient
  $R$ = desired reliability coefficient

Suppose we have a test with a reliability of .80, and wish to augment the reliability to .90 by adding similar items to the instrument. How many items do we need to add? Substituting in the formula we have—

$$n = \frac{.90(1-.80)}{.80(1-.90)} = \frac{.90(.20)}{.80(.10)} = 2.25$$

The test must be lengthened two and a quarter times to achieve a reliability of .90. If the original test has 50 items, we would need to add enough to total 112, or 62 more. To use this formula, one should meet reasonably well the assumptions on which it is based. In general, the added items must turn out to be equivalent in all respects to those in the original instrument.

Merely adding items does not necessarily increase the reliability. In fact, extreme increases in length can introduce effects of fatigue and boredom which actually reduce reliability.

At times it is more desirable to increase the reliability of an instrument *by shortening it*. This is especially desirable when there is only so much testing time available, so that lengthening the test is out of the question. This approach will work if there are a number of poorly discriminating items in the test. A dramatic illustration of this comes from the writer's own files. As a part of our regular service, we scored and item-analyzed the papers on a final examination in one of the social science fields. We then rescored the papers twice, using first those items with discrimination indexes above .20, and second, those with indexes above .30. The reliability coefficients for all three scores turned out as follows:

|  | Number of items | Reliability coefficient * |
|---|---|---|
| Total test ....................... | III | .81 |
| Composite (items with discrim. indexes above .20) ............... | 88 | .83 |
| Composite (items with discrim. indexes above .30) ............... | 53 | .85 |

\* Estimated by Kuder-Richardson Formula 20

Hence, a composite of fewer than half the items would have yielded a reliability higher than that of the total test! With such facts before him, the instructor could decide on the next occasion to give only the shortest version of the test or to add some other instrument or questions which would give him a more complete picture of student progress in the course.

Since the reliability coefficient used here throws light mainly on the homogeneity of the outcomes measured, one can legitimately question whether the test should be so shortened and made in effect more homogeneous. The answer in this case was in the affirmative, for the course was essentially a survey of facts and generalizations in the particular field. Logical analysis of the examination questions suggested to the instructor that he was not emphasizing objectives more complex than recall of information.

### Factors affecting reliability coefficients

Quite a few factors affect the size of reliability coefficients, and it is important to recognize such influences when interpreting coefficients.

Two deserve comment here: range of ability in the group and interval between testing. *The reliability coefficient is quite dependent on the range of ability in the group upon which computed.* The greater the variability of the group, the higher the reliability coefficient. This means that a test will work out differently, depending upon the particular group on which it is tried out. A test may have a high reliability coefficient when given to a group of widely varying ability in the functions measured, but a much lower reliability in a more selected group.

The reliability coefficient, as computed by the equivalent-forms and retest methods, also varies with the interval of time between testings. In general, the longer the interval, the lower the coefficient one may expect. Advanced books give more detail on these and other factors.

11. The odd-even reliability coefficient of a mathematics test is .73 when given to a group of college freshmen. Which coefficient below would approximate the reliability of the same test when it is given to a typical group of high school seniors?

   a) .63     b) .68     c) .73     d) .78

12. A fifty-item examination developed by an instructor contains five items answered correctly by all students in the group. How does the presence of these five items affect the reliability of the test?

   a) Lowers the reliability by reducing the effect of the other items.
   b) Raises the reliability by increasing the length of the test.
   c) Has no effect on the reliability of the test.

### Ways of improving reliability

Reliability may be improved by making changes of the following sorts in the instrument itself:

1. *Increase the length of the test by adding more items.* This is the usual way of improving reliability.

2. *Replace items that are too easy or too difficult* with items that are closer to the 50 per cent level of difficulty. The effect of this is to increase the *functioning* sample by adding items that contribute to discrimination.

3. *Replace other poorly and negatively discriminating items* which cannot be revised. This again has the effect of increasing the functioning sample of test items.

4. *Increase the number of alternatives per item,* if this seems called for. Four- and five-choice items are more reliable than two- and three-choice items.

5. *Improve the clarity and adequacy of the directions* to the instrument as a whole and to specific exercises within it. This helps eliminate misinterpretation and oversights.

Other ways of improving reliability relate to the actual administration and scoring of the instrument.

### OTHER STATISTICAL ANALYSES

In addition to the sorts of studies mentioned, various other statistical analyses may be conducted. Some of these, such as analysis for possible response sets and the intercorrelation of part scores, are of more value to the test specialist. But others, notably the analysis of distribution statistics, are of value to the nonspecialist as well.

### Analysis of distribution statistics

Questions concerning the difficulty of a test and its discriminating power can be answered by turning to certain distribution statistics. Two useful statistics are the mean and the standard deviation. The mean is the average score in a distribution of scores, while the standard deviation is a measure of the variation of scores away from the average.[3]

The mean, of course, gives some indication of the relative difficulty of the test as a whole. In general, the lower the mean, the more difficult the test.

The mean also gives some indication of the discrimination of the test. A test which is too easy or too difficult lacks discrimination. From the standpoint of effective discrimination, then, the best test is one which is neither too easy nor too difficult for the group. Again from the standpoint of effective discrimination, the best place for the mean is about midway between the highest possible score and the expected chance score.

Direct evidence of the discriminating power of a test comes from the standard deviation of scores. The larger the standard deviation, the greater will be the discrimination. For the typical general achievement test, a figure approximating one-sixth of the useful score range—that is, the difference between the highest possible and the expected chance score—seems to be a reasonable minimum value for the standard deviation.

13. If the purpose of a test is to measure mastery of fundamentals, or minimum essentials, would it be desirable for the mean and standard deviation to approximate the values suggested above? Explain.

14. Occasionally one hears an instructor comment about his test in words like the following: "This test *really* did a good job of measuring achievement. Look at that beautiful distribution of scores!—A few high scores, a few low scores, the rest spread out in between. A bell-shaped curve just like the books show."

   a) What major assumption was this instructor making?
   b) How sound is this assumption?

[3] The formula for the standard deviation is $\sqrt{\dfrac{\Sigma x^2}{N}}$, where $x$ is the deviation of any score from the mean, $N$ is the number of cases in the distribution, and the symbol $\Sigma$ means to sum over all the cases.

### Determining speededness

If a test is given under conditions which purport to be very liberal time limits, it is desirable to check the papers afterward to see whether this was actually the case. A simple method is to count the number of completed papers and to convert this figure into a per cent. A more elaborate method is to count the number of individuals reaching successive items on the test and to convert these into per cents. Such data allow us to determine whether the time limits were generous enough or whether the test was too greatly speeded.

## CONSIDERING BROADER CRITERIA

While an achievement test should meet technical standards as outlined in Chapters 4–6 and in this final chapter, we should not lose sight of the fact that it should meet broader criteria as well. Among other things, its *use* should foster the development of desirable study habits and self-evaluation on the part of students, the improvement of instruction, and the development of wholesome relationships between instructor and students.

Any testing device which has been subjected to the kinds of analyses just reviewed will truly have been put to the test. If it can pass these tests, then it must surely qualify as a first-rate piece of work.

If the device is to be used for such broader purposes as have been outlined, all this effort will be fully justified. You as the instructor will feel that your extra efforts have been amply rewarded in the satisfaction of a job well done, and in the realization that these efforts will have enriched the experience of those to whom all of this makes a difference—your students.

## REFERENCES

1. Bloom, B. S., Engelhart, M. D., Furst, E. J., Hill, W. H., and Krathwohl, D. R. *Taxonomy of educational objectives, handbook I:* cognitive domain. New York: Longmans Green, 1956.
2. Dressel, P. L., and Nelson, C. H. *Questions and problems in science:* Test item folio no. 1. Princeton: Educ. Test. Serv., 1956.
3. Ebel, R. L. Procedures for the analysis of classroom tests. *Educ. psychol. Measmt,* 1954, **14**, 352–364.
4. Fan, Chung-teh. *Item analysis table.* Princeton: Educ. Test. Serv., 1952.
5. Findley, W. G. A rationale for evaluation of item discrimination statistics. *Educ. psychol. Measmt,* 1956, **16**, 175–180.

6. Guttman, L. A basis for analysing test-retest reliability. *Psychometrika*, 1945, **10**, 255–282.
7. Kelley, T. L. The selection of upper and lower groups for the validation of test items. *J. educ. Psychol.*, 1939, **30**, 17–24.
8. Kuder, G. F., and Richardson, M. W. The theory of estimation of test reliability. *Psychometrika*, 1937, **2**, 151–160.
9. Lingenfelder, Louise M. The development of methods for constructing a diagnostic and placement examination over the general field in education. Unpublished doctor's dissertation, Univer. of Chicago, 1947.
10. Mosier, C. I. A critical examination of the concepts of face validity. *Educ. psychol. Measmt*, 1947, **7**, 191–205.
11. Rulon, P. J. A simplified procedure for determining the reliability of a test by split-halves. *Harv. educ. Rev.*, 1939, **9**, 99–103.
12. Tyler, R. W. Achievement testing and curriculum construction. In E. G. Williamson (Ed.), *Trends in student personnel work*. Copyright 1949 by Univer. of Minnesota Press.

## FURTHER READINGS

Bloom, B. S., and Broder, Lois J The analysis of mental processes rather than mental products, and, Variations in problems as revealed by problem-solving investigations. *Problem-solving processes of college students:* An exploratory investigation. Chicago: Univer. of Chicago, 1950. Pp. 1–21 and 41–66. Copyright 1950 by the University of Chicago.

Cureton, E. E. Validity. In E. F. Lindquist (Ed.), *Educational measurement*. Washington: Amer. Coun. on Educ., 1951. Pp. 621–694.

Ebel, R. L. Procedures for the analysis of classroom tests. *Educ. psychol. Measmt*, 1954, **14**, 352–364.

Thorndike, R. L. Reliability. In E. F. Lindquist (Ed.), *Educational measurement*. Washington: Amer. Coun. on Educ., 1951. Pp. 560–620.

*Technical recommendations for achievement tests*. Prepared by Committees on Test Standards, American Educational Research Association and National Council on Measurements Used in Education. Washington: Amer. Educ. Res. Ass., 1955.

# Index